# 100 THINGS
# SOUTH CAROLINA FANS
# SHOULD KNOW & DO
# BEFORE THEY DIE

# 100 THINGS
# SOUTH CAROLINA FANS
# SHOULD KNOW & DO
# BEFORE THEY DIE

Josh Kendall

TRIUMPH
BOOKS

Library of Congress Cataloging-in-Publication Data

Kendall, Josh, 1973–
    100 things South Carolina fans should know & do before they die / Josh Kendall ; [foreword by] Don Barton.
        pages cm. — (100 things...fans should know)
    Includes bibliographical references.
    ISBN 978-1-60078-850-5 (pbk.)
    1. University of South Carolina—Football—History. 2. South Carolina Fighting Gamecocks (Football team)—History. I. Title. II. Title: One hundred things South Carolina fans should know and do before they die.
    GV958.U585K46 2013
    796.332'630975771—dc23
                                        2013027116

This book is available in quantity at special discounts for your group or organization. For further information, contact:
    **Triumph Books LLC**
    814 North Franklin Street
    Chicago, Illinois 60610
    (312) 337-0747
    www.triumphbooks.com

Printed in U.S.A.
ISBN: 978-1-60078-850-5
Design by Patricia Frey
Photos courtesy of AP Images unless otherwise indicated

*For My Three Js:*
*Janet, Jones, Joseph*
*I Love You*

# Contents

# Foreword

Ask a hundred Carolina football fans to select their favorite player, coach, game, or season, and you would probably get 100 different answers. All of them are likely covered by Josh Kendall in this legendary tribute to Gamecocks football.

The hundred "chapters" in this book take you onto the playing fields and bring you face to face with those in the stadiums, plus related personalities and happenings behind the scenes.

Although championships by Gamecocks teams have been hard to come by, there has been no shortage of outstanding individuals, games, and seasons. A popular saying is that the most consistent aspect of Carolina athletics is inconsistency.

This countdown through 100 subjects provides a mini-history of the ups and downs, the ins and outs, the whos, whats, and whens of the Gamecocks. Older fans have an opportunity to relive some of the magic moments. Among them are Bobby Bryant's game-winning 95-yard punt return against North Carolina State in 1966 and Brandon Bennett's last-second dive over the line to beat Georgia in 1993.

Younger Gamecocks can learn about long-ago greats such as Steve Wadiak, Earl Clary, and South Carolina's first All-American, Lou Sossamon.

Recalled are players with, shall we say, distinct personalities who were memorable for who they were as much as for what they accomplished, such as Dom Fusci, Alex Hawkins, Steve Taneyhill, and Stephen Garcia.

And there are the legends, including Heisman Trophy winner George Rogers, Hall of Fame play-by-play announcer Bob Fulton, and legends-to-be Marcus Lattimore and Jadeveon Clowney, "The Hit" man.

The marks left by coaches Rex Enright, Paul Dietzel, Jim Carlen, Lou Holtz, and Steve Spurrier are chronicled, along with special moments in their careers at USC.

Kendall relates many more stories about people, games, and seasons that will satisfy the appetite of the most zealous Gamecocks supporters.

It is especially gratifying, because, when the final seconds tick off the clock, the Gamecocks always come up winners.

—Don Barton

# Acknowledgments

If you'll forgive me, I'd like to start here with the personal side. First, to my beautiful wife, Janet, who not only did everything else in the house while I waded into this book but is also my favorite editor, thank you, thank you, and thank you again. And to my boys, Jones and Joseph, thanks for being the most wonderful distractions a man could have. Finally, to Mom and Dad, thanks for everything.

To Don Gulbrandsen and Karen O'Brien of Triumph Books for the opportunity and their patience with the new guy, thank you. I truly appreciate it.

Now on to the book. I never could have completed this project without the help of two men—Don Barton and Mike Safran. I want to thank them for their time and their unfailing generosity. Gentlemen, your history lessons were always appreciated. Any omissions in this book are mine, not theirs.

And thanks to Steve Zuhkle at The Tech Stop in Indianapolis, Indiana, for telling me one cold February morning that 50 chapters, in fact, were not lost for all eternity.

There were others, too, who took the time to walk me through the vast spaces of South Carolina history I was not able to witness myself. Brad Edwards, Tommy Suggs, Todd Ellis, Ron Bass, and Steve Taneyhill, particularly, went out of their way to help, and I appreciate that.

To all the people I interviewed and included in this book—Steve Spurrier, George Rogers, Mike McGee, Mike Hold, Jeff Grantz, John Routh, Corey Miller, Rick Sanford, Del Wilkes, Sheldon Brown, Johnathan Joseph, Andre Goodman, Marcus Lattimore, Teddy Heffner, Jadeveon Clowney, Jarvis Jones, Bjoern Werner, Bobby Carroll, Ray Tanner, Ryan Brewer, Steve Spurrier Jr.,

Stephon Gilmore, Mike Farrell, Scott Kennedy, Stephen Garcia, Gary Garcia, Wes Bunting, Mark Richt, Brad Lawing, and Kevin Long—thank you.

Lastly, I owe a special debt to *The State* newspaper, whose archives were a huge resource for me as you will be able to tell and whose bosses allowed me the freedom and the time to write this book. Thanks Rick, Mark, and Henry.

# Introduction

By far, the best part of writing this book for me has been all the things I have a learned or learned more about. I'll just list a few highlights here:

- While my appreciation for Marcus Lattimore's career has only grown, I learned that George Rogers is the greatest Gamecocks player ever, and it's not really close.

- I learned that Tommy Suggs has been in the middle of pretty much every significant thing that has happened in South Carolina's football program in the last 50 years.

- I learned that both South Carolina coaches who were named National Coach of the Year were Ohio natives—Joe Morrison of Lima and Lou Holtz of East Liverpool. I don't think it means anything, but I did learn it.

- I learned that the media guides of the 1960s and early '70s listed not just players' highlights on the field but also their religion and marital status as the last two words of each biography. In 1970, junior defensive tackle Jake Wright was "Methodist. Single." No word on turn-ons and turn-offs, though.

- I learned that Del Wilkes was verbally committed to Clemson before he got one of the all-time great recruiting pitches in college football history from Jim Carlen. I also learned Wilkes probably should have a book of his own rather than just a chapter. I imagine he's seen some things.

- I learned that Joe Morrison spent 14 years playing in the NFL and all the time he was sneaking smoke breaks during games with the New York Giants. Who does that? The same kind of guy who wears all black in the Columbia sun, I suppose.

- I learned why Williams-Brice Stadium doesn't sway anymore, but I kind of wish it still did.
- I learned that Bobby Bryant doesn't get the appreciation he deserves.
- I was reminded three times of tragedy and how it touched Steve Wadiak, Derek Watson, and Kenny McKinley in different ways.
- And I learned, thanks to Ryan Brewer, that karma does sometimes kick in.

I learned much more than that, and I hope you do, too. I also hope you'll find me, whether it be in cyberspace or on the street, and tell me why I didn't give enough love to this person or gave too much to that one or discuss anything else that you please about this book.

# 1 Steve Spurrier—Winning at Last

It may seem odd to see such a recent addition to the school's long history in this spot, but the man who killed the Chicken Curse (we'll get to that later) deserves top billing.

South Carolina has played football for 119 seasons. Steve Spurrier has been there for eight of them, but he did what no one before him could do—turn the Gamecocks into a consistent winner, or any kind of winner really. His 66 wins at the school, versus 37 losses, are a program record and account for 12 percent of all the games South Carolina has won since its program began in 1892.

He not only owns the highest winning percentage at the school (64 percent) since World War II, but he's only the fifth of the 15 coaches in school history with more than 20 games of service to win more than he lost as a Gamecock.

Rather than be spooked by the school's historic lack of success, Spurrier was drawn to it when he accepted the job in 2005, one year after a discouraging two-season stint in the NFL, where he was 12–20 with the Washington Redskins.

"There was nowhere to go but up. I like those situations," Spurrier said. "There were a whole bunch of firsts we could achieve there at South Carolina if we could keep it going. I had a few buddies say, 'You can't win there. Nobody else has.'"

Spurrier did, piling up achievements never before seen in Columbia along the way. From 2005 to 2012, he added the following "firsts" to the school records books (deep breath time here): 11-win season (2011 and again in 2012); top 10 national finish (2011, 2012); six-win SEC season (2011); SEC East title

*Coach Steve Spurrier talks to quarterback Connor Shaw as D.L. Moore looks on during the first half of a game against Tennessee, on Saturday, October 27, 2012, at Williams-Brice Stadium in Columbia, South Carolina.* (AP Photo/ Richard Shiro)

(2010); defeat of a No. 1 team (Alabama, 2010); defeat of rivals Georgia, Tennessee, and Florida in the same season (2010, 2011); back-to-back wins over Tennessee (2010, 2011); road win over Florida (2010); road win over Tennessee (2005); five consecutive bowl appearances; undefeated SEC East season (2011); successful recruitment of nation's No. 1 high school player (Jadeveon Clowney); and five straight seasons with seven or more wins.

"If we could get it going the right way, we thought we could do it," Spurrier said. "I thought that it was a place that had not reached its potential yet. It was very similar to when I went to Florida in 1990; they had not reached their potential prior to that. I was lucky to be there at the right time in the right place. That's what coaching is all about—get somewhere at the right time in the right place with some good players. It took a few years to get really good players here."

Spurrier was 28–22 in his first four seasons (hardly the kind of success he had become accustomed to in a 12-year run at Florida that included six SEC championships and a national title), and he considered leaving after the 2008 season, which ended with consecutive losses to Florida, Clemson, and Iowa by a combined score of 118–30.

"We wanted to try to see what we could do at South Carolina. I just thought it was a state and a university with tremendous potential that maybe hadn't quite been run right," Spurrier said. "You always hope you can do it real quickly. I think we just didn't put together a team that was quite capable as quickly."

It finally turned around in 2010, which began a three-year stretch in which South Carolina was 31–9.

In December 2012, the 67-year-old Spurrier, who once predicted he wouldn't coach into his 60s, signed a two-year contract extension that pushed his deal through the 2017 season, and he said he just might finish out that contract, which would have him coaching until age 72.

"A lot of people tell me, 'You'll be there five years. What else are you going to do?' I sort of stop and think, 'Heck, you may be right.' All I know is when I was 55, I never thought I'd be coaching even in my 60s. Then you get to be 65," Spurrier said. "I don't see how retirement is all that much fun. I can't see that right now. So we'll keep pushing this thing, [and] maybe we can win us an SEC [championship] the next two or three years."

He added that his retirement, when it comes, could come out of the blue.

"When I leave, it's going to be, 'Bang!'" he said. "When it feels like the right time or there is something else I want to do, or this, that, and the other."

# 2 George Rogers— Heisman Trophy Winner

When the Tennessee Volunteers forced Coach Bill Battle out the door following a 6–5 season in 1976, it was cause for rejoicing in Knoxville, Tennessee. The way had been cleared for native son Johnny Majors, who had just won the national title at Pittsburgh, to return home and take over the reins.

For a high school running back in Duluth, Georgia, it was not such a happy time, though. For months—maybe for years, honestly—George Rogers had been planning to play his college football for the Volunteers.

"I had an aunt who always helped me out by giving me clothes and things and she worked for a doctor who was a big Tennessee fan, so I had a big attachment to Tennessee through that," he said.

His recruiting visit to the school clinched his decision.

"I was going to go to Tennessee," he said.

But Rogers didn't know Johnny Majors from Johnny Appleseed, so he threw open his recruiting process once again when Battle was dismissed.

"I wasn't going to go in on a coaching change," Rogers said.

Coaches from around the country flooded to then-tiny Duluth, trying to profit from Tennessee's loss. South Carolina coach Jim Carlen came to town outgunned. The Gamecocks were coming off a 6–5 season that seemed just like all the 6–5 seasons before it, but Carlen sold what he had to offer—a stage.

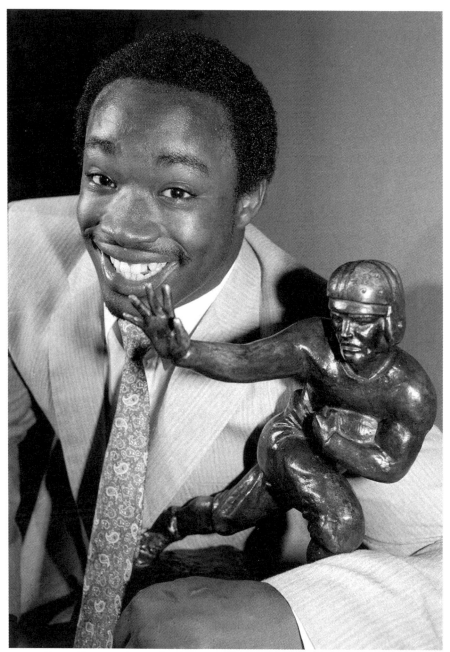

*George Rogers embraces the Heisman Trophy awarded him at the Downtown Athletic Club in New York City on December 1, 1980.* (AP Photo/Dave Pickoff)

"He said, 'Son, I know everybody is offering you everything, but we just want to give you a scholarship and to [have you] play your freshmen year.' When he said that, I was going to South Carolina."

Rogers just had to break the news to his family. The Gamecocks were a college football vagabond, an independent school that hadn't won more than seven games in a season since 1903.

"Believe me, when I said South Carolina, my whole family blew up. They said, 'No way,'" Rogers said.

At first, Rogers' mother refused to sign his scholarship papers. But she eventually relented, and Rogers was off to Columbia where Carlen made good on his promise of playing time and then some.

The Gamecocks did not win a title during Rogers' tenure, but no player could ask for more opportunity. He holds the school's career records for yards (5,204) and carries (954). He rushed for 623 yards as a freshman and 1,006 as a sophomore while sharing carries with Johnnie Wright.

Then two things happened that changed the course of Rogers' life and the future of South Carolina football. Carlen and the Gamecocks transitioned from the dual-back veer offense to the I-formation, which features one back. Originally, that back was going to be Wright, and the 6'2", 228-lb. Rogers was penciled in as the fullback.

"Lo and behold, Johnnie got hurt," Rogers said. "From there on, I was getting the ball a lot."

Rogers carried the ball 311 times for 1,681 yards in his junior season, and South Carolina reached the eight-win mark for the second time in school history.

"One thing you knew when you played the South Carolina Gamecocks is you didn't have to worry about what we were going to do. We were going to run the football," Rogers said.

Rogers' junior year made him a household name among college football fans and set the stage for 1980, when he carried the ball an astounding 324 times for 1,894 yards and won the school's only Heisman Trophy.

"George not only could run over you, he could outrun you," then-South Carolina quarterback Garry Harper told *The State* (Columbia, SC) newspaper.

The next year, Rogers was the NFL's No. 1 overall draft pick by the New Orleans Saints, going one spot ahead of a linebacker from the University of North Carolina named Lawrence Taylor.

When Marcus Lattimore came along in 2010, a debate would begin about who was the best running back in South Carolina history. (That's a debate Rogers wants no part of, by the way. "You have to look at the Duce Staleys and the Harold Greens, too," he said. "I don't try to be better than everybody else.") But there is no doubt about who is the most decorated running back ever to wear the garnet and black.

Among the lines on Rogers' resume are Heisman Trophy winner, South Carolina's first consensus All-American, 1981 NFL Offensive Rookie of the Year, 1988 Super Bowl champion (as a member of the Washington Redskins), and member of the halls of fame for College Football, South Carolina Athletics, South Carolina, Georgia, and the New Orleans Saints.

When asked how he'd like fans to remember his Gamecocks career, Rogers said, "I would tell them that I got my education at the University of South Carolina."

# 2001—Opening for Elvis and the Gamecocks

South Carolina began playing football in 1892. Richard Strauss composed "Also Sprach Zarathustra" in 1896.

But it took the confluence of Tommy Suggs and Elvis Presley in the early 1970s to bring the two things together and create one of the most iconic entrances in college football. The music, which rises higher and higher into a dramatic crescendo, is better known as "2001" because it was used in the 1968 movie, *2001: A Space Odyssey*. Elvis used the piece as his introduction music for concerts during the 1970s when Suggs twice saw him live—once in Columbia at the Carolina Coliseum and once in Louisiana while Suggs attended banking school at LSU. During the show in Louisiana, Suggs told friend Alex Miller, "I am going to take that back to Coach [Jim] Carlen because that is going to be our new entry song at Carolina Stadium."

So Suggs, a former South Carolina quarterback who has gone on to a 40-year career in the Gamecocks' radio booth, found a tape of the music and played it for Carlen, who was immediately on board... except for one key detail. Carlen wanted the school's marching band to perform it. Suggs explained it needed to be played over the stadium's loudspeakers, but Carlen insisted on the band. So in 1981, the South Carolina marching band played "2001" before two games. Few people in the crowd heard it, and it looked like the idea might die there.

Suggs stuck with it, though. When Carlen left after the 1981 season, Suggs took the music to Athletics Director Bob Marcum, who also loved it. But once again, there was a problem. Marcum didn't think the football stadium's antiquated sound system could play the music loud enough to inspire much of anything in the crowd. Marcum suggested they hold off one more year because a $120,000 sound system was being installed the following year, which turned out to be the only season in which Richard Bell served as head coach.

In 1983, the Gamecocks had a new coach and, at long last, a new theme song.

## The Nickname

South Carolina's athletic teams have been known as the Gamecocks since the early 1900s, and it remains one of the country's most unique nicknames.

Only South Carolina and Jacksonville State University in Alabama use the Gamecock as a mascot. It is a nickname that has strong roots in the state. Revolutionary War hero Thomas Sumter was known as "The Fighting Gamecock" during his time with the South Carolina militia. Actual gamecocks are the combatants in the mostly outlawed sport of cockfighting, which also has deep roots in South Carolina.

"Those early teams must have been a feisty and spirited group," according to the school's athletic website. "A gamecock, of course, is a fighting rooster known for its spirit and courage. A cockfight, which was a popular sport throughout the United States in the 19th century, would last until the death of one of the combatants. Cockfighting has been outlawed by most states for humanitarian reasons, but it is still held surreptitiously in many areas."

PETA (People for the Ethical Treatment of Animals) has asked the NCAA to ban the nickname.

"Our position is that since cockfighting is illegal in 48 states in this country and a felony in South Carolina—you go to jail, period—we don't think schools should be promoting this illegal act with their mascots," PETA's Dan Shannon told *The Birmingham News* in 2005. "Our problem with Gamecocks is it promotes cockfighting. That's not only illegal but tremendously cruel to the animals involved. We've been in contact with the presidents of these universities for several years. We've exchanged polite letters back and forth, very polite and respectful, but they have chosen not to change their names."

"Joe Morrison came and his first game at home we played the real '2001' as we know it now," Suggs said. "That's where the confusion came in that Joe Morrison started it. He did start it the way it is played now, but it wasn't his idea. It just happened to come on the first game he was here. The rest is history."

The music became synonymous with South Carolina football and remains so today.

"I travel all over the country and if people hear South Carolina football, two things come out of their mouth. They say, 'Steve Spurrier,' and they say, 'Man, that entrance to '2001' is unbelievable,'" said Todd Ellis, the team's play-by-play voice and a former South Carolina quarterback. "It's iconic. It still makes the hair on the back of my neck stand up when we play it. It's truly one of the trademarks of the University of South Carolina."

As the music peaks and the Gamecocks pour through a cloud of smoke onto the playing field, the crowd at Williams-Brice Stadium erupts.

"Clearly that's a wonderful call to arms for all the Gamecocks," former athletic director Mike McGee said. "I was at Southern Cal for nine years, and we had the Trojan band. It was supposedly one of the best in the country, and it was, and I often thought about how the Southern Cal fight song was well known, obviously. But there is a uniqueness about '2001.'"

The man who championed the song through many roadblocks knew it could be a point of pride for his school, but he never imagined it would grow to be what it has become today.

"I know there is an emotional pitch before a game starts, and I just felt like if we could do something to get the crowd up and get everybody emotional about the running on the field that it could eventually be one of the tops in the country. But I probably didn't realize [how] much national play it would get," Suggs said.

When Suggs watched a television replay of the 2012 South Carolina–Georgia game that matched the No. 5 and No. 6 teams in the country, he appreciated again the significance of the song when television announcers Brent Musburger and Kirk Herbstreit remained silent while it played.

"For about a minute and a half, two minutes, they said nothing," Suggs said. "They just said, 'Sit back and enjoy.'"

# 4 Black Magic in 1984

When Joe Morrison was asked by South Carolina's sports information staff to forecast the upcoming 1984 season, he said this, among other things:

"We should be an improved football team for 1984. The question will be how improved our opponents are. With the exception of a couple of quarters last season, we were pretty much a competitive football team. This year we want to be competitive every quarter we play. We can't take anyone lightly, but neither do I think anyone can take us lightly."

In August, when it appeared in the media guide, it sounded like typical coach speak. The Gamecocks were coming off a 5–6 record in 1983, Morrison's first year at the helm. Two months later, it sounded like Morrison had been sandbagging.

"That [season] was surprising," said Tommy Suggs, a former South Carolina quarterback who by that time had moved into the team's radio broadcast booth. "I just didn't see that coming. I felt like we had good talent but not great talent. That was a surprising year, which made it probably more euphoric and enjoyable."

The 1984 season would see the Gamecocks run out to a 9–0 record and the No. 2 ranking in the country. Along the way to the best start in school history, the 1984 team earned the nickname "Black Magic," a nod to Morrison's all-black attire and his habit of wiggling out of trouble with a win.

The sorcery started right away when The Citadel came to town to open the season. When the Gamecocks scored to take a 31–24 lead with 1:02 left in the game, it appeared they had finally subdued the underdog Bulldogs. Instead, Citadel's Mike Lewis took the ensuing kickoff back to the 18-yard line before being stopped by Chris Major.

With 22 seconds left, Citadel quarterback Robert Hill hoisted one last pass to the end zone, but it was intercepted by Otis Morris.

In *100 Years of Gamecock Football*, a video tribute to the Gamecocks released in 1992, narrator Ron Franklin said, "Plays like that would eventually be attributed to Black Magic."

After a 21–0 win over Duke, South Carolina got to the meat of its season, tackling a No. 12 Georgia team that had won three straight SEC titles earlier in the decade.

"There was a different type of feeling in the locker room before the [Georgia] game," offensive linemen Del Wilkes said on *100 Years of Gamecock Football*. "It was a quietness I had never been around. You could look in the guys' eyes and you could tell that this was something different."

What was different was the result. South Carolina hadn't beaten the Bulldogs since 1979, but it would triumph 17–10 that day thanks, of course, to more Black Magic. Backup quarterback Mike Hold had to replace injured started Allen Mitchell in the fourth quarter. At the time, Hold had participated in seven plays as a collegian, but he found Ira Hillary for a 62-yard gain to set up the game-winning touchdown.

"I've never been prouder of, or happier for, a bunch of individuals than I am for this football team tonight," Morrison said in his post-game press conference. "I thought last year that the [win over] Southern Cal was the biggest win my coaching staff had [enjoyed] in a long, long time. But I think this one is bigger."

As Gamecocks cheerleaders sprinted the sideline, waving black flags featuring a skull and crossbones and the words "Black Death," South Carolina would win six more in a row, including beating mighty Notre Dame in South Bend, Indiana.

"The hoopla, the frenzy that was going on was sick," Hold said. "I still get chill bumps when I think about it."

Those were heady times for the Gamecocks and their fans. One of Tommy Suggs' favorite stories from the season centers on the N.C. State game in the eighth week of the season. Suggs, a former quarterback who works in the team's radio booth, was riding to the game with John Lanahan, a former Notre Dame offensive lineman who at the time was a member of the Gator Bowl selection committee.

"John was telling me, 'One of the reasons we want South Carolina so much if we have a shot at them is because your fans are such quality fans. They are such respected fans. They are not a bunch of crazy people,'" Suggs said. "So we pull up to the stadium and all our fans are dressed in black like Joe Morrison, and they are throwing oranges at the N.C. State fans, [and] I'm saying, 'John, just forget that.'"

The oranges were a symbol of South Carolina's belief that it was headed to the Orange Bowl, a thought that seemed perfectly valid when the Gamecocks beat N.C. State 35–28 and Florida State 38–26. After trouncing the Seminoles, the Gamecocks moved to No. 2 in the nation, which remains the top mark in school history.

The magic ended on November 17 when unranked Navy upended South Carolina and its season with a 38–21 win in Annapolis, Maryland. The loss still stands as the most painful in school history.

The Gamecocks salvaged the year in the regular season finale against Clemson, and it took the last drop of Black Magic. South Carolina trailed 21–15 when it took the ball at its own 16-yard line with 3:07 left. Two minutes and 14 seconds later, Hold dove across the goal line for a 1-yard touchdown that tied the game at 21–21.

The ghost of Navy seemed to be alive when South Carolina junior Scott Hagler, dubbed "Mr. Consistency" in the Gamecocks' media guide, missed the extra point. However, the Tigers were flagged for being offside, and Hagler connected on his second chance.

"I still say [that] had it been reversed and we beat Navy and lost to Clemson, I don't think they would remember that year the way they do," Hold said.

# 5 Carolina-Clemson—The Rivalry

The rivalry started in 1889 with a man named Pitchfork Ben Tillman. And honestly, it's probably only gotten more heated from there.

Before he was elected governor of South Carolina in 1890 and then U.S. Senator in 1895, Tillman was a champion of South Carolina farmers who had grown weary of the fact that the state's flagship university in Columbia seemed more interested in taking boys off the farm than teaching them how to tend it.

"The agricultural element said that [the school was] spending farmers' money to educate lawyers," said Don Barton, a former South Carolina sports information director and a South Carolina athletics historian.

So Pitchfork Ben helped found Clemson in 1889, and "The Agriculture vs. The Aristocracy" was born. Legislation passed along with the founding of Clemson pushed down South Carolina's enrollment to 89 students, while Clemson opened its doors with more than 400.

South Carolina and Clemson would not play their first football game for another seven years, but "it was a rivalry before they ever hit the field," Barton said.

Jeff Grantz, who quarterbacked South Carolina to its most emphatic victory in the series (a 56–20 win in 1975 during which the Gamecocks scored a touchdown on every possession), grew up just outside Baltimore, Maryland. He made his recruiting visit to South Carolina during one of the Gamecocks' games against the Tigers.

"Right then I knew how big a rivalry it was, and I was never disappointed," Grantz said. "I think it's similar to Auburn-Alabama because you really don't have any professional football [in either state]. People in this state are a Carolina fan or a Clemson fan."

Clemson leads the overall series 65–41–4 and leads in tradition (17 conference champions vs. one), which has only served to make South Carolina's current four-game winning streak that much sweeter.

The Gamecocks won the first meeting in 1896 (12–6) but would win just two of the next 16 games. Since then, droughts have been more frequent than winning streaks for South Carolina. Through it all, however, the rivalry has never lost its fierceness.

In 2004, the teams engaged in an end-of-game brawl so raucous that each university withdrew its team from bowl consideration.

How can a small state produce such a hot-blooded rivalry? Precisely because it is a small state, Barton said.

"Being a small state makes it even more heated because we interbreed," Barton said. "You can hardly see a family that doesn't have both Carolina and Clemson, including mine. In fact, I was a rabid Clemson fan growing up [in Anderson]. I became a born-again Gamecock."

Tommy Suggs, who quarterbacked South Carolina to the 1969 ACC title and has worked 40 years in the football team's radio booth, had a similarly religious conversion. (Yes, it counts as religion here.) He and his family were Clemson fans when he grew up in Lamar, South Carolina.

Meanwhile, former Gamecocks quarterback Steve Taneyhill grew up in the 1980s halfway between Penn State and the University of Pittsburgh. In those days, the Nittany Lions and Panthers were two of the country's top programs and the rivalry was heated, but that game lost its sizzle years ago. Taneyhill doesn't believe Carolina-Clemson ever will.

Heading into his first rivalry game in 1992, Taneyhill asked his teammates, "What's this thing like?"

"I figured it out after the game and the ensuing months," he said. "You figure out that it's awfully important to a lot of people. Here we are 20 years later, and I still hear it. 'You can't do this, you're a Carolina guy.' It's a special, special thing for us."

Former Gamecocks quarterback Mike Hold, an Arizona native, also had to be indoctrinated into the rivalry upon his arrival in South Carolina. When friends first asked Hold about his favorite game from the 1984 season, he thought the answer was obvious.

"I'd always say Notre Dame. We won at Notre Dame," he said. "I quickly learned that Clemson was the right answer."

# 6 Marcus Lattimore— A Difference Maker

He walked away, gingerly at the time, on December 12, 2012, leaving behind a South Carolina career full of both historic production and unfulfilled potential.

Marcus Lattimore's Gamecocks career will be remembered less for its highs (National Freshman of the Year honors in 2010 and the school record in touchdowns) and lows (two devastating knee injuries) than for its lasting legacy.

"What he has done for us is the reason the University of South Carolina is not only a football program of significance but that our university is talked about around the country," Coach Steve Spurrier said on the day Lattimore announced his attention to skip his senior season and enter the NFL draft. "People know we have had some success, and it really all happened three years ago. It happened when Marcus Lattimore said, 'I'm coming to the University of South Carolina.'"

That happened on February 3, 2010, in Silver Hills Baptist Church in Spartanburg, South Carolina. The 6', 218-lb. Lattimore was the state's Mr. Football and considered one of the nation's top 10 high school prospects by every major recruiting service. At the time, it wasn't fashionable for an elite high school player to come to South Carolina, but Lattimore changed that.

"Very few guys do I remember where I was when he committed, and I remember where I was when Marcus committed," Spurrier said. "I was in my office with the TV on, like probably all you other Gamecocks, and we remember where we were when Marcus said he was going to sign with South Carolina."

According to Lattimore, he was lured to South Carolina because he wasn't going to be "the next" anybody—he was going to be the first Marcus.

"They know my skills and know what I can do," he said at his signing ceremony. "But I was never guaranteed a starting spot, I can tell you that. I think if I can come in and work hard enough, I can be out there the first game."

Lattimore didn't start his first game but came off the bench quickly to gain 54 yards on 14 carries against Southern Miss. The next week was his coming-out party, a 182-yard two-touchdown effort that steamrolled Georgia, and Lattimore was off to the races.

He would rush for more than 100 yards in a game 10 more times in his career, and he would finish tied for second in school history in that category. He finished his career with 2,677 yards, which is sixth in school history behind five players who all played four years with the Gamecocks.

Lattimore played in only 29 of the 40 games South Carolina played during his three-year career due to major knee injuries that ended his sophomore and junior seasons. The first came in 2011

*Marcus Lattimore (21) runs away from Kentucky's Mike Douglas (50) during the second half of a game in Lexington, Kentucky, on September 29, 2012.*
(AP Photo/Garry Jones, File)

when he tore the ACL in his left knee against Mississippi State and missed the final six games of the season.

After a ballyhooed return in 2012, Lattimore rushed for 662 yards in nine games before suffering one of the most devastating hits in South Carolina history in a victory over Tennessee—a direct blow that dislocated his right knee and resulted in a tear of three of his four major ligaments, including the ACL.

Volunteers wide receiver Zach Rogers called it "one of the worst injuries I've seen in person," and Lattimore said he thought his football career was over as he was wheeled off the Williams-Brice turf on a medical cart. However, somewhat amazingly, Lattimore suffered no irreversible damage from the injury and still felt ready to leave South Carolina for a shot at an NFL career after three seasons. He was selected by San Francisco in the fourth round of the 2013 NFL Draft.

Lattimore's impact on the South Carolina football program is not limited to the statistics he posted or the three seasons he played, Spurrier said.

"Let me tell you where we were three years ago. I had been here five years and, as some sportswriter said, I was a pedestrian 35–28 five years in," Spurrier said. "We were hovering around 7–6, 6–6, and we signed Marcus Lattimore. In the last three years we have won 30 games, won the Eastern Division, beat Georgia three, beat Tennessee three, beat Clemson three, Florida two out of three, first 11-win season, first top 10 ever."

Lattimore's signing helped pave the way for the Gamecocks to sign the next two Mr. Footballs in the state, including defensive end Jadeveon Clowney, the No. 1 prospect in the country. In addition, Spurrier often credited Lattimore's leadership from the weight room to the locker room as one of the most important factors in South Carolina's turnaround.

"Marcus, first of all, is one of my favorite players not because he is maybe the best running back I have ever coached, but because he is an unselfish player who wants to do what is best for the team," Spurrier said. "Not only is he a leader on the field, weight room, [and] conditioning, he [also] goes to class and he does everything the coaches ask [him] to do and then more."

"Lattimore's impact at South Carolina will live long past his playing days," Spurrier added.

"We will refer back, 'Remember how Marcus used to do this or that?'" Spurrier said. "Hopefully what Marcus has done here will continue and pass on to the other guys."

# 7 Cocky—More Than a Mindset

On February 6, 2013, Cocky—the strutting, yellow-beaked, bushy-tailed, costumed mascot of the South Carolina Gamecocks—was recognized on the floor of the South Carolina State House.

"He needs virtually no introduction, but for those of you who can't see, his name is Cocky," the speaker said to resounding cheers.

It was a much different reception than the Gamecocks' official mascot received the first time he was introduced. That came on October 18, 1980, in a homecoming game against Cincinnati. The university was transitioning from the unofficial Big Spur, a staple for two years after its creation by a student, to the new school-sanctioned version that season. However, the new Cocky costume was running late. So John Routh and his fellow Cocky, the two students who won the job in open tryouts before the season, used a modified version of the old Big Spur costume in the first six games of the 1980 season.

The unveiling of the Cocky costume came at halftime of the seventh game, against Cincinnati.

"We built this chicken roost that was supposed to be wheeled out from underneath the stands as the band was playing at half-time, and Cocky was going to pop out of the roost," Routh said. "Well, we built the chicken roost a little too tall and couldn't get it out from underneath the stadium. So when the P.A. announcer

## The Geralds

It's always a neat story when the son of a college football player signs to play with his father's alma mater. When two sons are good enough to make it, it's an even better story. When the two sons both carry their father's first name and are separated by five months, it's a doozy.

Gerald Dixon was a standout defensive lineman for the Gamecocks in 1990 and 1991 and went on to a 10-year career in the NFL. In 2011, his sons Gerald Dixon Jr. and Gerald Gervais Dixon were both members of South Carolina's signing class, and both were defensive linemen.

"I could see where this could get difficult," Gerald Sr. told the *Chattanooga Times Free Press*. "It's like the old *Newhart* show when Larry would say, 'This is my brother Darryl, and this is my other brother Darryl.' It's just going to be one of those things, but I think they will distinguish themselves by the way they play."

The brothers were born to different women and grew up near each other in Rock Hill, South Carolina.

"At that time, the mothers that I had the kids by wanted to name the kids Gerald," Gerald Sr. told the *Times Free Press*. "That was the name they were going to stick with. The first one was Gerald Jr. and the second was Gerald Gervais, so we kept it simple like that. They're great kids, and they've lived up to the name so far."

The Dixon boys, who are expected to become contributors on South Carolina's defensive line, are now known as Junior and G.

goes, 'Ladies and gentlemen, your new mascot Cocky!' there was nothing. So it didn't start well."

When Cocky did emerge, most fans were unimpressed. Their mascot had gone from a 7' barnyard rooster that looked like its fighting namesake to the fluffy, kid-friendly Cocky.

"A lot of fans wrote letters to the athletic department asking that Big Spur be brought back, so that's what we did," said Routh, now the director of the University of Miami Sports Hall of Fame.

The re-purposed Big Spur costume finished out the season, and it looked like the end for Cocky. However, during basketball season, the school's cheerleading advisor suggested the costume could be used for women's basketball games.

"She said, 'Why don't we just put lips and eyelashes on it and call it SuperChick?' So Cocky was remade as SuperChick," Routh said.

From there, Routh eventually took the cause to baseball coach June Raines.

"I said, 'We've got this costume. Would it be alright if I came out and did some games?' He was like, 'Sure, come on out, have some fun,'" Routh said.

So Routh scrubbed off the lips and eyelashes, and Cocky was born again. The Gamecocks advanced to the College World Series that season, and Cocky was such a hit that he was invited to Omaha, Nebraska, for the event. A few victories in Omaha and suddenly Cocky was a conquering hero.

"That started the ball rolling for Cocky," Routh said. "I am recognized as the original, and it's kind of neat that something has lasted this long. Every school loves their mascot, but Cocky has really become one of those eight or 10 really recognizable mascots."

Cocky is now everywhere the Gamecocks are…and plenty of other places, too. In 2003, he was the winner of the national Capital One Mascot Challenge. ESPN's Chris Fowler, the host of the network's popular *College GameDay* show, often refers to South Carolina simply as "Cocky" when updating the status of Gamecocks games.

"Very few mascots get that kind of recognition as the face of the university," Routh said.

Now Big Spur lives on only at Safran's Antiques in downtown Columbia, where owner Mike Safran has the menacing head perched high on a shelf. It's probably best left there, Routh believes.

"It wasn't a huggable, lovable mascot. It was tough looking. Big Spur scared a lot of kids," he said. "That was another reason [to change to Cocky]—to have something the kids could get attached to. The [Big Spur] tail stuck out about 5', and it had these metal rods in it. There were several cheerleaders who were knocked down by it when he turned too quickly and knocked a cheerleader in the head."

# 8 Joe Morrison—The Man in Black

Picture a man who is 6'1", 200 lbs., and a 14-year NFL veteran. He is standing at one end of South Carolina's practice field, dressed head-to-toe in black, with sunglasses too dark to see through and smoking a cigarette in the sweltering Columbia heat.

Meet Joe Morrison, the man in black.

"He was silent and strong," said former quarterback Todd Ellis, who played for Morrison from 1986–88. "You looked at him and you saw 14 years of NFL play and experience. He was a football player probably more than he was a football coach. He just oozed that experience."

Morrison, who was hired away from New Mexico, did what few men before him had been able to do—he won at South Carolina. He was 39–28 from 1983–88, and some people around the program believe he would have made the Gamecocks title contenders if not for his sudden death of heart failure on February 5, 1989.

"He was a player's coach. He took care of his players," said Corey Miller, who played linebacker for Morrison. "He knew how to relate to us. He was a pro guy. He coached South Carolina like it was a pro team. He loved his guys. It was awesome."

Athletics Director Bob Marcum had his eye on Morrison for a while before hiring him to replace Richard Bell.

## Cha-Cha Slide

It will never get the respect of the waltz or have the tradition of the tango, but for a few months in South Carolina, there was no more popular dance than the cha-cha slide.

It was a few steps of that dance between Coach Steve Spurrier and the mother of then-recruit Marcus Lattimore that was credited with sealing the deal in Lattimore's recruitment.

"Coach Spurrier has really loosened up," Yolanda Smith told *The State* newspaper. "I made the comment in the past where I felt he was unapproachable. He's made a 180. I had this coach doing the cha-cha slide with no music. He was just great. He had his arms open wide every time he saw me. He speaks to me personally. He's been so personable with us lately. He's really changed as far as myself. He came over to the hotel and sat around with us, and we had a really good time."

Lattimore would go on to sign with the Gamecocks.

"That's where my heart is," Lattimore said during his signing-day ceremony. "And [Spurrier] did the cha-cha slide with my mama."

Lattimore showed fancy footwork of his own later that year, leading South Carolina to the SEC East title with 1,197 rushing yards. He was named the National Freshman of the Year that season and left the school as its sixth-leading rusher in history (2,677 yards).

"Bob Marcum called me one night and said, 'I want you to go to dinner with me and someone. He's going to be our next football coach,'" said Tommy Suggs, a former South Carolina quarterback and 40-year veteran of the school's radio booth.

Morrison, who was joined at dinner by his friend and Pro Football Hall of Famer Sam Huff, told great stories that night, Suggs said. It might have been more words than Morrison spoke during his entire tenure at South Carolina.

"I knew that Joe was a man of few words, and I knew what he wanted to get out of his football program," Suggs said. "He was very determined in how he wanted it done."

Morrison was the Giants' captain for seven years, the team's Most Valuable Player in three seasons, and he had his No. 40 jersey retired. He spent three seasons coaching at New Mexico, where he went 4–7, 4–7–1, and then 10–1. Prior to his stint at New Mexico, he led Tennessee-Chattanooga's program. In 1984, he was named National Coach of the Year with the Gamecocks.

"There was a mystique about him," All-American offensive lineman Del Wilkes said in 1992 on *100 Years of Gamecock Football*. "He was a quiet man, a man of few words, and people like that are intriguing."

Morrison's tenure saw the high of the 1984 Black Magic season, which got its name partly from Morrison's wardrobe, and the low of 1988 season, which saw a steroid scandal and losses to Georgia Tech, Florida State, and Clemson by a combined score of 122–10.

He recruited and coached some of the greatest players in school history in Ellis, Miller, Wilkes, and wide receiver Sterling Sharpe. Ellis remembers Morrison's recruiting fondly.

"All these coaches called me all the time. For a year and a half, I never even answered the phone in my house, but Joe Morrison told me, 'I will call you every Friday morning at 7:30 before you get on that bus, and I'll never talk to you more than three minutes unless you want to ask me something.' And I am telling you that for a year he called me every Friday morning at 7:30, and we talked for two or three minutes," Ellis said.

Ellis believes Morrison might have turned his success at South Carolina into an NFL job had he lived.

"He certainly was more of a head coach administrator, but he knew the game," Ellis said. "He was not a big salesman. He's not like these guys today because you have to be part carnival guy, part CEO, part football player, and everything else."

# 9 Defensive Back U.

The modern line traces its roots back to Terry Cousin, but the history goes back further than that.

Bobby Bryant, who weighed 140 lbs. when he graduated from high school in Macon, Georgia, is actually the Godfather of one of the most impressive lineages in college football history. Bryant was drafted in the seventh round of the 1967 NFL-AFL Draft and played 13 seasons for the Minnesota Vikings, starting a streak of South Carolina defensive backs filling up NFL rosters that hasn't stopped.

Rick Sanford, now a Columbia chiropractor and talk radio host, continued the trend in the modern era of the NFL. Sanford was the first South Carolina player at any position to be selected in the first round (by the New England Patriots) of the NFL draft. It figures he was a defensive back.

Sanford was taken No. 25 overall in the 1979 NFL Draft and went on to play seven seasons in the NFL, six of those with the Patriots.

In all, 27 South Carolina defensive backs have been selected by the NFL, with 13 players chosen since 2002. Earl Johnson, Norman Floyd, and Brad Edwards, who played nine years and nearly won a Super Bowl MVP trophy, followed in the 10 years after Sanford.

Things really took off in 1997 when Terry Cousin signed a free agent contract with the Chicago Bears. Cousin played 12 years in the NFL, starting 69 games and making Gamecocks defensive backs a hot commodity.

"If you want to play at the next level and you play in the secondary, it should be a no-brainer," said former Gamecocks cornerback Sheldon Brown, who was taken in the second round of the 2002 NFL Draft. "If I was a parent, with the success rate of the

*Stephon Gilmore (rear) reaches above East Carolina's Joe Womack (82) to break up a pass during a game in Charlotte, North Carolina, on Saturday, September 3, 2011. South Carolina defeated East Carolina 56–37.* (AP Photo/ Bob Leverone)

DBs leaving here and going there, I would definitely want to send my kids [to South Carolina]. It's a tradition."

From 2004 through the 2012 season, Brown started at least 14 games each season for the Philadelphia Eagles and Cleveland Browns. NFL scouts and general managers know to look for South Carolina products in the secondary, according to Brown.

"Without a doubt, especially right now in this era because you have one after another that is learning from the guy in front of him," Brown added.

While safeties like Ko Simpson have gotten into the mix, too, South Carolina cornerbacks have carried most of the weight of the tradition. In 2011, five of the NFL's 64 starting cornerbacks were South Carolina graduates—Brown, Johnathan Joseph, André Goodman, Captain Munnerlyn, and Dunta Robinson. Chris Culliver was a rookie backup that season, as well.

In 2012, Gamecocks cornerback Stephon Gilmore was selected No. 10 overall by the Buffalo Bills. Fred Bennett, Stoney Woodson, Emmanuel Cook, Deandré Eiland, Willie Offord, Arturo Freeman, and Lee Wiggins have also been part of the history in one form or another.

"It just shows the type of players that the university produces year in and year out," Joseph said. "I think it's always going to keep going."

The standard set by past players at the position is one of the reasons Joseph thinks the streak won't stop anytime soon.

"That is a big factor in it. A lot of the reason I came here is because of Sheldon Brown and Dunta Robinson," Joseph said. "Those guys kind of paved the way for me. It's always about playing at a high level and being accountable on and off the field and setting a good example for the younger guys and being a role model. They schooled me and taught me the ropes."

Goodman was drafted in the third round in 2002 and played 10 years in the NFL before taking a job mentoring South Carolina student athletes.

"The fact that these guys have been able to take this position at this university and then transition it to the pros and have great success like they have had, there is a great sense of pride that comes along with that, something [recruits] start to recognize when they hit this campus," Goodman said. "Those are the guys I am rooting for on a regular basis because it gives you a sense of, 'I am still playing the game through them.'"

# 10 1980—George Rogers' Heisman Season

When George Rogers was in high school in Duluth, Georgia, he told friends that legendary Nebraska running back Johnny Rodgers was his cousin.

"At the time, I didn't know his name was spelled with a 'D'," Rogers said.

Making yourself seem related to the 1972 Heisman Trophy winner just seemed like a good idea. Earl Campbell, who won the 1977 Heisman Trophy, was Rogers' boyhood idol, and Rogers "had heard of that guy from Buffalo" (O.J. Simpson, who won the 1968 Heisman).

Until 1979, that was as close as George Rogers had ever come to thinking about college football's most prestigious award. Then Rogers finished his junior season second in the nation in rushing with 1,681 yards.

"That's when I started keeping up with, 'Where am I at with the rushing?'" he said. "I was like, 'Next year, I am going to lead the [country] in rushing.'"

And he did with 1,894 yards, winning the 1980 Heisman Trophy because of it. It took some heroic efforts along the way.

Tommy Suggs, who led South Carolina to the 1969 ACC title as a quarterback and then became the color analyst for the Gamecocks' radio broadcasts, remembers the 1980 season as his most pressure-packed as a broadcaster.

"I was pulling so hard for [Rogers], and we had such big games that year," Suggs said. "It was such a showcase atmosphere for him and for our school. The excitement was just unbelievable and so wonderful to be a part of it. The pressure built up every game. Just every game, he had to get more than 125 yards or something like that. It was really interesting."

The Gamecocks' schedule set up well for Rogers that season with marquee games at Southern Cal and at Michigan in the first four weeks of the season. He responded both times, rushing for 141 yards on 26 carries in a 23–13 loss to the Trojans and 142 yards on 36 carries in a 17–14 upset win over the Wolverines.

"I will never forget the game at Southern Cal. They had 11 men right up there, and they hit [Rogers] so many times," said Bob Fulton, the school's play-by-play radio voice, on *100 Years of Gamecock Football*. "At the end of the game, every Southern Cal player came over and congratulated George. That's worth something."

Rogers, who had the 33rd-best single-season rushing performance in NCAA history that year, had at least 108 yards in every game of the 1980 season. His lowest total, that 108-yard effort, came on 10 carries against Wichita State in the second game of the season.

He had 168 or more yards six times, including a season- and career-high 224 against Duke on October 11. Still, throughout much of the season, the race remained too close to call, according to national pundits, and a close ballot was expected.

However, Don Barton thought differently. Barton, South Carolina's former sports information director and an athletic department historian, saw two things that season that boosted Rogers' profile.

"Nobody would ever remember this, but I do distinctly. Jimmy the Greek loved George," Barton said. "Every week [Jimmy] would hype George Rogers. He liked George Rogers, and he would show film of what George Rogers did that weekend."

Rogers himself cinched the award, Barton believes, during a nationally televised special shown on ABC before the voting deadline. Rogers, Pittsburgh defensive lineman Hugh Green, and Purdue quarterback Mark Herrmann, the presumptive finalists, were interviewed.

"They said, 'Hugh Green, why do you think you should win the Heisman Trophy?' He said, 'Well, there hasn't been a defensive player to win it, and I think it may be a good time for a defensive player to win.' They came to George and said, 'What do you think?' He said, 'I agree with Hugh. I think it's time for a defensive player to win it.' I think that just melted [the voters]," Barton said. "George was such a genuine person, and he was serious. It wouldn't have bothered him not to win that Heisman Trophy. He would have been happy for Hugh."

On December 1, Rogers was awarded the 46th Heisman Trophy in a relative runaway, beating out Green's 861 points with 1,128 points.

## 11 Steve Wadiak—The Cadillac

There is no more fascinating or more tragic career in South Carolina football history than that of Steve Wadiak.

He may have been the Gamecocks' first bona fide college football star, and he might have achieved that status in professional football if not for the early morning hours of March 9, 1952, when he was killed near Aiken, South Carolina, in an automobile accident as he and friends were returning to Columbia from an out-of-town party.

The next day the *Rome News-Tribune* reported, "The car in which [Wadiak] was riding left the highway and turned over five or six times. Wadiak and five companions were thrown from the four-door sedan. His head badly cut, his neck broken, the university football captain died soon after at an Augusta, Georgia, hospital."

The driver of the car, Joel Ray, was tried before a jury regarding the accident and death on March 25, 1952. Ray was cleared of responsibility when the jury concluded the accident was "unavoidable."

At Ray's trial, Highway Patrolman W. McTeer was asked about the details of the wreck.

"I asked [Ray] how fast he was traveling at the time, and he said between 70 and 80. I got measurements from the skid marks, tire marks rather, at the scene of the wreck, and from where he started leaving the pavement to where he left the pavement and got on the dirt to where he first turned over was 425'. After he turned over the first time, he went 183' turning over; the marks on the ground were plain each time it turned over," McTeer testified. "From the people that showed me where Wadiak landed, it was 57' from the car to where he was picked off the dirt."

According to his testimony, McTeer attempted to determine if alcohol was the cause of the accident.

"If they were drinking, sir, I couldn't tell it," he concluded, although he noted there was a "one pint [alcohol] bottle out of the car and away from the crash."

The news stunned Columbia, which had adopted Wadiak, a Chicago native, as one of their own. The details of Wadiak's pre-South Carolina football career are as murky as those from the night of his death, and some people speculated he never even attended high school and was simply a product of the neighborhood football league in his hometown.

In fact, the only thing about Steve Wadiak that is cut and dry is the fact that he was an outstanding football player.

"Steve Wadiak was a great player," said Don Barton, a former South Carolina sports information director and a Gamecocks historian. "He did not have the supporting cast that they have now."

The Gamecocks never won more than five games a year in Wadiak's four seasons, but it was not his fault. He led the Gamecocks in rushing in each of those seasons and was named All-Southern Conference in 1950 and 1951.

"He had a style of running. He had football speed," Barton said. "He had a flair for shedding players. Some players have that knack. He sort of shocked you when you got there, and you just sort of peeled off."

Wadiak's finest moment came on October 19, 1950, during South Carolina's annual Big Thursday meeting against Clemson. The Tigers had won their first three games by a combined score of 116–0 when they came to Columbia to face Wadiak and the Gamecocks.

Wadiak, nicknamed "The Cadillac," would rush for 256 yards, which is still the third-highest total in school history. He powered South Carolina to a 14–14 tie with a Tigers team that would not lose that season.

"He had an unusual ability once that football was in his hands," said Hootie Johnson, a teammate of Wadiak's who would go on to serve as chairman of Augusta National Golf Club.

Four months after that Clemson game, Wadiak was suspended from school for "an infraction of University rules." That infraction, Barton said, was dating a woman whom Wadiak did not know was married at the time.

"Steve Wadiak has always been a hard-working, clean-living football player," South Carolina Coach Rex Enright said, according to the *Rock Hill (SC) Herald* on March 1, 1951. "He is now involved in an infraction of the University rules. When he is permitted to return to the University, he will certainly be welcome on the football squad."

Wadiak did return to lead South Carolina in rushing once more in 1951. He ended his South Carolina career with 2,878 yards, a record that would stand for almost 30 years.

"He was the kind of guy who could run over you or run around you," Johnny Gramling, the quarterback on the 1951 team, said on *100 Years of Gamecock Football*. "He had extreme balance. Coaches would say, 'You let Gramling and [other players] do what the heck they want. You just watch Wadiak and stop him, and you'll stop the whole shooting match.'"

In 1951, Wadiak became the first South Carolina player to have his number retired.

# 12 Tommy Suggs— A Gamecock Life

In 1961, when members of South Carolina's Sigma Nu fraternity pulled what is known as "The Prank," Tommy Suggs and his family were not all that amused.

The Prank poked fun at the Tigers, and in 1961 Tommy Suggs was a Tiger fan. That's hard to imagine these days because no one has been involved with the South Carolina program longer or in more ways than Suggs.

The relationship began in 1968. Suggs had lots of options coming out of Lamar, South Carolina, and at the beginning, the

## Ms. K

From 1969 until 1988, Sue D. Kurpiewski ruled The Roost, or at least its dining room.

Ms. K., as the adoring athletes knew her, was the head dietician at the athletic village known as The Roost. When Kurpiewski died in 2008, the Gamecocks were quick to line up with Ms. K stories.

"Oh, wow," 1980 Heisman Trophy winner George Rogers said. "I loved her so much. She was the only lady who fed me bologna."

Rogers often survived on bologna sandwiches growing up in Duluth, Georgia, and he maintained his taste for them in college.

"Everyone else would be eating steak before games, but I'd say, 'Ms. K, if I had a bologna sandwich, I'd run like never before,'" Rogers told *The State* newspaper. "And she'd have me five bologna sandwiches. If I missed lunch, she'd let me in the back door to get a sandwich. I used to pick her up off the ground and hug her to death. She was my sweetheart."

Ms. K took her duties seriously, according to former quarterback Todd Ellis.

"What a lady," Ellis told *The State*. "You could have 200 athletes in the cafeteria, and she was 100 lbs. lighter and 2' smaller than any of them, but if you were supposed to have [a special diet of] tuna or thin lean meat, she'd make sure it was that way. You did not want to mess with Ms. K."

---

Gamecocks were low on the list. For a while, his first choice was Lefty Driesell and a basketball scholarship at Davidson. The second choice was Clemson on a football scholarship.

Paul Dietzel had arrived in Columbia to coach the Gamecocks in 1966. While Dietzel's coaching record at South Carolina wasn't stellar, no one who met him would argue he wasn't a terrific salesman. Dietzel convinced Suggs to turn down Driesell and spurn the Tigers to sign a scholarship with the Gamecocks. For Suggs, that meant calling Driesell.

"Coach Dietzel turned me, and I promised Lefty Driesell that I wouldn't sign a college football scholarship until I finished my senior year of basketball. I went on and committed to Carolina, and I had to call [Driesell] on the phone," Suggs said. "He got angry about it, which I don't blame him."

There was one more competitor left, though. The New York Mets were considering drafting Suggs to play shortstop in their organization. The Mets pushed Suggs to come with them full-time and give up his scholarship.

"That's the only way they would take me and I wouldn't do that, so I ended up going to Carolina in football," Suggs said.

Suggs had plenty of offers to play football and would have had more if he had stood taller than 5'9". He was a PARADE All-American football player at Lamar High School and helped usher in the era of the forward pass at South Carolina. When Suggs got to school, Johnny Gramling's 1,045 yards in 1953 was the most a Gamecocks quarterback had managed in one season. Suggs threw for 1,544 in 1968, 1,342 in 1969, and 2,030 in 1970. His 4,916 career yards still ranks seventh in school history.

"I was lucky," Suggs said. "I played with some good guys and had some good games, got on some good rolls. Good career."

Suggs threw three touchdown passes on November 15, 1969, when the Gamecocks beat Wake Forest 24–6 to clinch the ACC title (still their only conference crown), and he left school without ever losing to Clemson, a big feather in the cap of any Carolina quarterback.

"He was a leader," Bob Fulton said on *100 Years of Gamecock Football*. "The ballplayers had great respect for him. He was not a tall quarterback. He was short, but he was a great scrambler, and if you needed something near the end of the game, he was the one to get it for you."

Until Todd Ellis arrived on campus to pull the trigger on the run-and-shoot offense, Suggs owned every significant passing record in school history.

Suggs' influence on the school didn't end with his graduation. Not only is he responsible for making "2001" the entrance music for the Gamecocks, but for the last 40 years, he has served as the color analyst in the Gamecocks' radio booth.

From his current vantage point, he marvels at the fact that at the end of the 2012 season only four teams in the country had been ranked in the Associated Press Top 25 for more consecutive weeks than his Gamecocks.

"That's unbelievable," Suggs said. "I wish my daddy could see it because he never thought it would happen. It's hard to understand at times. I keep telling our fans, 'We have to wear it well.' We have to get used to it, not be braggadocios but be confident and go continue this thing. It's special."

# 13 Steve Taneyhill— The Mullet Man

After spending months praying that Steve Taneyhill would chose their beloved Gamecocks, South Carolina fans weren't sure what they'd gotten themselves into when the quarterback from Altoona, Pennsylvania, finally arrived.

One of the most highly recruited players in the nation in 1992, Taneyhill narrowed down 80 scholarship offers to Alabama, Florida State, Miami, UCLA, and South Carolina.

"South Carolina didn't have a quarterback that had played coming back," Taneyhill said. "The opportunity to play right away probably won out over everything, wanting to get on the field as fast as I could. At that time the SEC was just about getting to be the best, and I just liked the thought of playing there."

*Quarterback Steve Taneyhill looks for a receiver during a game against Clemson on Saturday, November 18, 1995, at Williams-Brice Stadium in Columbia, South Carolina. Taneyhill threw his 29<sup>th</sup> touchdown pass of the season, breaking the Southeastern Conference single-season record set by Florida's Shane Matthews in l991. South Carolina lost to Clemson 38–17.* (AP Photo/Lou Krasky)

The Gamecocks and their fans liked it, too, although some of them had their doubts when Taneyhill arrived with a flowing blond mullet past his shoulders, earrings, and just the kind of attitude Carolina folks would expect from a Pennsylvania fella with hair past his shoulders and earrings.

"I have just always kind of done things my way. Not to come across as cocky or arrogant, and I know that is how it is perceived, but I have just always kind of done it my way and enjoyed doing it," said Taneyhill, now a successful head coach at Union County High School in South Carolina. "That's the thing. I think everything should be fun. You work hard, and you should have some fun. I know what the perception was, but in the locker room and with my teammates it was never really a big deal after the first week."

A little digging suggests it was probably the first win that actually convinced Taneyhill's fans and his teammates that they could fully embrace this brash young man. And that didn't come until the sixth game of the season. The Gamecocks started the season 0–5 before coach Sparky Woods handed the starting job to Taneyhill, who helped South Carolina to a 21–6 upset win over Mississippi State.

"I'm a believer now," tight end Boomer Foster told *The State* newspaper after the game. "He's said a lot of stuff in the papers, but he's the real thing."

As for the hair and earrings?

"He can wear a dress for all I care," wide receiver Asim Penny said after the Mississippi State game.

"All this stuff about my looks… I'm just a person," Taneyhill said that night. "It's a big issue down here. I don't understand. Back home, all the guys and girls have earrings. This is just me. I'm not changing me."

By that point, South Carolina would not have wanted him to change. Taneyhill led the team to five wins in its final six games,

## Thomas Dendy

In 2004, *The State* newspaper ranked the five best drives in South Carolina football history.

The first one on the list came on November 24, 1984, to cap a 22–21 come-from-behind win over archrival Clemson, and one of the key plays on that drive was an 18-yard scamper by sophomore tailback Thomas Dendy to move the Gamecocks to Clemson's 11-yard line.

South Carolina radio broadcaster Tommy Suggs can remember that drive to this day.

"It was Thomas Dendy just running over people," Suggs said.

Dendy did a lot of running over people at South Carolina. He didn't post any 1,000-yard seasons, but he led the Gamecocks in rushing four straight seasons (1982-85). Steve Wadiak and Brandon Bennett are the only other South Carolina players to achieve that feat.

Dendy's best game came in his freshman year when he gained 156 yards against Navy, and he rushed for triple digits five more times in his career, making him 10th in school history with six 100-yard games.

Dendy was drafted in the 11th round of the NFL draft by the Denver Broncos, but he did not make the team.

"I tried hard, but I just wasn't able to make it," Dendy later told *The Greenville News* while working at a youth camp in South Carolina. "That's something you try to teach them. When you have that opportunity, take advantage of it and do the best you can do. You may not be successful in the eyes of others, but if you did the best that you could do, then I consider it a success."

including a 24–13 upset of Clemson to snap a four-game losing streak in that series. Taneyhill was 19-of-29 for 296 yards and two touchdowns that night, and after one of his scoring passes, he ran to the middle of the field at Death Valley and mimicked putting his signature on the painted Tiger Paw. When the game was complete, Taneyhill gave a theatrical bow to the Clemson fans.

South Carolina fans were in love, and baseball caps complete with hair hanging out the back were soon hot sellers in Columbia.

Taneyhill never took the team to the promised land as some fans had hoped, but he did fill up the team's passing record books and lead South Carolina to its first bowl win, a 24–21 victory over West Virginia in the Carquest Bowl his junior season.

The two best passing days in school history belong to Taneyhill, who threw for 473 yards against Mississippi State in 1995 and 451 yards against East Carolina in 1994. He is second to Todd Ellis in career passing yardage with 8,782 yards, and his 62 career touchdowns are a school record.

"I can't just say one game [was my favorite]," Taneyhill said. "There were probably six or seven games in there that I will always remember."

People who saw Taneyhill play for the Gamecocks from 1992 to 1995 would have had a hard time picturing him as a head coach at a high school. He's not offended by that. He never would have dreamed it himself.

"My senior year, Coach [Brad] Scott said, 'You know, you'd be a great coach.' I said, 'Coach, I don't have enough patience,'" Taneyhill said. "And I didn't at first."

He learned though, and he won five state championships before arriving at Union County. In true Taneyhill fashion, he's still doing things his way. He has been a head coach in 12 of his 13 seasons in coaching.

"Coach Scott was right—I have been pretty good at it," Taneyhill said. "It's a great thing for a quarterback because as the quarterback, you're kind of in charge. The team is yours if you're a good, strong leader. The offense goes how you go, and then you get into coaching and now it's really your team. I don't know that I'd be a very good assistant coach."

# 14 1984 Navy Game

For the first 115 years of South Carolina football, the 1984 season was the most successful, and there was no close second.

Considering that, it's stunning and also sad to hear the quarterback of that team talk about his most vivid memory from that season.

"Anytime anybody talks about that season, they say, 'Reflect.' Well, I think, 'What could have been?'" Mike Hold said. "If that's the first thing that comes to my mind, then the next thing is what caused that? That's Navy."

It was November 17, 1984. No. 2 South Carolina was pitted against unranked Navy in Annapolis, Maryland. It remains the most famous—and bitterly so—game in school history.

"It was absolutely miserable," said Tommy Suggs, who quarterbacked the Gamecocks to the 1969 ACC title and thought he was watching the second title in school history as he took in the 1984 season from the radio broadcast booth.

This time, it was a national title that was on the Gamecocks' minds. And it was within reach the morning of November 17. No. 1 Nebraska was playing No. 6 Oklahoma. The Gamecocks were matched against a Midshipmen team that had won three games up to that point. The Orange Bowl was eyeing South Carolina and Nebraska for a national title matchup.

Riding their "Black Magic," the nickname derived from Coach Joe Morrison's all-black attire and the team's habit of winning despite all circumstances, the Gamecocks had looked Orange Bowl–worthy through their first nine games. The previous week they trounced No. 11 Florida State 38–26 in Williams-Brice Stadium to get to 9–0.

"Up to that point we were struggling to move up the rankings," Hold said. "It was always about respect. Now we beat Florida State, and we've got all the respect in the world. And then we go out and lose to Navy, the one game we were favored to win all year."

And the game wasn't particularly close. Navy led 14–7 at halftime and scored 24 straight points after the break to take a 38–7 lead on the way to a 38–21 win.

"They didn't take us seriously," Navy defensive lineman Eric Rutherford told *The Washington Post* after the game. "As we kept scoring points and coming up with big plays, they kept looking at each other and figuring they're undefeated [so] they would come back. It just got too late for them. I don't think they came to play."

No one on the Gamecocks' sideline could reasonably argue with that. South Carolina committed five turnovers, four interceptions, and a fumble. Rutherford had four sacks all by himself.

"I don't think they're adept pass blockers," Rutherford said. "The quarterback just ran around so much, we just stayed where we were and he came to us."

Navy—which was playing without six starters, including star tailback Napoleon McCallum, due to injury—would finish the season 4–6–1.

"I think we just overlooked them," South Carolina defensive back Joe Brooks told the Associated Press. "We were looking more to the Orange Bowl and Clemson. We almost had a big head coming into this game. We thought it was an easy game. The enthusiasm we have before a game just wasn't there. We were just dead on the sideline."

The South Carolina offense, which was ranked No. 6 in the country entering the game (448 yards per game), gained 388, and the defense allowed 352.

"I don't want to take anything away from Navy," Morrison said after the game. "They played very well and deserved to win. But we didn't play well."

As if to taunt South Carolina fans, a report from ABC television's Beano Cook surfaced that the Gamecocks had already been extended an invitation and had accepted a bid from the Orange Bowl, which would have been a violation of an NCAA rule. The bowl quickly denied the claim.

Later in the day, Nebraska would lose 17–7 to Oklahoma, further tormenting the Gamecocks. Rather than loving the miserable company, South Carolina was left to think about what might have been.

"We would have been No. 1 in the country," Suggs said wistfully. "We would have moved up to No. 1."

Washington took the Gamecocks' place in the Orange Bowl and knocked off Oklahoma 28–17 to finish No. 2 in the country. The Gamecocks went to the Gator Bowl, where they lost 21–14 to Oklahoma State.

"To come so close…," Hold said 29 years later.

# 15 Famously Faithful Fans

South Carolina football fans have been described in many ways—"long-suffering" and "hopelessly optimistic" are just a couple of the most frequent clauses. However, perhaps the adjective that suits them best is "there," as in almost always at Williams-Brice Stadium. The notion that South Carolina has never known anything other than packed stadiums even during its most dismal seasons is a myth, but there's no question the passion of Gamecocks fans has outweighed any reciprocation they have received in the win-loss column.

"There are a lot of schools with loyalty," former athletics director Mike McGee said, "but I'd put South Carolina with any of them."

The Gamecocks consistently rank among the nation's top 20 in attendance, and they averaged 80,001 people at each home game during the 2012 season. A better judge of fan faithfulness is the 1998 season. South Carolina, which finished 1–10 and fired head coach Brad Scott that season, averaged 74,744 fans for six home games that year.

In 2004, Steve Hummer of the *Atlanta Journal-Constitution*, described South Carolina this way:

"Here is a program more famous for what occurs in the stands at Williams-Brice Stadium than down on the grassy stage.

"'When you talk about South Carolina football, you think about one thing—the loyalty of our fans,' [Coach Lou] Holtz says, and off he goes on another filibuster.

"'You don't think about championships. You don't think about bowl wins [two in forever]. You don't think about comebacks. You don't think about winning big games. You think about our fans. Our fans here have been tremendous.

"'Yeah, they do deserve better, and they have for years.'

"So what happened after a second straight 5–7 season ended with a 63–17 loss to hated Clemson last November, one the 67-year-old Holtz called the most embarrassing game of his career?

"'The Gamecock Club this year set an all-time record in donations,' said the group's executive director, Jeff Barber. 'We passed $12 million in unrestricted money. And this will be the fourth highest season-ticket sales we ever had.

"'Other schools laugh at us because we're so optimistic. Since when is that a bad thing?' Barber wonders.

"Being a Gamecock fan means never having to say you've arrived."

Former South Carolina quarterback Steve Taneyhill can remember lean home crowds, particularly in 1992 when the Gamecocks started the season 0–5 in Sparky Woods' fourth season. Only 55,102 people showed up on October 17 to see South Carolina play No. 15 Mississippi State.

"You kind of expect that at 0–5, but it grew and grew and grew," Taneyhill said.

South Carolina upset the Bulldogs 21–6 that day, and the next time they played at home, 71,529 people showed up to watch the Gamecocks beat Tennessee 24–23.

"I think they have a very solid core of fans, maybe 50,000 or so, but I have been to games over there when things weren't going so well where they only had 55,000 or 60,000," said Teddy Heffner, who has seen three decades of South Carolina football games as a sports writer at *The State* newspaper and now as a radio talk show host on 560 AM The Team in Columbia.

"It's not just a football game—it's a social event in Columbia," Heffner said. "It's probably the biggest social event here. Of those 80,000 that are in the seats these days, I would guess 30,000 don't know what a first down is. Maybe I am being too harsh there, but a lot of them are there to be seen. I can remember the day when you went to the press box that you wore a coat and tie. I think that's not just true in Columbia but other places in the South with no professional team. It's the big thing here in town."

Even when pro football came to neighboring North Carolina in 1995 with the creation of the Carolina Panthers, it didn't make a dent in the Gamecocks' fan base.

"Most South Carolina fans could care less about the Carolina Panthers," Heffner said. Gamecocks football "is the thing that is going on. There is a lot of prestige in being a season ticket holder and going to ball games. It's something to do on Saturdays during football season."

In 2012, South Carolina set a school record when 85,199 fans packed Williams-Brice Stadium beyond its official capacity of 80,250 to watch the No. 6 Gamecocks beat No. 5 Georgia 35–7.

# 16 George Rogers vs. Herschel Walker

On November 1, 1980, Sanford Stadium in Athens, Georgia, was the center of the college football universe. The home-standing Bulldogs were ranked No. 4 in the country. South Carolina was ranked No. 14.

But the 66,200 people in the stands and the national television audience on ABC mostly wanted to see two men—senior Gamecocks running back George Rogers and freshman Bulldog running back Herschel Walker.

Keith Jackson, the voice of college football at the time, and Ara Parseghian, the former Notre Dame coach, were in the booth calling the game for television. South Carolina radio color analyst Tommy Suggs rode to the stadium with Parseghian.

"We went out to the stadium early, earlier than normal, just to get ahead of the rush," Suggs said. "We sat there and talked I know for an hour, just talking about college football and this game. I think both of us were just hoping that it would be a good ball game and wouldn't be disappointing, and boy was it a great ball game."

To be fair to the more than 150 or so other players on the field and sideline that day, it wasn't a great game simply because of Rogers and Walker. The South Carolina defense twice stopped the Bulldogs on downs at the 1-yard line. Georgia place-kicker Rex

## Lee Corso

Lee Corso may not have understood the passion, or the long memories, of South Carolina fans in 2005 when he said no one, not even new hire Steve Spurrier, could win an SEC championship with the Gamecocks even if given "400 years" to do it.

He does now.

Corso, a popular former college football coach and host on ESPN's *College GameDay* show, said he would "crawl across the field on my hands and knees and kiss his ring" if Spurrier won an SEC title at South Carolina.

Corso's statement immediately became a rallying cry for the Gamecocks and their fans. South Carolina boosters created a website titled LetsShowCorso.com that allowed users to throw virtual footballs at Corso. A video on the site also showed Corso predicting South Carolina would not beat the likes of Georgia, Tennessee, and Clemson, along with clips of the Gamecocks doing just that. That video even appeared on the video screen at Williams-Brice Stadium before the game.

While Spurrier had his fun with the prediction, he asked his team's fans several times to treat Corso well on subsequent visits to Columbia.

"I want to encourage our fans and our students to be a class act this weekend," Spurrier said. "The whole nation will be watching. I think the last time [ESPN was] here, some of our students or fans were giving Lee Corso some grief, and I know he did say it's almost impossible to win the SEC here. But I guarantee you he would love to see South Carolina win it. He would love to crawl across Williams-Brice Stadium and salute the fans. That's what he said he'd do if we ever win it. But he was just trying to mention how difficult it was since we have not really been that close in our history. Lee Corso is a good person and a good man. I guarantee you he roots for us most of the time."

Corso probably wasn't rooting for the Gamecocks on December 4, 2010, however, when they played Auburn in the SEC Championship Game. Corso said before the game that he still stood by his promise, but the Tigers saved him from it with a 56–17 win.

Robinson hit two field goals of more than 50 yards, including a 57-yarder, that proved the difference in the 13–10 Georgia win.

But it was Rogers and Walker everyone came to see, and they did not disappoint. Rogers, who would go on to win the Heisman Trophy that year, carried 35 times for 168 yards, his 18th straight game with more than 100 yards. Walker, who would go on to win the national title that year, had a Georgia-record 43 carries for 219 yards, including a 76-yard touchdown.

"Should have beat Georgia, and of course I fumbled," Rogers said 33 years later.

The fumble came at Georgia's 16-yard line with 5:22 left to play, and the Gamecocks never threatened again.

"We were going in to get them again. We were going to score. We were going to beat them," Suggs said. "It just didn't work out, but it was a great ball game, good gosh."

In the postgame press conference, South Carolina coach Jim Carlen blamed himself for putting too much on Rogers' shoulders.

"It was a dumb play on the part of Coach Carlen to put George back in the game, as tired as he was," Carlen said. "We can't expect George Rogers to do everything. We just didn't throw the ball well enough to complement our running game."

The Gamecocks completed two passes that day, and by the end of the game Rogers' right hand was so swollen it looked like a balloon, according to Suggs.

"Georgia No. 1 was a pretty good football team and hit pretty hard, and George ran kind of straight up. His hands were more susceptible to getting hit when people made tackles," Suggs said. "He just got pounded a lot. They hit him on [his hand], and [the ball] came loose. I felt so sorry for George because his hand was all beat up."

After the game, Walker deferred to his elder, saying Rogers should be the Heisman Trophy winner.

"I need some more experience before I can get everything down pat," Walker said afterward. "I shouldn't even be compared with George Rogers. If I was voting for the Heisman, I'd vote for George. He's the senior. He's shown what he can do over four years. I still don't know what my capabilities are yet. Whatever you do, please don't write about just me."

As if the game needed another subplot, it was the first time Rogers' father had seen him play in person. George Rogers Sr. had spent the previous eight years in prison after being convicted of murder, and one of his first trips after parole was to Athens to see his son play.

"They got him to come up to Athens," Rogers said. "I saw him smiling. I know he was cheering me on. I got to see him after the football game. I wanted to show him that I was a pretty good football player."

# 17 Lou Holtz—Championship Pedigree

When Mike McGee fired Brad Scott in 1998, he knew he wanted to hire Lou Holtz.

Accomplishing that would be a long and winding road. McGee and Holtz had known each other for more than two decades at that point and had coached against each other four times when Holtz was at North Carolina State and McGee was coaching Duke. (Holtz posted a 3–0–1 record in the head-to-head matchups.)

Holtz, an assistant coach for the Gamecocks in 1966 and 1967, had been on a lot of wish lists in Columbia since winning the national title in 1988 at Notre Dame. It took all the effort McGee could muster to get that wish fulfilled.

*Lou Holtz (left) and Florida coach Steve Spurrier (right) chat prior to their game on November 10, 2001, at Williams-Brice Stadium in Columbia, South Carolina. Florida defeated South Carolina 54–17.* (AP Phot/Lou Krasky)

In all, Holtz turned down the job three times before finally accepting, and he even called McGee the morning of his introductory press conference in Columbia to say he was having second thoughts, McGee told *The State* newspaper.

"Beth and I were up praying last night about this, and we think maybe this is not the right time," Holtz told McGee that morning. McGee responded, "Lou, [my wife] Ginger and I have been praying about this for two months, and we know it is."

Holtz had been out of coaching for two seasons when he was hired at South Carolina. He spent the downtime working as a college football analyst at CBS, and his CBS broadcast partner, Tim Brando, helped pique Holtz's interest in the South Carolina job, according to Brando.

"I told him, 'That's a hell of a job,'" Brando told *The State*. "I could see that triggered a reaction. 'Why do you say that, Tim?' he asked me. I told him they packed the house for bad football, they were in the SEC, and their alumni pour every cent into the team. I said I thought it was a great place for a guy who could recruit outside the state."

While Holtz mulled over the offer, McGee began to at least consider Frank Beamer, Butch Davis, Tommy Bowden, and Jim Haslett for the job.

Eventually, however, the 61-year-old Holtz walked onto a stage set up on the Williams-Brice Stadium field on December 3, 1998, to be announced as the Gamecocks' 31st head coach. Five thousand fans attended the news conference.

"When I left the University of Notre Dame, I honestly felt I would never coach again," Holtz said. "My heart is now here at the University of South Carolina. My effort and dedication is to you… Our goal is to win the national championship."

Holtz's son Skip came along with his father as the offensive coordinator with an understanding from the administration that he would be given consideration for the head coaching job when Lou Holtz left the school.

Publicly, Holtz said the biggest factors in his decision to take the job were the challenge of winning at a place where many people said no one could do it and the ability to have almost total control of a program.

"People were saying, 'You can't win at South Carolina,'" Holtz told *The State*. "I had a lot of coaches, some in the SEC, tell me not to come here, that you can't win here. They said there are enough other jobs where you could win. You're fighting too big a hill. You've got a reputation, you can go to other places. A combination of things intrigued me. I told my wife I wanted to do it one more time where everything would be in accordance with my thoughts, my feelings. I wouldn't coach it all, but my philosophy would be prevailing."

At the beginning, it looked like the people who said Holtz couldn't win at South Carolina were right. He didn't win at all in his first year—not once. The Gamecocks were 0–11 in 1999 but managed the second-best turnaround in NCAA history the next year by going 8–4 and winning the Outback Bowl 24–7 over Ohio State.

Holtz would post a 9–3 mark the next season with another win in the Outback Bowl, but that was the high-water mark of the Holtz tenure in Columbia. His final three seasons featured five, five, and six wins, and he left following the 2004 season with a 33–37 record at the school.

# 18 Bob Fulton—The Voice

In college football towns across the country, but especially in the South, the home team's play-by-play radio announcer is almost universally known as "The Voice of the (fill in the blank)."

Larry Munson was "The Voice of the (Georgia) Bulldogs." Jack Cristil was "The Voice of the (Mississippi State) Bulldogs."

Bob Fulton was just "The Voice." During 41 years of broadcasting South Carolina football and basketball games, Fulton saw some ugly times, but he made it all sound beautiful with a baritone voice that still represents Gamecocks sports for many generations of South Carolina fans.

Former South Carolina sports information director Don Barton was part of the group that hired Fulton in 1952 following his work on Major League Baseball broadcasts.

"It was the easiest decision we ever made," Barton told *The State* newspaper after Fulton's death in 2010. "Bob's voice was head-and-shoulders above everybody else's. God gave him a voice that he doesn't give many people."

Nine football coaches, 10 basketball coaches, and 13 athletic directors came and went at South Carolina while Fulton called the Gamecocks action. He worked 436 South Carolina football games and 1,156 basketball games. While the teams weren't always successful during that time period, Fulton did preside over many of the school's athletic highlights, from the career of legendary basketball coach Frank McGuire to the Heisman Trophy season of running back George Rogers.

"Bob loved Carolina, and he was a major part of the university," Tommy Suggs, the school's longtime color analyst and a former Gamecocks quarterback, told *The State*. "In the 23 years I worked with him, he was Carolina athletics. He was special. God, he was special."

A native of Pennsylvania, Fulton spanned South Carolina athletics from 1952 to 1995, with a two-year break in 1965 and 1966 when he left the school to work at Georgia Tech before being lured back to Columbia. (That two-year stint isn't remembered well in South Carolina, but it helped Fulton influence one of college football's most enduring national voices. Keith Jackson, the longtime college football play-by-play voice for ABC, grew up in Carrollton, Georgia, listening to Fulton's Yellow Jacket broadcasts.)

"He was the soundtrack of many people's lives," former South Carolina quarterback and current play-by-play voice of the Gamecocks Todd Ellis told *The State*. "We all know how important football is to the fans, and that passion came through in Bob Fulton."

Fulton tutored Ellis when Ellis took over the South Carolina booth in 2003, and Fulton tried to pass along his trademark style—always with the home team but never too partisan, an anti-Munson in Southern football.

Ellis "told me he was going to say, 'It's our ball,'" Fulton told *The State*. "I said, 'No, you should say it's Carolina's ball.' People know that you are from Carolina and you're certainly going to show more excitement when Carolina does something good as opposed to when the opposition does something good. You can be a little more biased, a little more excited about the home team."

Fulton's final game for the university was the 1995 Carquest Bowl, a 24–21 win over West Virginia that was the first bowl victory in South Carolina history. That win also gave Fulton a record better than .500 in his broadcasting career as the Gamecocks finished 213–211–12 with Fulton at the mic.

Fulton's voice was so iconic to Gamecocks that he sold custom fantasy tapes to fans after his retirement, inserting a fan's name into a sports scene.

"I enjoy it because it gives me a chance once again to do play-by-play, and in a sense it's like re-creating a game. I also try to work with announcers from time to time, and I enjoy doing that. I'm just in a stage of my life where I want to pay people back who have been so good to me all around the state," Fulton told the school's alumni magazine in 2009.

Along with memories, he also left behind a trail of broadcasters influenced by his style and the kindness he showed colleagues. One was Jim Powell, now the play-by-play voice of the Atlanta Braves.

"Bob treated me with way more respect than I ever deserved. He was as classy a colleague as I've ever worked with," Powell told *The State*. "Bob became an iconic announcer because he just called the games. The Gamecocks were first and foremost. It was never about him."

# 19 Jadeveon Clowney— The Beast

He made South Carolina fans wait, and then he made it worth the wait.

Jadeveon Clowney was the No. 1 high school football player in the country in the recruiting class of 2011. There was no argument about this fact. In fact, the 6'6", 256-lb. defensive end was the best college football prospect in more than decade, according to most analysts.

And Clowney grew up in Rock Hill, South Carolina. The Gamecocks used that home-field recruiting advantage, as well as a strong relationship between South Carolina defensive coordinator Ellis Johnson and Clowney's grandfather, John, to take the early lead in Clowney's recruitment. But that didn't stop every other school in the country from showing serious interest.

Just when it looked like Clowney was headed to South Carolina, archrival Clemson made a strong push and convinced Clowney to delay his decision. While every other major college football prospect made their choice on the National Signing Day on February 2, Clowney waited until February 14, his birthday and Valentine's Day, to make his decision public.

The delay gave Gamecocks fans heartburn, but it gave Clowney the spotlight all to himself on February 14. ESPN broadcast his announcement decision from South Pointe High School live as more than 100 media members, coaches, teachers, and classmates sat in the school auditorium.

When Clowney announced his decision to attend South Carolina, he became the first No. 1 high school recruit to sign with the Gamecocks, and he set off a wave of hyperbolic predictions about what he would do in a garnet and black uniform.

Head coach Steve Spurrier, himself a Heisman Trophy winner and the coach of more than 50 players who were drafted into the NFL, called it "sort of scary reading that we were going to sign a player of that caliber."

Clowney's high school coach Bobby Carroll predicted Clowney would only spend three years at South Carolina before heading to the NFL.

"I have had several NFL guys, former players and coaches, say that he's like the LeBron James of football. He could probably go out and start in the NFL straight out of high school," Carroll said. "He might not be able to play every down, and he'd have to get a little bigger and stronger, but I really think he could do it."

The most amazing thing about that statement is how few people refuted it. Recruiting analysts said they had never seen such a combination of size and speed in high school. While Clowney didn't make good on his prediction that day that he would be a regular starter as a freshman, he made an immediate impact on the program.

Sharing time with veterans Devin Taylor and Melvin Ingram, Clowney had eight sacks in his first season, including two each against Georgia, Vanderbilt, and Nebraska. It was his sophomore season when Clowney broke out, smashing the school's single-season record with 13 sacks and making himself a household name.

After a foot injury slowed him though the middle of the season, Clowney closed with such a kick that he entered the 2013 season as a serious Heisman Trophy candidate—quite an accomplishment considering no defense-only player has ever won the award.

*Jadeveon Clowney puts on a South Carolina hat on Monday, February 14, 2011, at South Pointe High School in Rock Hill, South Carolina, after announcing that he will play football for the University of South Carolina.*
(AP Photo/The Herald, Andy Burriss)

In the final regular season game of the season, Clowney set a South Carolina single-game record with 4.5 sacks against Clemson. Against Michigan in the Outback Bowl, Clowney didn't have a sack, but he did have a hit so hard against Michigan running back Vincent Smith that it knocked off Smith's helmet and was instantly christened across the country as simply The Hit.

At the end of his sophomore year, Clowney was a finalist for every major national defensive award in college football, and he spent a week in December flying across the country for awards banquet after awards banquet along with a handful of more veteran college football players who were also finalists for the awards. To a man, those older players were amazed by Clowney's freakish athletic ability.

"There's no ceiling for him," Georgia linebacker Jarvis Jones said.

"He's a beast," Florida State defensive end Bjoern Werner added. "I love watching him because he's so explosive. He's only a sophomore. That's what makes it scary."

Clowney was a consensus All-American as a sophomore and won the Hendricks Award, which goes to the nation's top defensive end. He made it clear as well that his junior season would be his last at South Carolina, and some columnists and radio talk show hosts around the country even suggested Clowney should consider sitting out his junior season to eliminate the risk of injury since several NFL analysts projected he would be the No. 1 overall NFL draft pick in 2014 no matter what his junior-year production turned out to be.

Clowney dismissed all that talk, however.

"I don't think about getting injured," he said. "Stuff happens all the time. You can get injured just walking somewhere, fall off a curb. I will play my game, give it all I've got every play. I haven't gotten hurt yet. I don't plan on it, knock on wood."

Clowney's success on the field was also a boon to the Gamecocks off the field.

"When you think about the University of South Carolina, you think about Jadeveon Clowney, too," athletics director Ray Tanner said. "[The athletics department is] just a part of the university, but our presence across the country is a big deal, and Jadeveon has enhanced that in a very big way."

# 20 The Fire Ants

Many days during the practices of the 1984 season, offensive lineman Del Wilkes would look to the opposite end of South Carolina's practice field and shake his head.

"Those poor suckers," he said to himself.

What Wilkes was seeing was the preparation of the Gamecocks' "Fire Ants" defense, which helped propel the 1984 Black Magic season.

"They weren't a very big group physically, so everything with them had to be about tenacity, speed, getting to the ball, getting to the ball as a group, flying around," Wilkes said.

South Carolina defensive coordinator Tom Gadd was credited with creating the defense, but it was fellow defensive assistant Bill Michael who named the group, Gadd told *The State* newspaper. The defense, which was clad in its all-garnet home uniforms of the day, flew to the ball during a 38–14 win over Southern Cal in Williams-Brice Stadium in October 1983.

"We were grading films, and the kids were really hustling, getting to the ball," Gadd told *The State*. "Bill Michael said, 'They look like a bunch of fire ants.' Sid Wilson [South Carolina's sports information director] was there. Next thing you knew, he'd started calling them that in press releases, and it just mushroomed."

Gadd had a very clinical way of grading the effort of his Fire Ants.

"Whenever a play would end, the last frame of film before it would go to the next play, he would count to see how many jerseys were in the frame there, and if you weren't one of the guys around that football, you were going to have to run or do up-downs or be punished in some way," Wilkes said. "He ran the snot out of those guys."

## Educating a Fan Base

As part of building South Carolina's football program, Coach Steve Spurrier found himself not only coaching players but at times fans in what he expected from his program.

The first time came on September 28, 2006. In Spurrier's second season, the Gamecocks hosted No. 2 Auburn and nearly upset the Tigers before falling 24–17. Many of the fans at Williams-Brice Stadium, pleased with their team's effort, applauded the team as it exited the field.

Spurrier was not happy.

"They sort of clapped as the guys left the field. So I said, 'Please don't do that again. Please don't clap when you lose a game. There's no moral victories in any sport,'" Spurrier said recalling the incident. "A lot has changed at South Carolina [since then]. I got a couple good friends that have been there for 30, 40 years and so forth. One of the guys said, 'We used to come to the ballpark hoping for a good game. If we're playing Florida, Georgia, Tennessee, we were just hoping for a good game, not get blown out. Now we sort of come to the ballpark thinking we're going to beat those guys. We're sort of mad if we don't.' I said, 'That's the way you're supposed to feel—mad or a little upset if you don't beat them.'"

Spurrier took the fans to task again in 2012 following a 48–10 win over East Carolina during which many fans left at halftime.

"I hope we are not reverting back to the days when football wasn't very important around here and the pregame party and the postgame party were more important than the game itself," Spurrier said. "I'm hoping our Gamecock fans will treat the game as the most important part of their Saturday football day. But it didn't appear that way yesterday. Hopefully, the people that leave will feel a lot of embarrassment. I know it's a lot of students, but maybe the students need to feel embarrassed."

That's what Wilkes was seeing when he looked down those torturously hot practice fields in 1984.

"There were times in practice I would look down there and they did nothing but condition and run," he said. "I thought to myself, 'Thank God I am not on defense. I don't think I could do that.'"

Linebacker James Seawright was the leader of the Fire Ants, earning All-America honors from the Associated Press and Football Writers Association of America in 1984 after recording 133 tackles. Seawright finished his Gamecocks career with 369 tackles and left the school after that season considered the greatest linebacker in its history.

"He was one of the guys I watched growing up," former South Carolina defensive lineman and linebacker Corey Miller said of Seawright. "Really good inside linebacker—not overly big but a sideline-to-sideline type of guy, good tackler. He was kind of the standard. If you want to be a Carolina linebacker, you would kind of mimic his play."

Led by Seawright, the Fire Ants held the first five opponents of 1984, including Georgia and Pittsburgh, to less than 300 yards.

Twenty-five years later, Gamecocks defenses were still being compared to the Fire Ants. When Ellis Johnson showed up to coach South Carolina's defense in 2009, he was asked if his group mirrored the famed Fire Ants in any way.

"That was a pretty fast group. They could really run. Of course, I think we are [fast], too," Johnson told *The State*. "But at this point, we haven't proved it week in and week out down through an entire season. I don't know if you can put us in that bracket. We might be just another bunch in this league. But we're fast. We're not exceptionally big, but we can run. And I think we have to be able to sometimes compensate for our size."

Sound familiar?

"I think in fear of being punished, fear of having to run all day in practice, they flew around the football," Wilkes said. "While they weren't an imposing group physically, they made up for it in just flying to the football and everybody hustling."

# 21 Big Thursday— The Rivalry's Beginning

In the late 1800s, the South Carolina State Fair was looking for more oomph.

"The main event they had was the horse races on Thursday," said Don Barton, who was South Carolina's sports information director from 1950–59. "They needed something to draw a crowd besides the horse races, so they proposed that Carolina and Clemson play a game."

Thus, Big Thursday was born. The upstart college football programs played on the state fairgrounds, and early fans paid a quarter for entrance and often watched from their automobiles.

"It was a state holiday, and it was a fashion show," said Barton, who has written a book on the South Carolina-Clemson rivalry called *Big Thursdays and Super Saturdays*. "Dress shops in Columbia did more business on Big Thursday than they did for Easter. The girls would come wearing hats. Their boyfriends or husbands would buy the corsages to wear. It was a fashion show."

The newspapers of the day reflected that claim.

In 1933, merchants including Belk, R. L. Bryan Co., Haltiwanger's, J. C. Penney Co., Sylvan Brothers, Reyner's Jewelers, and James L. Tapp ran ads in *The Columbia Record* newspaper. One such ad read:

"Our employees want to go to the Fair tomorrow—they want to see the big game [Carolina and Clemson]. We want them to go. We know our customers will be sympathetic with our decision to close our stores on Thursday—we are confident they would prefer to wait until Friday to make their purchases."

In 1939, the Society Chatter section of *The Record* discussed the preparation needed for Big Thursday.

"Just about everyone in Columbia has a list of must do's before the Carolina-Clemson game. Get one of those cute hooded gabardine rain coats in case, a couple pairs of mesh stockings as a protector against the sticky weeds surrounding the stadium, little canvas chairs without feet… they have arm rests and a back that practically rubs one's aching spine, a good foundation cream and a new moss-green bonnet that goes beautifully with everything from red to black. Then have Bill's pants pressed, get a feather for the hat you are trying to make last another year, be sure Bill doesn't leave the tickets in his pants pockets, get a thousand eggs and a bunch of bacon for the out-of- towners dropping by after the game, see there is plenty of gas in the car, for Bill will forget of course."

The Esso gasoline company paid each year to have Big Thursday filmed and would show highlights the next week in local movie theaters before the feature started.

The Big Thursday games themselves supplied plenty of great stories. In 1946, a slew of counterfeit tickets led to mass confusion at the gates and eventually the fans, whether they had real or fake tickets, overran the gates to watch the game.

"The people occupied every bit of that thing except the playing field itself," Barton said. "In fact, they had to stop the game a couple times to move people off. Jimmy Byrnes, former secretary of state, governor at time, he saw the second half of the game on his hands and knees looking out through the legs of the players."

In 1958, coming off back-to-back shutout wins over the Gamecocks, Clemson coach Frank Howard said he would tip his hat to South Carolina coach Warren Giese if the Gamecocks managed to score a touchdown.

South Carolina scored several in a 26–6 win, and Howard tipped his hat after each score.

"My head was getting sunburned," Howard said after the game.

The Big Thursday tradition ended after the 1959 game when Clemson decided it no longer wanted to see all the game's attention and revenue go to Columbia rather than the Upstate.

Barton attempted to capitalize on the tradition's end with a special game program that was sold for "the outrageous price of a dollar," he said.

"Howard said, 'Now don't you go buying any of those programs down there because Carolina is getting all the money,'" Barton said. "They couldn't sell a program over on the Clemson side. People ordered programs after the game, so we sold them all anyhow."

The only time the teams played on a Thursday after the 1959 game was in 1963 after their regularly scheduled Saturday game was postponed by the assassination of John Kennedy. Clemson won that game 24–20 on Thanksgiving Day.

# The Two Careers of Todd Ellis

In 1992, as South Carolina celebrated its 100th year of collegiate football, Bob Fulton was asked for his thoughts about Todd Ellis.

"He rewrote the passing record book here at South Carolina, but what I will remember about Todd Ellis way down the line, if I last that long, is the outstanding person he was," said Fulton, the school's legendary play-by-play voice, on *100 Years of Gamecocks Football*. "He was a gentlemen and just a wonderful representative of the university. [He] still is."

Fulton didn't know at the time that "way down the line" Ellis would take the seat Fulton once filled as the play-by-play voice of the Gamecocks, bookending a career that has become synonymous with South Carolina athletics.

That career started in 1985 when Ellis, one of the top high school quarterbacks in the country, signed with the Gamecocks. South Carolina head coach Joe Morrison had hinted but not promised that the Gamecocks would abandon their run-first offense for a style more suitable to Ellis' arm. At first, Ellis wondered if it would actually happen. During Ellis' redshirt season, the Gamecocks stuck with the veer. But in 1986, when Ellis took the reins as the starting quarterback, Morrison did make the switch and footballs were flying in Columbia.

The offense and its freshman quarterback quickly meshed, and 1986 resulted in 3,020 passing yards from Ellis, 1,096 more than the Gamecocks amassed in the air in 1985. *The Sporting News* named Ellis a second-team All-American after the season.

In 1987 he threw for a South Carolina single-season record 3,206 yards, and he remains the only passer in school history with back-to-back 3,000-yard seasons. More importantly, the Gamecocks started winning, finishing 8–4 after a loss to LSU in the Gator Bowl.

The 1988 season saw another eight wins but less passing yards for Ellis, who finished with 2,353 yards. The 1989 season—during which the Gamecocks were reeling from the unexpected death of Morrison, and Ellis missed four games due to a knee injury—he threw for 1,374 yards, and the Gamecocks finished 6–4–1.

When his career was finished, Ellis owned every significant passing record in school history, and he remains the school leader in passing yards (9,953) and passing attempts (1,350). He is second in school history in passing touchdowns (49) and completions (747).

"The two things that stick out to me personally, just flat out great times, are beating Georgia twice and beating Clemson in 1987 at home in the first real ESPN night showcase game where they played '2001' and we were both ranked in the top 15," Ellis said. "Mostly my memories are about the players I played with and cutting up in the locker room and riding to practice on the bus and so on."

Ellis was selected in the ninth round of the 1990 NFL Draft by the Denver Broncos, who were coached by another former South Carolina quarterback, Dan Reeves. But the Broncos cut Ellis during training camp, and he did not catch on with another NFL team.

"Coach Reeves said he'd like to have played me more, but it just didn't work out. He was straightforward with me," Ellis told *The State* newspaper after he was let go by the Broncos. "He said he thought I had the tools to play in the NFL, but I need to be in a place where I can play more than I was going to at Denver. Part of my downfall was I spent most of my time on the sideline, learning without doing. The most consecutive plays I got [in practice] was six, and that was only once. Usually it was only two or three in a row. It's hard to learn and improve like that."

After returning to Columbia and earning a law degree from South Carolina, Ellis became the sideline reporter for the school's radio broadcast team. In 2003 he took over play-by-play duties, a job that he holds today. He also operates a law office in Columbia.

"I think since [graduation] I have better understood how South Carolina has struggled to have consistent years of very, very good play, and I think I understand that fully now, and I also appreciate those great moments when we are shining and things are going well because I know how hard that is," he said. "I don't know if it's just getting older, but there are times that it's harder to lose now than it was when I was a player."

# 23 Pops Frisby— Famous at Forty

Hundreds of players have worn South Carolina's garnet and black jerseys since the organization first fielded a team in 1892, but none have ever felt the spotlight like Tim Frisby.

In fact, no college football player in the country was more famous in the fall of 2004 than "Pops."

Frisby, a 20-year army veteran, walked onto the Gamecocks' football team that year at the age of 39 and, after a month of obscurity, became a national talking point. At the height of his fame, South Carolina received more than 100 media requests for an interview.

Frisby appeared on *The Late Show with David Letterman*, *The Tonight Show with Jay Leno*, *Good Morning America*, and almost every sports broadcast in the country.

"It's not something I sought out," Frisby told *The State* newspaper. "I thought I could come in here and try out and, if I was capable of playing, play. Really my first three or four weeks in the program where I was unnoticed, that was great. I just wanted to play."

He first did on September 25, 2004, when he played the final four plays of a 17–7 win over Troy during Lou Holtz's final season as head coach.

"I have a lot of respect for the guy," Holtz told *The State*. "A Ranger, 20 years in the army, six kids. He loves this team. I thought it would be good to get him in. I'm sorry we could not throw it to him."

There was little not to love about Frisby's story. A native of Allentown, Pennsylvania, he bypassed a scholarship offer from Tennessee State out of high school to join the army.

"I said I'd do a three-year tour, and it turned into 20," Frisby told Leno.

Along the way, he participated in Ranger training, served during the Gulf War, and had six children with wife Anna. When he left the army, Frisby returned to Columbia where he had served at Fort Jackson from 1984–88, enrolled at the university, and joined dozens of other students during walk-on tryouts for the 2004 team.

Frisby faced NCAA hurdles on the way to the field. His high school days came before the NCAA Clearinghouse was formed to certify the eligibility of all college athletes, and the resulting confusion made him ineligible for the first three games of his career.

"Tim is certainly not the typical college football player," NCAA spokesman Erik Christianson told *The State* at the time. "People take different paths in life, and now he has this opportunity in front of him, and we were happy to help him with his request."

Frisby received an ovation from his teammates at practice the day he was ruled eligible.

"It's an amazing story, and he's got a marvelous attitude. He comes out, and he works," Holtz told *The State*. "He really does some nice things. He's not out of place out there for a 39-year-old."

Throughout his two years at the school, Frisby emphasized that he came to school to be a football player, not a sideshow

"I didn't want to be one of these guys talking about it. 'Hey, this guy's no good. I could be out there playing,'" he told *The State*. "Until you're out there doing it, then you'll see how good these guys are or how good you are. You have to measure yourself against it. I didn't come into it just to take one shot at it and leave it alone. If I'm here, I want to compete and play and try earning the [playing] time. I'm not just out here to gain a story."

Being 20 years older than his teammates did present challenges, he acknowledged along the way.

"I'm up on the line of scrimmage [at practice] and the cornerback will say, 'I'm going to get a drink, I'll catch up with you,'" Frisby told Leno.

Frisby, who got his Pops nickname from wide receivers coach Rick Stockstill, caught the only pass of his career in 2005 when he hauled in a 9-yard reception in a 45–20 win over Troy in Steve Spurrier's first season on the job.

Frisby left the Gamecocks after the 2005 season with two years of eligibility remaining, and he looked into selling his story for a Hollywood movie.

"Pops is a good walk-on player who contributes a lot," Steve Spurrier told *The State*. "He's been a wonderful guy, does everything. He's been a good teammate of all the guys."

Frisby returned to Columbia in 2007 and graduated with honors.

# 24 "If It Ain't Swayin', We Ain't Playin'."

It ain't swayin' anymore, but there was a time when Williams-Brice Stadium itself moved to the rhythm of "Louie, Louie."

The swaying motion was first noted on the east side of the stadium during South Carolina's 38–14 win over Southern Cal in 1983. The first time quarterback Todd Ellis saw it was in 1986 when he had just led the Gamecocks to a fourth-quarter lead over traditional power Nebraska.

"When we went up in the fourth quarter and got ahead of Nebraska, I looked up and you could literally see the top deck moving," Ellis said on *100 Years of Gamecock Football*. "I'll never forget that."

Many of the people in and under those stands will never forget it either. While the movement was a point of pride for most Gamecocks fans—many of whom adorned their automobiles with bumper stickers that read, "If it ain't swayin', we ain't playin'"—it was a cause of concern for some.

Engineers assured the school and its fans at the time that the swaying of the 72,400-seat stadium was normal and posed no danger.

"Structurally, if you've got the whole student body out there jumping up and down constantly for 75 years, you might have some metal fatigue," John Trussell, assistant director for stadium insurer Insurance Reserve Fund, told *The State* newspaper. "But with only six or eight games a year, it will fall down from old age long before that."

Still, the school's board of trustees decided a change must be made for the stadium to host events other than football games. While the Gamecocks' fans might understand that the stadium was perfectly safe, the reasoning went that concert-goers might not and could panic when the stadium swayed.

The first change was banning bands from Virginia Tech, Georgia Tech, and Clemson from playing "Louie, Louie," the song that was being played by the South Carolina marching band when the stadium swayed during the 1986 Nebraska game. The Gamecocks band did not play the song again after that incident at the request of school officials.

At the time, Trussell denied a report that Insurance Reserve Fund had requested the banning of the song.

"There's no provision in a policy saying, 'Thou Shalt Not Play "Louie, Louie,"'" he told *The State.*

The Rolling Stones were another victim of the sway. The Stones had asked South Carolina permission to play a 1989 concert at Williams-Brice but were turned away at least in part because of concerns about the stadium's movement during a rock 'n roll concert.

"We moved students out of the [upper decks of] the stadium because they were stomping their feet and rocking the stadium [to

"Louie, Louie"], and you can imagine what might happen at a rock concert," Michael Mungo, chairman of the board of trustees, told *The State* newspaper at the time.

In 1990, $300,000 worth of supports were added to the east side of the stadium to prevent the sway.

"It will be stiffened so there will be no motion," Dennis Pruitt, South Carolina vice president for student affairs, told *The State*. "It will make the stadium useful for all other uses."

Studies at the time showed the upper east deck moved up and down more than an inch at times when the movement of the crowd was synchronized in exactly the right way. Engineers likened the movement to a diving board that moved at the end furthest from its support base. Ten struts were added connecting the upper deck to the east side's base to stop the movement.

The upper west side deck, built before the east side's top level, never moved like its counterpart because it was anchored by the stadium's press box.

State engineer Jay A. Flanagan reported the "addition of braces… would not improve the serviceability of the upper stands," but school officials nonetheless felt safer with the struts.

School president James B. Holderman told *The State* that the work was approved in order to allay "the concern registered among people who are sitting there on it or below it… and crowd control has been the great concern."

On September 25, 1994, the Rolling Stones played a concert during the opening leg of their Voodoo Lounge Tour at Williams-Brice Stadium. No swaying was reported.

# 25 1969—Still the Only Title

"The Year of the Rooster, the 4,677[th] recorded year on the Chinese lunar calendar, was a good year for the Fighting Gamecocks."

This is how the school described its 1969 season in the 1970 media guide, and it was indeed a good year for the Gamecocks. South Carolina, led by quarterback Tommy Suggs and fullback Warren Muir, won the 1969 ACC title, the team's first and still only overall conference championship.

"Relatively speaking, it was as big then as it probably would be winning an SEC title now," Suggs said. "It was huge."

Suggs completed 109-of-196 passes for 1,342 yards and seven touchdowns that season as the Gamecocks finished 7–4 overall and 6–0 in the conference.

Muir led the team in rushing with 969 yards and was named an All-American, while Coach Paul Dietzel was named the ACC Coach of the Year.

"Coach Dietzel had a real good recruiting year my year and a couple years after. We didn't have enough depth, but we had some really good players," Suggs said. "We started jelling I think at the end of my sophomore year."

South Carolina finished 4–6 in 1968, but it won three of four down the stretch and finished the season with a 7–3 win over Clemson.

"We played some great teams close [in 1968]," Suggs said. "We got better and better, more confident. So when we started the year, we felt like we could be pretty good but we hadn't been there. We were fairly young and we had to jell on and off the field, and we started doing that. Once we started winning, we got more and more confidence. We won a couple close ones, blew out a couple people. All of a sudden, we kind of woke up and there it was. So it was somewhat of a surprise, but at the same time we felt like we had enough talent to be good."

The 1969 season opened with a game against Duke in which Suggs posted more than 200 yards of total offense to lead a 27–20 victory. A week later, they held on to beat North Carolina 14–6 to set up a game against SEC foe Georgia.

The Bulldogs won 41–16, which marked a trend for the season as the non-conference schedule was not nearly as good to the Gamecocks. They also lost that season 29–14 to Tennessee and 34–9 to Florida State.

"We were in the ACC then, which was good football, but we'd still go out and get spanked by Georgia and get spanked by Tennessee and Florida State and those people," Suggs said. "That still bothered us, and we had to overcome that and come back and play in the ACC, but it was nice to win it and we deserved it. We were better than anyone else that year."

The most exciting win of the season came against Virginia Tech. The Gobblers (yep, they were called the Gobblers then) took a 16–14 lead with a minute to go in the game on a touchdown but missed the extra point. Billy DuPre, described in the 1970 media guide as "the littlest Gamecock of them all," kicked a 47-yard field goal with nine seconds remaining for a 17–16 win.

After back-to-back losses to the Seminoles and Volunteers, South Carolina traveled to Winston-Salem, North Carolina, to take on Wake Forest in 33-degree weather in a game that would decide the ACC crown. Fortunately for South Carolina, Suggs always loved to play the Deacons. He had thrown four touchdowns against Wake Forest the previous year, and he added another three more on that night to pace a 24–6 win.

"It was huge," Suggs said. "There were a lot of people at the airport when we came back."

Suggs has called the 1969 Clemson game, a 27–13 win that did not factor into the conference race, one of his favorite because it represented the culmination of all his team accomplished in 1969.

The season put South Carolina in the Peach Bowl where it lost 14–3 to a West Virginia team coached by Jim Carlen, who six seasons later would replace Dietzel as South Carolina's head coach.

# 26 Rex Enright—Ushering in the Modern Era

Can you name the former South Carolina football coach who played for Knute Rockne at Notre Dame and Curly Lambeau with the Green Bay Packers and coached not just the Gamecocks' football team twice but the Gamecocks' basketball team two seasons and the University of Georgia basketball team for eight seasons?

If you said Rex Enright, you're right, and you're probably impressed. Enright, a Rockford, Illinois, native, coached South Carolina's football team from 1938–42, took a break to serve in World War II, and returned to coach the Gamecocks from 1946–55. Until Steve Spurrier topped his record in 2012, Enright was South Carolina's winningest football coach with 64 victories.

While his resume was impressive, the man was even more so, according to South Carolina historian and former school sports information director Don Barton, who worked under Enright at South Carolina.

"He was just a great person," Barton said. "The only thing they would say negative about Rex was he was too good for his own good."

After games, Enright would entertain and inform media members covering the school at his home. There were more losses

## The Obituary

On October 10, 2012, J. Philip "Phil" Self, 66, passed away. A lawyer in Atlanta for 35 years, Self was a graduate of the University of Georgia and its law school. His obituary, printed in *The (Macon, GA) Telegraph*, his parents' hometown paper, was brief—only 250 words. Thirty-one of those words were these:

"Phil was a diehard Georgia Bulldogs fan and was a season ticket holder for decades. It is a shame that the last game he saw was the tragedy last Saturday night."

"The tragedy" was South Carolina's 35–7 win over the Bulldogs on October 6. The Gamecocks were ranked No. 6; the Bulldogs were ranked No. 5. It was the biggest game in the history of Williams-Brice Stadium based solely on team rankings, and it was a blowout.

Self died four days later. Don't let anybody tell you football is not a life-and-death matter in the South.

than victories during the Enright years (69 versus 64), but that doesn't diminish Enright in Barton's eyes.

"The problem with Coach Enright is we never had the materials," Barton said. "Rex was a very good coach, but he had no depth. He was good at getting people up for a specific game, like the Clemson game."

Enright beat the Tigers more than they beat him (8–6–1), which is not always the case with South Carolina coaches, and he boasted a 7–2–1 record against Clemson in his second stint with South Carolina. Barton said the Gamecocks would practice under strict security and at a different location (Capital City Park) the week of the Clemson game. One year, Enright took South Carolina's players out of town to spend the night prior the Clemson game, which is commonplace in modern college football but was unusual in the 1940s.

"I don't think he was doing anything different. He was just sort of setting a stage," Barton said. "Enright won a lot of big games. I don't how true it is, but he was famous for winning some games he shouldn't win and losing games he shouldn't lose."

In 1953, the Gamecocks beat a previously unbeaten West Virginia team 20–14. In 1954, South Carolina beat traditional power Army 34–20.

Those games were balanced by losses against Fordham and Duquesne. Enright's best season was 1953 when the Gamecocks went 7–3 and 2–3 in the ACC. The losses that season were No. 10 Duke, No. 2 Maryland, and Wake Forest.

After his 15 seasons as head coach and in failing health, Enright retired in 1955, naming Warren Giese his successor and taking over as athletics director. Enright served five years at the top of South Carolina's athletics department after retiring as head coach. The school's new administration building, which was used until 2012, was named in his honor—the Rex Enright Athletics Center. Enright retired as athletics director in 1959 and died a year later due to ulcers and a heart condition.

As embedded as his name is with South Carolina history, his brushes with other sports history are perhaps more impressive. At Notre Dame, he not only played for Rockne but also just missed being one of the famed Four Horsemen. Notre Dame's Four Horsemen were nicknamed and made famous by sportswriter Grantland Rice, who gave the name to the Fighting Irish's offensive backfield of Elmer Layden, Harry Stuhldreher, Don Miller, and Jim Crowley in a story for the *New York Herald Tribune*.

Enright actually held Layden's job as Notre Dame fullback the year before and the year after the Four Horsemen were immortalized in 1924, according to Barton. In fact, Barton often mentioned the fact in publicity material he sent out about Enright.

"Two or three years before he retired, Rex said, 'Don, I think I'm through understudying Elmer Layden,'" Barton said.

# 27 The Turnaround

The linchpin game came on September 9, 2000.

The 21-game losing streak—the 10 straight losses in 1998 that ended Brad Scott's career combined with the 0–11 of Lou Holtz's 1999 season—had been snapped the week before with a 31–0 win over New Mexico State, and the goal posts at Williams-Brice Stadium predictably came down.

However, The Turnaround was truly sparked the next week when No. 9 Georgia came to town. The Bulldogs were expected to win the SEC East and even contend for the national title but left Williams-Brice stadium with a 21–10 loss after the Gamecocks intercepted would-be star quarterback Quincy Carter five times and controlled the ball offensively.

"I'm sure when everybody around the country sees this score, they're going to say 'What? Look at that score.' Fans are going to be coming out of the woodwork," South Carolina defensive lineman Cleveland Pinkney told *The State* newspaper after the game. "I'm sure this puts a big shock into everybody."

It put a shock into the Bulldogs, including Georgia defensive lineman Richard Seymour, a Palmetto State native who crossed the state line to play for the Bulldogs.

"It's tough losing to an inferior team," Seymour told *The State*. "This is devastating."

For the Gamecocks, though, it was a historic performance that jumpstarted an 8–4 season and a trip to the Outback Bowl on January 1, 2001. The eight-game turnaround, from winless to eight wins in back-to-back years, is the second biggest turnaround in NCAA history.

*South Carolina football fans tear down the goal post after beating ninth-ranked Georgia 21–10 on Saturday, September 9, 2000, at Williams-Brice Stadium in Columbia, South Carolina.* (AP Photo/Bruce Flashnick)

Running back Ryan Brewer arrived just in time to suffer through the 0–11 season but then went to back-to-back Outback Bowls. He credits Holtz's recruitment of talented players who cared about the game for the turnaround.

"We were bringing in guys who were top-notch," Brewer said. "We were bringing in kids who loved the game and wanted to play hard."

The Gamecocks would win seven of their first eight games in 2000, the only loss coming 27–17 at Alabama, and they were ranked as high as No. 17 that year, snapping a streak of six straight seasons in which they didn't appear in the Associated Press Top 25. In fact, the six weeks in which South Carolina was ranked during the 2000 season was twice its total time spent in the Top 25 in the previous 11 seasons combined.

The 2000 regular season ended on a down slope as the vaunted "Orange Crush" section of the Gamecocks' schedule—three straight games against Tennessee, Florida, and Clemson—resulted in three straight losses. But South Carolina salvaged the feel-good story with a 24–7 win over the Buckeyes in the bowl game.

Mike McGee, then the Gamecocks athletics director and the man who hired Holtz, said he could see progress even during the 0–11 season.

"You look back at those games and virtually every one of those games was competitive," McGee said. "It wasn't like we were getting run over. We were getting better and better."

Brewer agreed, although they may have been the only ones who saw it. The Gamecocks scored more than 14 points just once and lost seven of their eight SEC games by at least 15 points during the 0–11 season.

"We knew we were getting somewhere," Brewer said. "We knew we were growing even though we got beat. We could feel that something special was about to happen, and we turned that corner the next season."

After the 0–11 season, South Carolina's overall winning percentage was .492 (466–482). Since, it is .611 (99–63).

"Since then it seems like we have been on the right track, maybe a few dips here and there, but it has grown to where it is now," Brewer said.

And it all started by beating the Bulldogs.

"You talk about loyalty, support, enthusiasm—we get all of that from our fans. And we get the expectations, too," Holtz told *The State* after the win. "We've won two games. My goodness, we just lost 21 in a row. We had high expectations when we came here. I don't think we're as good as some people think, and we're not as bad as I think. This was one game. We've got to continue to improve. I'm making no promises we'll even win another game from here on out."

They did, though.

# 28 Brandon Bennett— Over the Top

No South Carolina football player has rushed for more yards in a game than Brandon Bennett's 278 against East Tennessee State in 1991, but it's a 1-yard run two years later for which Bennett will always be remembered by Gamecocks.

"They're in that inverted wishbone, like a Power-I thing," legendary Georgia play-by-play voice Larry Munson said on September 4, 1993, as South Carolina lined up for the next-to-last play of the game with the seconds slipping away fast. "And Taneyhill gives it to him, and he dives and we hit him and stop him short of the goal line. We tackle him on about the 1- or 2-foot line as Bennett leaps. Watch the clock… 18… 17… 16… lay down you guys… 14… 13… 12… lay down… 11… 10… 9…"

The Bulldogs didn't lay down, though.

"Bennett, a great athlete, leaps over the pile and broke our hearts with two seconds to go," Munson concluded.

The Gamecocks beat the Bulldogs 23–21 in the season-opener on the play that 30 years later is still remembered by South Carolina fans as "Brandon Bennett, Over the Top." It's also remembered, strangely enough, by the Gamecocks for Munson's iconic call of the action. South Carolina had its own legend in the radio booth that day in Bob Fulton, but Munson's pleading and dejection still symbolize the play best in Columbia.

"I have gotten that call sent to me through email so many times," Bennett said. "It was a great call. He announced the heck out of that play. It's funny that their announcer is the one we listen to from that day."

What the players remember from that day, at least until the final play, was the heat. Sanford Stadium was a sauna—so much so that South Carolina's coaches had all the players take off their jerseys, shoulder pads, and undershirts at halftime just to cool down, according to quarterback Steve Taneyhill.

Taneyhill should be given some credit for one of the most exciting plays in school history because it might never have come down to such a thrilling finish had he turned the right way on the handoff attempt on the play before Bennett's dive.

"I turned the wrong way on a play at the goal line, and we've got to hurry back up to the line," Taneyhill said. "It's kind of a free-for-all getting everybody set up and getting everybody back ready. I'm just hollering, 'Same play, same play.'"

It was South Carolina's go-to play on goal line that season.

"That was our play—Brandon up in the air because he had such explosion," Taneyhill said. "We played a lot of basketball back then and Brandon could do anything on the basketball court… [he could] jump up there and dunk it."

Bennett used that kind of body control on that play, spinning in midair to slip past the only Georgia defender to make contact after he leapt into the air.

"How he spins in the air is what I remember," Taneyhill said. "As soon as I hand it to him, I spin back around because I want to watch. That was a crazy game."

That yard was one of only 72 the Gamecocks gained on the ground that day, and that game served as the biggest win of head coach Sparky Woods' career at South Carolina. The Gamecocks would go on to finish 4–7, leading to Woods' firing.

Bennett would go on to wrap up one of the greatest careers in South Carolina history the following year. His 3,055 career yards stand second in school history behind only George Rogers.

While the 1993 Georgia game was Bennett's most exciting contribution to Gamecocks lore, his performance against East Tennessee State on October 5, 1991, deserves a spot, too. A true freshman, he was filling in that day for injured starter Rob DeBoer.

"As a freshman, I was just hoping to go out there and not fumble the ball and be productive," Bennett said.

He finished with 278 of South Carolina's 362 rushing yards that day.

"To have a game turn out as that one did was huge, and it gave me a lot of confidence," he said. "They told me [my stats] afterward. I knew I was having a great game. You are just hoping to be able to get in there and touch the ball one or two times, so to be able to get in there and have that type of a career day was great."

# 29 The Recruitment of Todd Ellis

How badly did Joe Morrison want Todd Ellis to come to South Carolina?

Well, the Gamecocks head coach, famous for his quiet professionalism and all-black attire, showed up unannounced at Ellis' front door on December 23, 1984, dressed as Santa Claus and carrying a jumbo inflatable scholarship paper wrapped in ribbon.

"I'm at the house, and my father at 10:00 at night or 10:30 says, 'I have to go get some gas, I'll be right back,' which is strange. But he goes and a little while later he comes in the back door, and about that time I hear a knock on the front door," Ellis said. "My brother opens the front door, and I hear this, 'Ho, ho, ho, little boy, is your brother here?' And a guy comes in the front door in a full Santa Claus suit."

Morrison had flown from Jacksonville, Florida, where the Gamecocks were preparing to play the Gator Bowl, and had been driven straight to Ellis' home.

"My mother fed him a plate of turkey, he drank two Michelob Ultras, and he turned around and flew back to Jacksonville," Ellis said.

Morrison was so stoic that Ellis did not often tell that story publicly until after the coach's death because he knew it would embarrass Morrison. But there was no shame in chasing Todd Ellis on the recruiting trail in 1984. Every other coach in the nation seemed to be doing it.

Ellis was the quarterback at Page High School in Greensboro, North Carolina, and one of the first high school quarterbacks in the South to play in the run-and-shoot offense. Ellis was his state's first 3,000-yard passer, and Page won the state title in 1980 and 1983, tied for the title in 1984, and finished second in the state in 1982.

"I had gone through a metamorphosis and finally realized that a touchdown pass got you as many points as a touchdown run," Page's coach Marion Kirby told the *Raleigh (NC) News & Observer*. "We had some great receivers, and Todd worked harder than anyone I've coached on his mechanics."

Ellis' huge numbers led to huge attention. He started with 75 scholarship offers and methodically worked his way down to 12 schools that received in-home visits. From there, he decided where he would take the five official visits allowed by the NCAA—South Carolina, Georgia, LSU, Stanford, and North Carolina. The Gamecocks certainly weren't an early leader, but the home-state Tar Heels weren't either.

According to Ellis, former North Carolina coach Dick Crum "is incredibly boring, and their offense was boring."

After Ellis' visit to Stanford, he developed such a crush on the Cardinals that his mother was convinced he was heading west. When Georgia coach Vince Dooley made his in-home visit with the family, Ellis' mother picked up Dooley at the airport and begged him during the ride to the house to convince her son to stay in the South.

"She started crying and said, 'I don't care what you have to do. You can lie to him if you need to, but you've got to get him or he's going to go to Stanford,'" Ellis said.

But Dooley didn't lie, Ellis said, or that might have ended the recruitment because he did like most of what the Bulldogs were saying. What Ellis didn't like was Dooley telling him he shouldn't plan on throwing the ball more than 20 times a game when Georgia had perfectly good running backs who would be happy to take the ball out of his hands. Strike the Bulldogs off the list.

Ellis had a similarly good feeling about LSU, but he figured if was going to go as far as Baton Rouge, Louisiana, he might as well keep going to Palo Alto, California, and his first love of Stanford. So it came down to Stanford and South Carolina.

Ellis was having a hard time pulling the trigger on a cross-country relocation, and he had developed a close relationship with Morrison and Gamecocks defensive line coach Jim Washburn, who recruited North Carolina for the Gamecocks. Plus, the 1984 Black Magic season had shown Ellis proof that Morrison could win games in Columbia.

And Morrison clearly wanted Ellis (who was ranked the No. 4 player in the country by the one newspaper) enough to leave his team and its bowl preparation and come through Ellis' front door in a giant red suit.

"He was the man in black and somebody who was very conservative, and he comes to the front door [and] offers me that? Wow," Ellis said.

Six weeks after Morrison's stunt, the February 14 *Los Angeles Times* included this sentence: "One of the top prep quarterbacks, Todd Ellis of Greensboro, North Carolina, who threw for 3,110 yards and 19 touchdowns, signed with South Carolina."

This time it was Santa who got the gift.

# 30 Mike Hold—Black Magic Signal Caller

Not even Mike Hold knows exactly how or why he ended up in Columbia after a high school and junior college career on the West Coast.

It started on December 5, 1982, when Joe Morrison was named head coach at South Carolina after three seasons at New Mexico. But Morrison didn't just bring Hold on his journey.

Instead, Morrison's defensive coordinator Joe Lee Dunn took over the New Mexico State program. Dunn didn't recruit Hold to New Mexico either, but he called Morrison and said, "'If you need a quarterback, there's a kid at an Arizona junior college you might want to take a look at.'"

Morrison did need a quarterback. In fact, he needed a lot of players. Having started at South Carolina late in the recruiting cycle and not having a lot of tradition to sell in the first place, Morrison was searching for overlooked gems.

"[Morrison] actually didn't recruit me, but when Joe Lee Dunn stayed back to be the head coach at New Mexico, he recruited my junior college. He didn't recruit me, but he called Coach Mo," Hold said.

The Gamecocks were the only major college football school to offer Hold a scholarship, but he still considered staying closer to home and walking on at Arizona State. If George Rogers had not won the Heisman Trophy in 1980, Hold would not have known a single thing about the Gamecocks or the entire state of South Carolina before he received his first recruiting letter.

"Yeah, there was a lot [of trepidation], and it was mainly just because I didn't know a whole lot about South Carolina," Hold said. "I was more focused on trying to stay home. There was some anticipation—I don't know, some negative thoughts about coming—but once I got here and got settled in and made friends, it was easy."

South Carolina's football history would not look the same if Hold had stayed home. Hold redshirted in 1983 and was the Gamecocks' leading passer in 1984 (1,385 yards) and 1985 (1,596 yards). He remains the No. 12 passer in school history with 2,981 yards and 15 touchdowns.

It is the 1984 season—the Black Magic year—for which Hold will always be remembered. He shared time with Allen Mitchell much of the season but got the starting nod in the regular season finale against Clemson as the Gamecocks tried to bounce back from a heartbreaking loss to Navy the week earlier.

It didn't start well that night for Hold and the Gamecocks. They fell behind 21–3, but after Hold rushed 22 times for 75 yards, only completing six passes for the game, South Carolina escaped with a 22–21 victory. Hold carried the ball on the Gamecocks' final three offensive plays—a 2-yard run around the right end, a 7-yard sweep to the left, and a 1-yard touchdown run with 54 seconds remaining that proved the difference.

After a senior season that was not nearly so dramatic, Hold played two games for the Tampa Bay Buccaneers in 1987, throwing two touchdown passes in eight career completions.

He then joined the upstart Arena Football League (AFL) and stayed on in some capacity with the organization for 13 years. He quarterbacked eight different AFL teams and remains in the league's record book tied for third in an auspicious category—most times sacked in a rookie season (24). He went on to serve as head coach for the AFL Carolina Cobras in 2003. He also coached the Augusta, Macon, and Mahoning Valley teams in the Arena League's second division.

Hold left the Arena League in 2000 and became the associate athletics director for business and football operations at Newberry College in Newberry, South Carolina, and he can go virtually nowhere in the state to this day without being reminded of his Black Magic season.

"Had I gone to Arizona State, I don't care if you had won a national championship, I would have never had the opportunity to experience the last 25 years that was built around that 1984 season," Hold said. "At Southern Cal, you win a national championship, well, cool. It wasn't like that here. That was the one thing that validated me coming here."

# 31 Tiger Killer Gressette

The obituary of Tatum Wannamaker Gressette ran in the *Charleston Post and Courier* on July 20, 1997:

"Tatum Wannamaker Gressette, 97, a former head football coach and athletic director with The Citadel from 1931–1940, a former assistant to the president at the University of South Carolina and a retired teacher, died Saturday in a local hospital."

And that wasn't the half of it. The obituary also noted that Gressette left this earth as the member of four separate halls of fame. During his life he was inducted into The Citadel Hall of Fame, the University of South Carolina Hall of Fame, the South Carolina Golf Hall of Fame, and the South Carolina Athletic Hall of Fame.

He is also credited with helping form South Carolina's Gamecock Club, which raises funds for the school's athletic teams, and he was the director of the state's retirement system.

And all those accomplishments came after his playing days, when he earned the nickname "Tiger Killer," according to Mike Safran.

"[Gressette was] just a remarkable man, really was," said Safran, owner of Safran's Antiques in Columbia and the owner of the largest known collection of Gamecocks memorabilia. "I enjoyed knowing Tatum. He was sharp as a tack at 97."

In Gamecocks football, there can be no greater nickname than Tiger Killer, and Gressette earned it in 1920 and 1921 against the archrival Clemson Tigers.

When Gressette arrived from tiny St. Matthews, South Carolina, the Gamecocks hadn't beaten Clemson in eight years. In fact, they were 3–13–1 all-time in the series at the time.

Gressette changed that luck in 1920 when he hit a 25-yard drop kick field goal for the only points in a 3–0 win over the Tigers.

"There were these buildings in St. Matthews that he would practice drop kicking between, and it became known as drop kick alley," Safran said. "He was just an incredible fella. Knew Knute Rockne. Knew the people of the day. Whenever I would visit with him, I'd feel like I was stealing from a library. The stories he was telling, you'd have sensory overload."

Former South Carolina sports information director Tom Price, in his book *Tales from the Gamecock Roost*, wrote that it remains the only successful drop kick in Gamecocks football history.

"I [told my teammates that] if you'll keep those fellas off me for two seconds, I'll get us three points," Gressette said on *100 Years of Gamecock Football*. "I knew I could because my leg was grooved. Sure enough, I put it down and it went in."

Gressette only played one more season, serving as captain of Sol Metzger's team in 1921 when the Gamecocks beat the Tigers 21–0. For his two years of service, and 2–0 record against the Tigers, Gressette was named to the school's all-time Pre-World War II team as one of four backs. (In a strange twist that in some ways is typical of the nature of the South Carolina–Clemson rivalry, Gressette's son and namesake would go on to attend Clemson College.)

Gressette told Safran that he was likely the first South Carolina football player to be paid to attend the university. He told Safran he was given $800, the equivalent of more than $10,000 today, in 1919.

"They brought me to Carolina to help them defeat Clemson," Gressette said. "We wanted to beat Clemson just as bad then as the players do now. And we did."

Most Gamecocks would call it money well spent.

# 32 Paul Dietzel—A Salesman

Ron Bass was thrust into action by an injury to starting quarterback Jeff Grantz.

South Carolina was getting ready to host North Carolina at home in a night game, and Bass was nervous when head coach Paul Dietzel instructed his players to head to the stadium and file into a large room underneath the stadium.

"He turned off the lights, and he had us all lay down and I guess meditate, for lack of a better word," Bass said. "That's what we did. We were resting and meditating. His advice was to go through the plays, go through them in your head. What do you do in different situations? We were in that room in the dark for an hour. We came out and were very relaxed and focused."

Today, the technique is widely used and is called positive visualization. In 1974, Bass and his teammates didn't know what to call it, but they won the game 31–23.

Former South Carolina quarterback Tommy Suggs, who was recruited by Dietzel, said the former coach was always ahead of his time.

"He was a great visionary," Suggs said.

Dietzel won the 1969 ACC title with the Gamecocks, the only conference championship in school history, but he finished with a 42–53–1 overall record from 1966–75.

"He may not have won as many football games as a lot of people wanted, but he sure did some things for the athletics program that were vitally needed," Suggs said.

Dietzel, like most major football coaches of his time, was also the school's athletic director, and that role took more and more of his time as his career evolved at South Carolina.

*Paul Dietzel, South Carolina's head football coach shown in 1973.* (AP Photo)

"You didn't have all these sports, so it was easier, but you still had a lot of work in addition to being a head football coach," Suggs said. "Coach did things here no one else could have done."

Dietzel was vital in raising money for expansions of Williams-Brice Stadium. He is also responsible for building The Roost athletics complex and Carolina Coliseum.

"Paul Dietzel was always one of my favorite people. I have never met a man who was more positive in his thinking than Paul was," the school's longtime play-by-play voice Bob Fulton said in 1992 on *100 Years of Gamecocks Football*. "He was interested in a lot of things outside coaching football."

After one particularly disappointing loss to Virginia Tech, Dietzel used his postgame television show to sell used Astroturf from the field to raise money for the school's various building projects.

"And he sold it, too," former South Carolina sports information director Don Barton said. "Dietzel was definitely about [public relations]."

Dietzel's hiring was big news in Columbia. He had been named the National Coach of the Year after guiding LSU to an unbeaten season in 1958, and he had experience working under legends like Paul "Bear" Bryant, Vince Lombardi, and Sid Gillman.

"It was big-time to get Paul Dietzel," Suggs said. "He was a great salesman… He had great recruiting years—just got a little off focus and got to be an athletics director more than a football coach—but he was a very good salesman."

Dietzel, who never repeated his darkened room pregame preparation plan during Bass' career, was more of an administrator than a game-planner as head coach.

"He wasn't the offensive coordinator; he wasn't the defensive coordinator," Bass said. "He really took an interest in special teams more than anything else. That allowed the players to really work with the assistant coaches who were over their position. I don't know if that's like it is now. I see Steve Spurrier as a very involved coach, especially with the quarterbacks and receivers, too. Coach Dietzel, he delegated a lot more. I think that made him a good coach."

Dietzel, who flew B-29 airplanes in World War II, retired in Louisiana and became an accomplished watercolor painter.

"He was a good guy," Suggs said.

# 33 Williams-Brice Stadium

It has been called some unkind things, most notably an upside-down cockroach, but it's been home to South Carolina for almost 80 years and it's getting more and more comfortable.

What is now Williams-Brice Stadium, the home of the Gamecocks, began life as Municipal Stadium in 1934. It's construction was a dual project between the city of Columbia and the Works Progress Administration, which built a wooden wall around the field and stands as part of the federal government's attempt to put the nation's labor force back to work after the Great Depression.

The land for the stadium was purchased from a Columbia dairy, and early aerial photos show milk cows grazing just outside the gates. It seated 17,500 fans on September 29, 1934, when it hosted its first football game. The Gamecocks beat Erskine 25–0 and the next week officially dedicated the stadium with a 22–6 victory over Virginia Military Institute. It grew in fits and spurts from there, being named Carolina Stadium in 1941 after the city gave the stadium to South Carolina. But the most significant change came in 1971.

It was that year that Thomas H. Brice made a donation from the considerable estate of himself and wife Martha Williams-Brice, whose family operated the Williams Furniture Company in Sumter, South Carolina. Martha Williams-Brice died in 1969 but had made arrangements for the donation in her will.

"Tom Brice actually owed us that money," South Carolina historian and former Gamecocks sports information director Don Barton said with a smile.

Brice lettered at South Carolina from 1922–23, and in 1923 he fumbled in the South Carolina–Clemson game, setting up the Tigers' winning touchdown in a 7–6 South Carolina loss.

When Phil Lavoie fumbled during a South Carolina–Clemson game in the 1950s, he was chagrined to learn it was his only contribution to the football team that was noted in Barton's book on the Big Thursday rivalry between the schools.

"Phil said, 'Of all the great seasons I had at Carolina, all you had about me was I fumbled in the Carolina-Clemson game,'" Barton said. "I said, 'If it makes you feel any better, they named the stadium after somebody who did the same thing.'"

The improvements made possible by the Williams-Brice donation came during Paul Dietzel's coaching tenure. Dietzel dubbed the arena "not very attractive" and set out to find the money for a facelift.

The first problem was finding a willing donor. That was accomplished with the Williams-Brice family.

"They both loved Carolina a lot," Columbia lawyer Tom Brice Hall, the grandson of Thomas Brice and Martha Williams-Brice told *The State* newspaper in 2009 when the stadium celebrated its 75th anniversary. "I can't drive by the stadium without thinking about my grandfather. It's an honor to have the name up there."

The second problem was getting the donation past tax laws, which Dietzel said came with the help of Sen. Strom Thurmond and Rep. L. Mendel Rivers.

"I remember Strom asked Rivers, 'How do we get this through?'" Dietzel told *The State*. "And he said, 'Well, we'll stick it in this bill, and no one will pay attention.' And that's how we got it."

The Williams-Brice donation was in the $3.5 million range.

"That would give you a concession stand now," Barton said.

In fact, the bill for the facility kept going up and up while its stands went up and up. In 1982, an upper deck was added that took the capacity to 72,000. Another upgrade was needed when the Gamecocks entered the Southeastern Conference in 1992.

The school added club seats, luxury suites, and a new press box in 1995 at a price tag of $9.9 million. In 1996, it took another

$10 million to increase the capacity to 80,250 where it sits today, making it the 20th largest college football stadium in the nation.

The seating stopped there, but the improvements did not. In addition to significant infrastructure upgrades, the school also spent $6.5 million on a 36' x 124' video board that gave Williams-Brice the third largest in-stadium screen in the SEC.

On Gamecocks game days, Williams-Brice Stadium is the fourth-largest city in the state, and the school ranked No. 17 in the nation in home attendance in 2012 and finished that season with an 11-game home winning streak, the third longest in school history. From 2008–12, South Carolina was 27–3 during a 30-game span at home.

# 34 Steve Spurrier's Swagger

South Carolina wanted the "Evil Genius" when it hired Steve Spurrier in 2005. The Gamecocks were hoping for "Steve Superior."

Spurrier picked up both of those nicknames during a 12-year coaching career at Florida, during which he won six SEC championships and one national title, adding insults to his opponents' injuries with his barbed tongue.

This is the man who once pointed out that you "can't spell Citrus without UT"—a shot at his then-archrival Tennessee's habit of finishing second to him in the SEC—and wondered publicly what happened to all those supposedly great football players who signed with Georgia on the Saturdays when his Gators regularly beat the Bulldogs. He also said Florida State's familiar "FSU" logo really stood for Free Shoes University, and the *Lexington (KY)*

*Herald-Leader* once filled the front page of its sports section with a graphic containing just the Spurrier barbs aimed at the Wildcats.

That's the guy South Carolina wanted, a coach who would beat the rest of the SEC on Saturday and remind them of the score on Sunday. Unfortunately, that's not the man they got for the first five seasons. South Carolina was 35–28 during that time. In 2007, the Gamecocks rose to No. 6 in the country before losing five straight to end the season.

Steve Spurrier was, of all things, humbled. And quiet. Then things started to turn around. The Gators made headway on the recruiting trail, started beating some of their most frequent opponents, and turned around the Clemson series. Suddenly, Steve Spurrier had his swagger back.

The culmination of the return of "Darth Visor" came at the expense of the in-state rival Tigers. Uncharacteristically, it wasn't Spurrier who started this back-and-forth battle of barbs… although some Clemson fans will never believe that.

It began after the Gamecocks beat Clemson 34–13 in 2011. South Carolina play-by-play announcer Todd Ellis, a former Gamecocks quarterback, quoted Spurrier on the air after the game and then added his own barb at the end, saying, "As Coach Spurrier says, we may not be LSU or Alabama… but we ain't Clemson folks."

The "but we ain't Clemson folks" was Ellis' addition, but it didn't appear that way when the football program's official Twitter feed (@GamecockFB) posted this: "'We aren't LSU, and we aren't Alabama. But we sure ain't Clemson.'—Steve Spurrier."

Clemson coach Dabo Swinney was not a fan of that and responded with one of coaching's all-time greatest rants against an opponent. Among the highlight's from Swinney's nearly five-minute diatribe:

- "After five years, I think [Spurrier] had 35 wins and a new contract and all that kind of stuff. After five years at

Clemson, if I only have 35 wins, there is going to be a new coach here and there should be because there is a different standard."

- "I guess I'd have to say I agree with him. I'd say he's right. They are not Clemson, and they are never going to be Clemson to be honest with you, and no three-game winning streak is going to change that. It's not the first time they've won three in a row, and it won't be the last time. It might be 50 more years."

- "I have a lot of respect for Coach Spurrier, but I am going to defend my program. I am going to defend my players, my coaches, and I'm going to defend Clemson University because I believe in it."

- "There are a lot of rivalries out there. This is more of a domination, and that's a fact. My kid's grandkids won't live long enough to ever see this really become a rivalry. It is what it is."

- "I have respect for their program, but South Carolina is not Clemson. There are a lot of differences. This is a place that has won a national title, 17 conference championships. We've won more bowl games than they've ever been to. I think our program has 100-plus more wins than South Carolina. That's reality."

- "He's exactly right. They ain't Alabama. They ain't LSU, and they certainly aren't Clemson. Carolina is in Chapel Hill, and USC is in California and *the* university in this state always has been, always will be Clemson. You can print that, tweet that, whatever."

At the time, Spurrier said he wasn't bothered by Swinney's statements and had no intention of getting into a verbal altercation with the Clemson coach. As the months passed, though, he couldn't seem to help himself.

He subsequently made a dismissive reference to Clemson's habit of calling its stadium Death Valley and called most of what Swinney said about South Carolina "garbage" and "b.s." after Swinney offered a compliment to Marcus Lattimore.

Spurrier's swagger was back.

# 35 Jim Carlen—"Opinionated and Obnoxious"

Jim Carlen didn't pull punches.

As South Carolina's football coach and athletics director from 1975–81, Carlen was remembered after his death in 2012 as a fierce defender of his players and just plain fierce at times.

"Like so many people that we know in high places, including presidents of the university, presidents of the United States, they become their own worst enemies and self destruct," said Don Barton, a former sports information director at the school and an athletic department historian. "I considered Jim Carlen a friend. I liked him, but I could understand some of his detractors because he was blunt."

They were saying the same things even before Carlen died at the age of 79 at his South Carolina home.

"Probably the problem Jim had above everything else was his problem with the media and with some of the fans," South Carolina's legendary play-by-play voice Bob Fulton said in 1992 on *100 Years of Gamecock Football*. "I always liked Carlen because he never talked out of both sides of his mouth. If he didn't like you, he would tell you, and he probably told some people he should not have told."

Carlen compiled a 45–36–1 record at South Carolina, and his tenure featured some of the program's highest points, including a

56–20 win over Clemson in his first game against the Tigers and George Rogers' 1980 Heisman Trophy winning season.

It also included its share of low points, including losing five of his last six to the Tigers and losing to Pacific and Hawaii in the final three games of the 1981 season, which would be his last. Carlen did not go quietly, though. He let it be known he didn't think much of the decision, and when university president James Holderman was sent to prison for misappropriating funds 22 years after presiding over Carlen's dismissal, Carlen told *The State* newspaper, "I stood up for what I thought was right, and it cost me dearly. People back then said I was the one who was wrong; I wonder what some of them think now."

Carlen's greatest contribution to the school without question was the recruitment of Rogers who said Carlen was the only major college football coach who didn't offer him an improper incentive to come to school. Carlen became a father figure to Rogers, who had grown up without his father. As such, Carlen fiercely protected his star, perhaps to a fault.

"When George won the Heisman Trophy and flew back into the airport in Columbia, there were several thousand people out there to meet him. What did [Carlen] do? He rushed George out of there to the car instead of stopping and saying something on behalf of George," Barton said. "It was as if they were meeting a stranger on the plane. He quote 'protected' George from the media."

Carlen—whose seven-year tenure at the school is topped only by Rex Enright (15 years), Paul Dietzel (nine years) and Steve Spurrier (eight years through the 2012 season)—replaced Dietzel and inherited a team that fit his own thoughts about football.

"We had been a staff for a long time. We understood that you convince the players to play as hard as they could play, don't promise anybody anything, and those players played hard for us. Guys who were average or less got to where they were better than average," Carlen said in 1992 on *100 Years of Gamecock Football*. "I

## Sandstorm

When South Carolina marketing director Eric Nichols added "Sandstorm" to the list of music played during games at Williams-Brice Stadium, he had no idea what he was starting.

"We play songs and watch the student section and see what they react to," Nichols told *The State* newspaper.

The students and everyone else reacted passionately to "Sandstorm," a sans vocal techno piece written by Finnish artist Ville Virtanen. It has become a rousing staple during South Carolina home games with fans bouncing and waving white towels along with the song before kickoffs and after touchdowns.

"To see 80,000 people jumping, I would be lying if I didn't say how it warms my heart," Virtanen, who goes by the name Darude, told *The State*.

Darude wrote "Sandstorm" in 2000, and it quickly became a hit in dance clubs around the world.

"I'm not a musician by trade," he told *The State*. "I make music block by block, like a building, seeing how things fit."

One thing is clear—South Carolina and "Sandstorm" fit.

---

think you play defense. You keep the other team from beating you. And you play the kicking game. Then I think you get a running game that you can control to keep your defense from being on the field all the time."

Carlen stuck to those principals, said running back Kevin Long, a star on Carlen's 1975 team.

"He was a disciplinary, but he was fair and he was always concerned about the players," Long said. "I visited him before his death, and up until his death he was still concerned about his players."

Carlen remained in South Carolina after his firing and was rarely shy about offering his opinions on the Gamecocks' decisions. When Steve Spurrier was hired in 2005, Carlen told *The State* he thought it was a fantastic hire.

"He's opinionated and obnoxious," Carlen said, "so we're two of a kind."

# 36 Quite a Recruiting Run

As the dreadful early 2000s turned into the much rosier 2010s, South Carolina's football turnaround was built on three pillars—the coaching acumen of Steve Spurrier, a drastic overhaul of the team's facilities, and players.

Of the three, the players were the strongest foundation, and it all started at the top. The Gamecocks' long track record of mediocrity has always been highlighted by how few times the team was able to land a marquee football talent. The problem for South Carolina was twofold. For starters, the Palmetto State's population of 4.7 million ranks 12th among states with SEC schools. (By comparison, the Atlanta metropolitan area, which sits 60 miles from the campus of Gamecocks rival the University of Georgia, has around 5.2 million people.) That means South Carolina only occasionally produced elite college football talent, which brings up the second problem. For the first 100 years of its football-playing history, South Carolina could not convince those players to become Gamecocks.

"There has been a history of great players in this state," South Carolina recruiting coordinator Steve Spurrier Jr. said. "We just haven't gotten any of them."

That started to change in 2009 as South Carolina began a four-year stretch of signing the state's high school Mr. Football each season. The momentum from that change powered a three-year stretch in which South Carolina won its first SEC Eastern Division title and 31 games.

The reason this run of success with prep stars was such a boon for the Gamecocks is because of the talent the state began to produce. While the state's overall production of players went down during that time period, its number of players with superstar potential went way up, according to Rivals.com national recruiting analyst Mike Farrell.

Stephon Gilmore, a quarterback from Rock Hill, started the trend by signing with South Carolina despite heavy interest from in-state rival Clemson. Gilmore would go on to be the No. 10 overall pick in the 2012 NFL Draft as a cornerback.

"I could have went to Alabama, LSU, all the big schools, but I wanted to start something new at South Carolina and come here and try to get a winning team," Gilmore said.

Things got even better the next two years as running back Marcus Lattimore and defensive end Jadeveon Clowney were tabbed Mr. Football and signed on to play for Spurrier. Lattimore, widely considered one of the top three high school running backs in the nation in 2010, would be the National Freshman of the Year in his initial season and go on to set the school's career touchdown (41) and rushing touchdown (38) records. Clowney, the top recruit in the country at any position and one of the most highly regarded players of the 2000s, signed with the Gamecocks in 2011 and set the school's single-season sack record in 2012 (13) while being named a consensus All-American, one of only four in school history.

"You look at the state of California, Texas, Florida, there's not a player down there who compares to those two individuals or Gilmore," said South Carolina offensive line coach Shawn Elliott, one of the Gamecocks' top recruiters "We're always going to have 10 guys across the state who can play Division I, but it seems like here lately we are getting the best of the bunch.

"There's a difference between landing one of the best players in the country and landing one of the best players in the state. It's great that it just so happens to be the same in the last couple years. In the past, you didn't have that elite athlete who was coming out. Now you are in pretty good shape, and that helps turn things around pretty quickly, especially when they can play early."

South Carolina completed its recruiting four-peat by signing wide receiver Shaq Roland in 2012. Roland was the state's Mr. Football but did not receive quite the same hoopla as the previous three such honorees.

"Why did we get a Clowney or a Lattimore? Because we were playing good football and those guys wanted to be a part of this program," Spurrier Jr. said. "Obviously, it steamrolls. When something good happens, something really good happens and it keeps happening. You have to keep winning. Bad things happen quick, too, and it can go downhill real quick, too."

Scout.com director of scouting Scott Kennedy said the signing of Clowney alone might have been enough to change the national perception of South Carolina and its football program for years to come.

"Clowney really sort of took it to the next level for them," Kennedy said. "Any time you have the No. 1 player in the nation in your state and you make sure he stays home, people take notice."

# 37 Harold Green—Mr. Versatility

As a child, Harold Green traveled the world as the son of a career Air Force officer, but he finally landed in Summerville, South Carolina, and South Carolina's football history is better because of it.

Green—a 6'2", 222-lb. running back at Stratford High School—joined the Gamecocks in 1986 and left four years later as the second-leading rusher in school history behind only Heisman Trophy winner George Rogers. Green's 3,005 career yards on 702 carries still stands third in school history.

"He was the silent assassin," said former South Carolina quarterback Todd Ellis, who played with Green throughout his career. "The guy never complained. You could give him 30 carries or five, and he did his job. He made more moves laterally in a 5-yard span than anybody I had ever seen. Just a tough-as-nails tailback."

Green's best season was 1987 when he gained 1,022 yards on 229 carries. His 11 career 100-yard rushing games is tied for second in school history.

"I thought he was one of the toughest players I ever played with, and it proved to be that way when everybody discounted him when he got banged up a little bit and he goes and plays in the [NFL] for nine years and probably could have played longer," Ellis said.

Green also caught 94 passes in his career for 859 yards and remains 14th in school history in receptions.

"He was brilliant in the screen game," Ellis said.

Green's best game as a Gamecock came on November 14, 1987, when he gained 172 yards on 27 carries against Wake Forest. Green gained 100 yards in the second half of that game to power his team to a 30–0 win.

"We had to settle down, come back, and get things rolling," Green told the Associated Press after the game. "We caught on to what they were doing. I think Wake Forest played us a little bit more toward our passing game, which most of our opponents do. When we get the breaks to run the ball, we do. It turns out to be a pretty good gainer on the offensive side of the ball."

In 1990, Green was drafted in the second round of the NFL draft, No. 38 overall, by the Cincinnati Bengals. From 1991–95, he started at least 10 games for the Bengals, and he finished his professional career with 4,365 yards on 1,151 carries.

"He's the kind of guy who would go along and make two or three yards, then bang, he'd make 45 yards and set the team up for a touchdown," Cincinnati head coach Sam Wyche told the Associated Press. "That's his history. It can happen with him. He doesn't have the speed of a Bo Jackson, but he's got the threat of breaking a big play like that."

Bengals quarterback Boomer Esiason told the Associated Press that Green was "a diamond in the rough."

"He's a truly gifted athlete who catches, blocks, and runs," Esiason said.

Green also played for the St. Louis Rams and Atlanta Falcons to finish his NFL career. In 2002, he was elected to the South Carolina Athletics Hall of Fame.

"It's a great honor, especially understanding that there are a lot of athletes who have come through this university with a lot of accolades," Green told *The State* newspaper. "A lot of athletes have paved the way for guys like myself. To me, it's icing on the cake to stake claims right here in your backyard at your alma mater."

Green—who owns a share of Columbia auto dealer Pro Bowl Motors along with former South Carolina teammates Gerald Dixon, Sterling Sharpe, and Otis Morris—briefly served as a part-time career development assistant in the athletic department's administration.

"I can remember being a freshman coming in here and not realizing what the expectations of being a student athlete are," Green told *The State*. "I help them understand the demands. You've got to get yourself acclimated. The opportunities come very short term. The demands are great, and the dividends can be great, too."

# 38 Del Wilkes—Paving the Way

In 1984, Del Wilkes became the second consensus All-American in South Carolina history, but it almost never happened.

Wilkes was born in Columbia but moved to Calhoun, Georgia, as a child. He returned to the Columbia area the summer before his junior year and quickly became a standout offensive lineman at Irmo High School.

"It seemed like everything that happened to me athletically snuck up on me," Wilkes said. "It seemed like everything caught me off guard. I remember at Irmo when I was told I had made the Shrine Bowl [which pits the best high school players from North Carolina against the best from South Carolina], it just completely caught me off guard. I didn't expect that. I thought there was probably a team full of players that deserved that, and I didn't think I was one of them."

But he was, and college coaches were noticing. In the fall of 1979, Wilkes took a recruiting visit to Clemson, where he had developed a strong bond with Tigers head coach Danny Ford and assistant coach Jimmye Laycock.

"When I took my official visit to Clemson, went to the game, and the next morning over breakfast with Coach Laycock and Coach Ford, I committed to go to Clemson," Wilkes said.

Wilkes returned home that day thinking he would be a Clemson Tiger. The next day, he was at his grandfather's house to watch *Monday Night Football*, a tradition for the pair.

"That Monday night his phone rings—this is when your phone was on the wall, you couldn't walk around with it—and he came back and he said, 'Coach Carlen is on the phone. He wants to talk to you,'" Wilkes said.

Jim Carlen was the head coach at South Carolina and well known as a persuasive recruiter. He was not happy with Wilkes.

"He said, 'Look son, I know your mom and dad and you come from a good family. Why would you want to go up there?' He said, 'You come from good people. You don't want to go up there. They are a bunch of outlaws and rebels.' In a matter of just a few minutes, he talked me out of it, and I never regretted it. I am glad I went to South Carolina."

It didn't start smoothly, however.

"I can remember when I got to Carolina and we started fall practice, the first two or three days it was just the freshmen, and then the second or third day the upperclassmen starting practicing with us. I can remember when I had to start practicing against guys who were seniors in college, and here I am not far removed from being a senior in high school," Wilkes said. "They were much bigger, stronger, faster. I thought to myself, 'My God, these people have made a mistake, and it's not going to take them long to figure out I don't belong here.' I just thought, 'I don't stand a chance. I will never be able to compete at this level.'"

But Wilkes got more experience—and he got bigger and stronger with the help of steroids, as he told *USA Today*—and he soon learned he could compete at the collegiate level. He learned that in practice against another South Carolina All-American, defensive end Andrew Provence, who set the school's single-season record for sacks with 10 in 1982.

"If I could compete against Andrew Provence, then I felt like I had a chance," Wilkes said. "I felt like Andrew was one of the best defensive linemen in the country, and I knew there weren't going to be any guys who were any quicker, any faster, any stronger. Andrew was a stud. When I was able to go out in spring ball or two-a-days and I could pass block Andrew or I could run block Andrew, that's how I decided, 'I do have a chance. I am going to be able to compete.'"

Wilkes' career culminated in the 1984 Black Magic season, when he paved the way for quarterback Mike Hold and company as the Gamecocks won eight games and reached the No. 2 ranking in the country at one point. After the season, the Associated Press, Walter Camp Foundation, and the Kodak Coaches All-America team named Wilkes a first-team All-American.

Of the 1984 team, Wilkes said, "It was a group of guys who had been together a long time and were sort of tired of getting our butts beat and decided we wanted to be good."

## 39 The 2010 Season— Winning the East

In its first 116 years of football, South Carolina won one title, and there were those who didn't think another one would ever come.

The Gamecocks captured the 1969 Atlantic Coast Conference crown, but their ACC days were long behind them in the 2000s. They had entered the rough-and-tumble world of the Southeastern Conference (SEC), and they didn't show any signs of competing in the league in their first 15 years as members.

Then came the 2010 season. The 2009 campaign had ended with a disappointing 20–7 loss to Connecticut in the PapaJohns. com Bowl, but there was a new hope with the arrival of a freshman running back named Marcus Lattimore.

Here's how the season played out:

**September 2:** South Carolina beat Southern Miss 41–13 in Lattimore's collegiate debut. The young back scored two touchdowns, and sophomore wide receiver Alshon Jeffery had 106 receiving yards.

**September 11:** Lattimore became an SEC star by bowling over Georgia for 182 yards on 37 carries in a 17–6 South Carolina victory. "Marcus has a knack for finding a little crease," Coach Steve Spurrier said.

**September 18:** The Gamecocks dispatched in-state FCS school Furman 38–19. "Glad the game's over, and we don't have to play them again for another 25 years," Spurrier said.

**September 25:** In one of the best games (if not best results) of the season, South Carolina fell 35–27 to eventual national champion Auburn. Quarterback Stephen Garcia fumbled twice in the fourth quarter, and each time Tigers quarterback Cam Newton capitalized with a touchdown pass. Newton's performance that day—176 rushing yards and five total touchdowns—started his run to the 2010 Heisman Trophy.

**October 9:** Top-ranked and defending national champion Alabama came to Williams-Brice Stadium and left as stunned 35–21 losers at the hands of the Gamecocks. Garcia threw three touchdown passes and Lattimore had three scores of his own in South Carolina's only win against a No. 1 team. "I think this game was meant to be," Spurrier said.

**October 16:** As stunned as Alabama was to leave Columbia with a loss a week earlier, the Gamecocks were equally as surprised to be sent home from Commonwealth Stadium as losers to the Kentucky Wildcats. The 31–28 loss was Spurrier's first loss ever to the Wildcats. "Give Kentucky credit," Spurrier said. "They kicked our tails."

**October 23:** Filling in for an injured Lattimore, senior Brian Maddox rushed for 146 yards as the Gamecocks beat Vanderbilt 21–7.

**October 30:** The Gamecocks took a big step toward the division title with a 38–24 win over the Volunteers that was highlighted by Jeffery's 70-yard touchdown catch. "He doesn't look like he's fast, but no one seems to catch him from behind," Spurrier said.

**November 6:** South Carolina didn't lose control of its own destiny in the East, but it did lose a little pride, getting whipped 41–20 by Arkansas. "We didn't have much tonight," Spurrier said. "The way we played, you wonder how we won six games already this year."

**November 13:** After Florida's Andre Debose returned the opening kickoff 99 yards for a touchdown, it was all Gamecocks in The Swamp. Lattimore rushed 40 times for 212 yards, and the South Carolina defense made the Gators look silly in a 36–14 win that clinched the Eastern Division crowd and set off a raucous scene in the Gamecocks' locker room.

"It was kind of neat in the locker room to look at Ladi Ajiboye there and say, 'Ladi, we're going to Atlanta,'" Gamecocks coach Steve Spurrier said. "He is from Atlanta. We have a lot of players from Atlanta. That was our recruiting pitch all along. Our goal is to win the game in Atlanta. That's still our goal, and we have a chance. Obviously, it won't be easy against Auburn [in the SEC title game], but who knows what could happen if the ball bounces your way."

Garcia and Spurrier, who had a rocky relationship throughout their time together, embraced in the locker room.

"Last week in the press conference, somebody asked if this would be the same old South Carolina," Garcia said. "I don't want to say that we shut anybody up yet because we still have two games left, one of them being against Clemson, but I think it was a huge win for us."

**November 20:** There was no letdown after the Florida victory as the Gamecocks pummeled Troy 69–24.

**November 27:** Jeffery had another 100-yard game as the Gamecocks beat Clemson 29–7. It gave them their first back-to-back wins over the Tigers in 40 years.

The season didn't end the way South Carolina had hoped as a surging Auburn team pummeled the Gamecocks 56–17 in the SEC Championship Game, and Florida State prevailed 26–17 in the Chick-fil-A Bowl, but the season will always be remembered as a great one in South Carolina.

# 40 Brad Scott— Seemed So Right

Brad Scott should have been the guy.

Hired on December 7, 1993, to replace Sparky Woods and become South Carolina's 30th head football coach, he had the right pedigree and all the right answers.

"The headline in the paper the next day was, 'USC finally gets it right,'" said Teddy Heffner, longtime South Carolina sports writer and sports talk radio host on 560 AM in Columbia. "Brad Scott was considered a great hire at the time. He was the offensive coordinator for the national champions. South Carolina fans really felt like this was going to be a really, really good hire."

Scott came to the Gamecocks from Florida State—and fresh off an appearance in the national title game at that. He sincerely believed he had just taken a great job.

"I've had opportunities in the past, but I chose to turn them down because of the great situation I had there [at Florida State]," he said at his introductory news conference. "I can promise you one thing—when I got the call to find out if I was a little bit interested in South Carolina, I nearly jumped out of my chair. We'll be wide open. I think one of the things that we have explored a little bit over the last two years is the attack theory of offensive football."

He soon hit the road for the football coach's annual summer speaking tour, and he kept hitting all the right notes.

"I feel that I'm a good fit for the state of South Carolina," he told one group of fans, according to *The State* newspaper. "I'm a small-town guy who grew up with high moral values as far as being involved in my church... loving the competition that athletics offers, loving the outdoors, hunting, and fishing. And I'm learning here now about NASCAR."

## Billy Gambrell

For some, Billy Gambrell's name has been lost to history. For Dan Reeves, it never will be.

Reeves, a former South Carolina football player who played for the Dallas Cowboys and then found fame as an NFL head coach, called Gambrell the best all-around athlete he ever played with.

"By far," Reeves told the *Athens (GA) Banner-Herald* upon Gambrell's election to the Athens Athletic Hall of Fame in 2000. "He could dunk a basketball, run the football, play wide receiver, return kickoffs and punts. There wasn't anything he couldn't do."

That included track, where Gambrell was the ACC's indoor long jump champion in 1961. A Georgia native who is also a member of the South Carolina Athletic Hall of Fame, Gambrell rushed for more than 1,000 yards in his Gamecocks career; he led South Carolina in rushing in 1962 with 582 yards.

"I grew up at the YMCA. It was a wonderful place to play, and we played a lot of sports. That's just the way I was raised. That's what I wanted to do," Gambrell told the *Banner-Herald.* "So no, I never really thought of it as being that big of a deal. At South Carolina, we played offense and we played defense. There were no specialists. You were just expected to play."

Gambrell's best moment at South Carolina came on November 11, 1961, when he had 14 carries for 62 yards, caught five passes for 71 yards, scored a touchdown and a two-point conversion, and intercepted a pass in a 21–14 win over Clemson.

When the fall rolled around, Scott inherited one of the best passers in school history in quarterback Steve Taneyhill.

"I was excited because in high school I was in the shotgun and here comes a guy saying, 'We're going to get in the shotgun,'" Taneyhill said. "I had to refocus. Anytime a new coach comes in, the first thing he says is, 'Nobody has a starting position. I am evaluating everybody.' That's something that Coach Scott said that has always stuck with me. When a new coach comes in, he hasn't seen you, and it's time to prove yourself all over again. I was the guy, my ego was pretty good, but I had to refocus and rework."

Their relationship soon blossomed, however, and they remain friends now that Taneyhill has gone on to a successful high school coaching career in South Carolina.

The early returns were just what everyone expected. An offense that had gained more than 400 yards twice in 1993 did it four times in 1994, and Scott won seven games his first year, getting the Gamecocks to just the ninth bowl in school history.

However, that was the highlight of Scott's career. The next three years saw four, six, and five wins. And then came the 1998 season. South Carolina beat Ball State 38–20 in the season-opener and then lost 10 straight games, leading to Scott's firing after the season.

"[Athletics Director Mike] McGee has his own set of expectations for me, and I seem to have failed to meet those," Scott told *The State* newspaper the day he was fired. "But there was never a time where voices were raised or anything like that. I've got great respect for Coach McGee, and I think he respects me. He's always supported me and given me anything I asked for. It's a tough decision he had to make. It's a bottom-line decision."

Scott told the newspaper he expected 1998 to be a rough season when he made the decision to play young players in an attempt to build for the future

"It came down to a 1–10 season," he said. "Why else do you renew a guy for five years a couple of years ago if I wasn't doing a good job, especially with the significant renewal they gave me, and the financial package? If it was looked at over a five-year period... I don't believe that was the case. I think it really came down to going 1–10. If I was making the decision, it would have been a very hard decision to make. I think there's some folks out there who support me."

The number of South Carolina people supporting Scott dwindled quickly as he soon accepted a job as an assistant coach at archrival Clemson, where he served until retiring after the 2011 season.

"There are a lot of South Carolina fans who will never forgive Brad for going to Clemson. Hell, Carolina fired him—what's he supposed to do? He got another job offer, and he took it," Heffner said.

In one of the quirks of fate that are sprinkled throughout the history of SEC football, the man who replaced Scott as Florida State's offensive coordinator in 1994 was Mark Richt. Seven years later, Richt would be hired by one of the Gamecocks' chief rivals, Georgia, where he has won 118 games, two SEC championships, and six SEC East titles in 12 years.

"Think what the history difference might be if Brad Scott had gone to Georgia and Richt had come to South Carolina," Heffner said, "although I'm not sure South Carolina was really ready to win on the big-time stage then."

# 41 The Suspensions of Stephen Garcia

Steve Spurrier finally had his quarterback—Stephen Garcia.

The player who would turn around South Carolina's football fortunes announced his decision to play for the Gamecocks on December 7, 2006, at Jefferson High School in Tampa, Florida.

Garcia was considered a four-star prospect by the major recruiting services. His combination of passing and running ability were going to give Spurrier what he hadn't had at South Carolina—a signal-caller physically gifted enough to lift South Carolina into contention in the SEC. Alabama wanted him, Oklahoma wanted him, and Ole Miss wanted him, to name a few. But South Carolina got him.

Gamecocks fans immediately fell in love with the 6'3" 214-lb. player with his combination of talent and confidence. With hair

*South Carolina's Stephen Garcia (5) looks to pass during the SEC East game between the South Carolina Gamecocks and the Vanderbilt Commodores, played at Williams-Brice Stadium in Columbia, South Carolina, on September 24, 2011. South Carolina won the game 21–3 to go 4–0 on the season.*
(Cal Sport Media via AP Images)

down to his shoulders and a fascination with Greek mythology, Garcia exuded the gunslinger mentality so often attached to elite quarterbacks.

"I think he's got a lot of great things to look forward to," Jefferson High School coach Mike Fenton said at Garcia's announcement. "If he does what he's supposed to do, I really believe we'll maybe be seeing him play [in the NFL] one day."

But the "if he does what he's supposed to do" part was always the problem for Garcia. He enrolled early, in January 2007, in order to compete in spring practice, but it only gave him a head start on getting into trouble.

In February 2007, one month after arriving on campus, Garcia was arrested in Five Points, the main student nightlife section of Columbia, and charged with drunkenness and failure to stop on police command. He was suspended indefinitely by Spurrier, but the suspension was lifted the next day, and a trend was born.

Garcia would be suspended five times during his South Carolina career, but he never missed any game time due to that discipline. In March 2007, two weeks after his first arrest, Garcia was arrested again for vandalizing a professor's car. In March 2008, he was suspended from the team's summer drills after being charged with underage drinking. In March 2011, Garcia was suspended from a week of spring practice after a team rules violation at the previous December's Chick-fil-A Bowl, in which he threw no touchdowns and three interceptions. After that incident, Garcia vowed he was starting anew and would stay on the right side of the rules. Two weeks later, he was suspended indefinitely after disrupting a leadership event during which an organizer claimed Garcia smelled of alcohol. He was reinstated in time for fall practice.

Garcia's problems made national headlines, and more than one college football columnist suggested Spurrier should take a harder stance with his would-be star.

"He's a little different type individual, and he has made some lifestyle changes," Spurrier said in June 2011. "We'll see if he can continue."

Through all of these peaks and valleys, the quarterback played, and many times he played well. Garcia started 34 games at South Carolina, including 28 in a row, both of which are a record for a Spurrier quarterback. Garcia threw for 7,597 yards and 47 touchdowns, which both rank third in school history, but his career ended in sad if not unexpected fashion.

Garcia did not start the first game of his senior season after losing a preseason competition for the job to sophomore Connor Shaw. However, after Shaw struggled against East Carolina, Garcia entered the game and led a 56–37 comeback win. But he never capitalized on that momentum and was replaced again by Shaw after two games in which he totaled six interceptions. Fewer than two weeks after losing his starting job, Garcia was dismissed from the team by Athletics Director Eric Hyman after failing a substance test.

"We are all saddened that this has occurred," Spurrier said at the time. "We all feel like we've given Stephen numerous opportunities to be a student athlete here at South Carolina. Obviously, he has chosen not to follow the guidelines of his reinstatement contract. We wish him the best."

"We remind all of our student athletes that there are consequences for their actions," Hyman said. "For Stephen to return to and remain with the football squad this fall, we agreed on several established guidelines. Unfortunately, he has not been able to abide by those guidelines and has therefore forfeited his position on the roster. We wish him the best of luck as he moves forward in life."

By the time Garcia's South Carolina career came to a close, even his father thought the split might be good for both parties.

"He kind of made his own bed, and this is the culmination of some of those earlier mistakes," Gary Garcia said. "He's upset that he's not finishing what he came here to do, and that's win an SEC championship, but he is also maybe kind of relieved to get a little bit out of the eye of the storm and take a breath of fresh air."

Garcia would return to campus a final time five months later to compete in the team's pro day, a gathering of all players leaving the school and attempting an NFL career.

"Every time I think about it, it's upsetting that it happened and the way it happened," he said. "I am proud of the team. It's still rough, though. It's unfortunate it took me this long to finally get my head straight, but it has happened and I feel great. I think this thing really turned out well. I hope it turns out better."

The kid who once seemed destined for an NFL future was down to his last strike, but there were still those who thought he could pull it out.

"Honestly, when I watched him, I was kind of shocked with how talented he was," National Football Post analyst Wes Bunting said. "You see the inconsistency on television, but he is a really talented kid who can move around. He can make all the throws. From a talent standpoint, absolutely this guy can play in the NFL. Does he make some bad decisions? Absolutely."

The 2012 NFL Draft came and went without anyone selecting Garcia or even offering him a free agent contract. Instead, he spent the season as a backup quarterback for the Montreal Alouettes of the Canadian Football League.

# 42 Sterling Sharpe and the No. 2

South Carolina announced the retirement of Sterling Sharpe's signature No. 2 jersey on December 17, 1987. Twenty-two years later, South Carolina almost took it off the shelf against his will.

First, the fun part of the story. Sharpe came to the Gamecocks from Glenville, Georgia, and immediately found a home not just in Columbia but also in the run-and-shoot offense. As a wingback at South Carolina for four seasons, Sharpe caught 169 passes for 2,497 yards and 17 touchdowns. He led the Gamecocks in receiving in 1985, 1986, and 1987 and was the school's all-time leading receiver when he left school.

He was named a first-team All-American in 1987, and he is still third in school history in catches and yards.

Despite all those honors, Sharpe said he was surprised when Coach Joe Morrison announced at the team's postseason banquet in 1987 that no one else at the school would ever wear the No. 2.

"I couldn't believe it," Sharpe told *The State* newspaper. "I was really shocked. This had never crossed my mind. I thought this only happens to the great ones. Steve Wadiak was a great one, and George Rogers won the Heisman. This is a lot higher honor for me than being named an All-American or anything else."

Morrison, who had his jersey retired by the New York Giants, did not downplay the significance of making Sharpe one of only four South Carolina players to have his jersey retired.

"Something like this happened to me back in 1972," Morrison told *The State*. "Over the years it means more and more to you. I'm thankful for the opportunity of having had a player like Sterling Sharpe and being able to retire his jersey."

Sharpe was not finished being lauded. When he entered the 1988 NFL Draft, he joined one of the best groups of pass-catchers to enter the league in the same year. While the 1988 draft was not viewed at the time as a strong one, almost every analyst expected the wide receivers to be stars. And they were right.

Sharpe, Notre Dame's Tim Brown (the Heisman Trophy winner), and Miami's Michael Irvin were considered the top wide receivers in the nation, but no one could predict in which order they would be selected.

Hurricanes head coach Jimmy Johnson liked his guy, but he also liked Sharpe. When South Carolina was preparing to play the Hurricanes in 1987, Johnson called Sharpe "more dangerous than Tim Brown."

Many people felt Sharpe—6'1", 200 lbs., and blessed with a 4.4-second 40-yard dash speed—would be the first of the trio selected.

"I would be very surprised if Sterling Sharpe lasted past the 10th pick in the first round [of the NFL draft]," ESPN's Mel Kiper Jr. told *The Christian Science Monitor* before the draft. "'He's very tough, very consistent. He has big-league ability—game-breaking-type skills. He's going to be a fine player in the NFL, a guy with Pro Bowl ability."

Morrison predicted his star would be one of the top five players selected.

"He was our big-play guy," Morrison told *The Christian Science Monitor*. "When things got tight, he was the one we were looking to get the ball to. Sterling understood that the defensive folks were keying on him, yet he went out there time after time and made things happen—even when they were putting two and three men on him. He still had the ability to get loose."

As it worked out, Brown would be taken first, with the No. 6 overall selection. Sharpe would have to wait just more one selection more before going No. 7 to the Green Bay Packers.

The Packers were happy with their choice. Sharpe played seven seasons in the NFL, was chosen for five Pro Bowl teams, and finished with 595 catches for 8,134 yards and 65 touchdowns.

Sharpe credited his time in the Gamecocks' offense with helping prepare him for the NFL.

"The run-and-shoot puts a lot of pressure on the position I play," he told *The Christian Science Monitor*. "We were running backs. We were linemen. We were receivers. So I think that has prepared me for the NFL, because I can take a lick from linemen or linebackers, but I can also avoid contact."

Sharpe retired from the NFL following the 1994 season, and the next time his name came up in Columbia, the subject was not as happy. When highly recruited wide receiver Alshon Jeffery committed to play for the Gamecocks in 2009, he said Coach Steve Spurrier had told him the school would un-retire Sharpe's No. 2 so that Jeffery could wear it at South Carolina.

Sharpe was not happy to hear that news. He told a Columbia radio station that Spurrier had asked him twice for his blessing to use the number and that both times he refused to give it.

"Once they gave me that honor, I don't see how in the world they would audition or petition for me to give it back," Sharpe said to WNKT radio in Columbia. "I haven't done anything to add to those numbers, but I definitely didn't do anything to warrant having it taken down and having someone else wear it. If it happens, I will go through a mourning period. My guts will definitely be ripped out."

In the end, Jeffery wore No. 1 during his three-year South Carolina career.

# 43 Dan Reeves—On to Bigger and Better Things

Dan Reeves didn't win many games at South Carolina, but Tom Price thought even then that the Gamecocks' quarterback had a bright future in the game.

With Reeves at quarterback from 1962–64, South Carolina won eight games total. Still, Price could see something special in Reeves.

"He had a magnificent football mind as far as analyzing other teams, picking out plays," Tom Price, South Carolina's longtime sports information director, said in 1992 on *100 Years of Gamecock Football*. "When he was 19 years old, he could study film and tell the coaches things that would happen that you could exploit, and they would always work out."

Reeves' plays worked out pretty well in the NFL where he won 201 games and coached the Denver Broncos and Atlanta Falcons to a combined four Super Bowls. Reeves also played in two Super Bowls with the Dallas Cowboys and went three more times as an assistant coach with the Cowboys. Reeves' nine total appearances in football's biggest games are an NFL record.

A Georgia native who starred in football, baseball, and basketball in high school, Reeves was lured to the Palmetto State by another Georgia native, legendary South Carolina track coach Weems Baskin, who also served as an assistant football coach.

"Everybody was promising me everything, but Coach Baskin wasn't like that," Reeves told *The State* newspaper. "He was a straight shooter, an honest man who told you the way things were, not what he thought you wanted to hear. [Head football coach] Marvin Bass was the same way. He told me the same thing Coach Baskin did, that they had recruited six or seven quarterbacks, and if I played, it would be because I was the best they had. But they needed to know what I was going to do. My dad asked me what I thought, and I said, 'I'd like to play for these men.' He said, 'That's exactly what I'd do.' I couldn't sign quick enough."

Reeves led the Gamecocks in passing in 1962 (930 yards), 1963 (657 yards), and 1964 (974). He was not drafted into the NFL but was signed by the Dallas Cowboys, where he was converted to running back and rushed for 1,990 yards and 25 touchdowns during an eight-year NFL career. Reeves threw 32 passes in the NFL, completing 14 of them for 370 yards and two touchdowns.

"Back in '65 when I came in the league as a free agent and barely made the football team, then all of a sudden I became a player coach in '70... that was the furthest thing from my mind," Reeves told *The State* in 2003. "Thirty-nine years of being in the NFL and making a living doing something I played as a kid—I'm very lucky."

Bass was dismissed after Reeves' final season, but the old quarterback didn't forget his old coach. Bass served from 1982–92 on Reeves' staff with the Denver Broncos.

"My wife probably had one of the best [compliments] I ever heard her pay anybody," Bass told *The State*. "She said if Diogenes [the Cynic], in his search for the honest man, had come across Dan Reeves, his search never would have been that long. That's the kind of person Dan Reeves is. He's just a person who is good to be around, who has such a good attitude about everything in life."

Like Price, Bass quickly became enamored with Reeves' football acumen.

"He has an unbelievable mind for the game," Bass told *The State*. "When he played for me he was always a coach on the field, so we left him alone. He can see plays and weaknesses much sooner than most. He was such a great competitor. He would never quit on anything."

In 2009, Reeves filmed a promotional video for the school's alumni association titled *My Carolina*.

"*My Carolina* is an opportunity and a chance to reflect back on four great years of my life, being able to go to a tremendous university that gave me a chance to get an education and I could do something, play football and baseball, something that I really enjoyed doing, and it actually led to 39 years in the NFL," Reeves said. "*My Carolina* is something that has been very important to me."

# 44 Lou Sossamon— First All-American

Lou Sossamon was South Carolina's first football All-American, but his most vivid on-field memory does not revolve around the sport.

"One of the fondest memories I have is [when] I was on the field playing and Rex Enright—he was our coach, a wonderful man—but during the game he called timeout [and] called me over to the sideline," Sossamon said in 2011 when he and teammate Dom Fusci sat down for a video interview. "My wife was a cheerleader, and we had just started dating. [Enright] called me over the sideline and said, 'Louis, you are supposed to be playing football out there, not watching the cheerleaders.'"

Lou and Kat Sossamon were married for 65 years, from 1943 until her death in 2008, and it is a story of South Carolina football royalty in many ways. Kat Edgerton was the daughter of Red Edgerton, a Columbia physician who was the Gamecocks' head football coach from 1912–15.

The Sossamon family roots are firmly planted in Gaffney, South Carolina, where his father founded *The Gaffney Ledger*, a newspaper the family still controls today. Lou Sossamon, 92, played center and linebacker for the Gamecocks from 1940–42.

He was named All-Southern Conference in 1941 and 1942 and a second-team All-American in 1942, the news of which reached him during a fraternity dance after the season.

"Football gave me a scholarship to the University of South Carolina during the Depression, and I had two sisters coming behind me, so I was very fortunate to be able to go to school and not spend any of my father's money," he said. "So my two sisters got a chance to go after I did. It meant the world to me to go to the University of South Carolina. I met so many fine people who have been a joy in my life."

"[Sossamon] was the best, believe me, and as far as football players, he deserves to be on the all-time great team," Fusci said. "He's the best center we ever had."

Sossamon served in the navy from 1943–46, playing on several military teams, then he joined the New York Yankees of the upstart professional All America Football Conference for the 1946 season. He played with the Yankees through 1948 alongside future Dallas Cowboys coach Tom Landry, among others.

"I wouldn't say I was proud of this, but I will tell you about it," Sossamon said. "We were playing the Los Angeles Dons in the Los Angeles Coliseum in Los Angeles, California, and I was going to [run] downfield after I had snapped the ball to the punter. They always taught the centers [that] when you hear the thud of the kick, you look back and see if you can find the ball so you know where to go. I looked back and about that time this boy hit me in my stomach and I went down. I was spitting up a little blood. I got over to the bench and I told a friend of mine named Dewey Proctor from Furman, and Dewey said, 'What's wrong?' I said, 'I don't know, Dewey, but if I can get back home, I'm not ever going to leave there. I don't want to come back here anymore.'"

He returned to Gaffney where he served as publisher of the *Ledger* and was also a member of South Carolina's board of trustees. Sossamon is a member of both the South Carolina Athletics Hall of Fame and the State Hall of Fame.

"It was just a wonderful time in my life, and I can't thank the people enough for giving me so much assistance," he said. "I feel guilty not being able to thank so many of them now because they are gone."

# 45 Marcus Lattimore— Bulldog Killer

Few opponents have done more through the years to snuff out the embers of optimism at South Carolina than the Georgia Bulldogs. And few if any players in school history are more beloved than running back Marcus Lattimore.

The fact that one of their greatest players tormented one of their most bitter foes for three straight seasons only makes Lattimore's legacy that much greater in the Palmetto State. In the second game and first start of his career, Lattimore buried the Bulldogs under 37 carries and 182 yards.

It was the second highest total ever by a South Carolina freshman running back, trailing only Brandon Bennett's 278 yards against East Tennessee State in 1991, and it lifted the No. 24 Gamecocks to a 17–6 win over No. 22 Georgia.

On the clinching drive of the game, which resulted in a 24-yard field goal with 1:12 remaining, Lattimore carried the ball eight out of 10 plays and gained 19 yards.

## Joey U.

So far, no South Carolina quarterback has achieved much success in the NFL, but in the mid-1990s, the Gamecocks assured themselves a connection to one of the best in professional history.

In 1995, Joey Unitas, the son of Pro Football Hall of Famer Johnny Unitas, transferred from Ohio Wesleyan and walked on to the Gamecocks' football team.

"I'm definitely real proud of my dad and all his accomplishments," Joey Unitas told *The State* newspaper. "But if I say that I want to try to be as good as him, that's a ridiculous statement. He's known as one of the greatest. I can put pressure on myself to succeed, but any pressure put on by people on the outside who say, 'Why aren't you as good as your dad?' That's totally unfair. He's Johnny Unitas. I'm Joey Unitas. Ability-wise, I'm no Steve Taneyhill at this point. But I'm sure we have the caliber coaches here who can help me and work with me. I have three years to do it."

Unitas spent most of his time as South Carolina's scout team quarterback in practice. He saw action in six games and threw one pass, an incompletion. Then he went to Hollywood to pursue a career as an actor. In 2001, he appeared in the movie *The Princess Diaries*.

"We finally smartened up and said, 'Run Marcus Lattimore every play,'" South Carolina coach Steve Spurrier said. "Obviously, Marcus is a very, very good running back. He can hit a crack. He can break tackles. He can run forward, and he can hold onto the ball. He is obviously a big-time running back."

The performance introduced Lattimore to the national football scene and jumpstarted him on his way to National Freshman of the Year honors. Georgia coach Mark Richt saw it all coming that day as Lattimore ripped through a defense coordinated by first-year assistant coach Todd Grantham.

"He'll be one of the best in our league for years to come and probably play on Sundays, too," Richt said. "It doesn't take a rocket scientist to figure out what the story of the game was—No. 21 for them. Marcus Lattimore was certainly the most dominating player in the game. Coach Spurrier did a nice job of planning for that young man to carry the ball and just keep feeding him."

South Carolina coaches credited Lattimore with nearly 40 broken tackles, and more than half his yardage that day came after Georgia defenders had made first contact.

The game not only helped vault South Carolina into the SEC race, it also gave Spurrier a chance to take part in one of his favorite pastimes—jabbing at Georgia, which had just hired Grantham away from the NFL to help shore up its defense.

"That little inside zone play? The NFL doesn't run that play," Spurrier said. "That's a new little scheme [for Grantham], I guess. I'm sure they knew we were going to run it, but they didn't stop it much."

The zone read that South Carolina ran so often against the Bulldogs was the mainstay play of Lattimore's Byrnes High School team, and the Gamecocks had installed it that season as a way to take best advantage of his talents. His 37 carries that day rank fourth in school history.

"I wasn't expecting this… but that's what I'm used to," Lattimore said. "I ran that play four years in high school."

Georgia didn't stop it much the next year, either. With 12 months to figure out a way to handle Lattimore, the Bulldogs watched him rush 27 times for 176 yards in 2011. In 2012, Lattimore added another triple-digit day to his resume against the Bulldogs with 24 carries for 109 yards.

That gave Lattimore an average of 155.7 yards per game in three games against the Bulldogs and, more importantly, a 3–0 lifetime record against Georgia, a team that had beaten South Carolina 46-of-62 times prior to Lattimore's arrival on campus.

Richt was quick to credit Lattimore's bruising running style for turning the tide in the rivalry.

"It can wear you down physically, but it wears you down emotionally, too," Richt said. "If you block for 2 yards twice, it's third-and-6, but if your back can get you 2 yards after contact, it's third-and-2. That's what he can do as well as anybody I can remember in a long time. When a team can control the ball, especially through the run, that's about the simplest and safest way to move the ball. And if you can hand the ball off nine out of 10 times and keep the chains moving and score points, you are going to win a lot of ball games that way."

# 46 A Steroid Scandal

One of the darkest times in South Carolina's football history came to light on October 24, 1988, when *Sports Illustrated* ran an article, co-written by former Gamecock Tommy Chaikin, claiming more than 50 South Carolina football players were regular steroid users and that the coaching staff knew about it.

The Gamecocks were not far removed from one of the best seasons in school history—the 1984 Black Magic season, which saw eight wins and a No. 2 national ranking at one point in the season.

"It tainted it a lot. It was just a bad situation," said Tommy Suggs, a former South Carolina quarterback who is a 40-year veteran of the Gamecocks' radio broadcast team. "I think that tainted some people's feelings of where we were going as a football program."

Head coach Joe Morrison died of a heart attack less than four months after the issue hit newsstands. Chaikin claimed that Morrison was aware Chaikin was using steroids while on the team, and said Morrison learned from team physician Dr. Paul Akers, who was told by Chaikin in 1985.

"About this time Dr. Akers asked me if I was on steroids. I told him I was but asked him not to tell anybody," Chaikin said. "He turned right around and told Morrison, who called me in to find out who else was taking them. I told him I wouldn't talk about anybody else. Morrison looked at me and said, 'Don't do it anymore.' That was it."

Akers told *The State* newspaper he had no recollection of that conversation with Chaikin.

"The gentleman from *Sports Illustrated* asked me the same question, and I'll tell you the same thing I told him—I honestly don't recall such a meeting," he said.

South Carolina player Kevin Hendrix told *The State* that Chaikin and two other former players took steroids and that it was common knowledge among players on the team.

"It was no big secret. But I just think it was their little group," Hendrix said. "They were on them when I came here [in 1984]. They lived for that stuff. They'd have a bad workout and go back and shoot up all kinds of stuff."

Chaikin indicated that at least one assistant coach at the school encouraged the steroid use, but player Matt McKernan told *The State* that no coach or staff member at the school ever encouraged steroid use to him.

"The only thing they ever said to me was, 'Don't take them,'" McKernan said. "They don't condone them. They are not our personal guidance counselors, but they do try and see we don't get into trouble."

University president James B. Holderman issued a statement in the wake of the article: "The University of South Carolina deeply regrets the personal tragedy of Tommy Chaikin. Since earlier this year, the university has taken a variety of positive steps to strengthen our drug-testing and wellness program and assure that, as far as possible, such a tragedy should never reoccur here. New personnel and a comprehensive program, which includes testing for a wide range of drugs including steroids, are now in place. *Sports Illustrated* has asked if anybody is listening. The University of South Carolina has been for some time and has responded in a positive fashion. King Dixon, our athletic director, has universal confidence and will handle these matters in a straight-forward and expeditious manner."

Four South Carolina assistant coaches—Tom Gadd, Keith Kephart, Tom Kurucz, and Jim Washburn—were indicted on criminal charges in relation to the episode. Kephart and Washburn pleaded guilty to importing steroids, and Kurucz pleaded guilty to distributing drugs to athletes, according to the Associated Press.

Kephart told *The State* he suspected some steroid use among the players.

"I called all the linemen in and told them, 'I don't want to know what you're using, but cut it out,'" Kephart told the newspaper. "I offered them counseling and told them I could give them alternatives, amino acids and vitamins. We spent a ton on those. I always informed Coach [Morrison] when I held a meeting with any of the players; he always wanted us to let him know when we met with players. I told him we'd had an informal meeting in reference to steroids. I told him I thought it had been taken care of, that I felt the type of kids they were that they'd follow my advice and could see [steroid use] would be detrimental to them. He trusted me on that. He didn't want [steroids] around. He told me to keep him posted. He said if there was anything he needed to do to let him know. But after that, it didn't come up again."

Assistant U.S. Attorney John Barton told the AP that Morrison was never a focus on the investigation.

"I'll say two things about Joe Morrison," Barton said. "We interviewed Joe Morrison. He was cooperative. He was never a target in the investigation.

"There was not a program of coaches actively providing players with steroids. We never saw a pattern and practice of that. What you saw prosecuted... was the extent of the total involvement of coaches, players, and steroids."

# 47 Bobby Bryant— Dual Sport Star

The "Freshman 15," those extra pounds college freshmen are notorious for gaining, were a blessing for Bobby Bryant.

Bryant was an excellent athlete coming out of Macon, Georgia, in 1963, but he hardly made a ripple in the college football recruiting pool. That was probably because he was barely heavy enough to splash the surface at all.

At 6'1" and 140 lbs., Bryant's only major college football scholarship offer was from South Carolina, so he packed his bags and came to Columbia.

"I was pretty good in all sports [and a] pretty good football player, too. But I was real skinny," Bryant said. "Fortunately, I gained about 15 lbs. the first couple years and got up to 155–160 lbs. By the time I was a senior, I was a 170-lb. defensive back."

And a very good one. Bryant, a member of the South Carolina Athletic Hall of Fame, was named a first-team All-American in 1966 by the *New York Daily News* and the *Detroit Sports Extra*. When Bryant's college football career began, players were still playing both offense and defense, but by his junior season the two-platoon system had taken hold.

Still, Bryant made an impact on two areas of the game—as a defensive back and kick returner. He still holds the school record with a 98-yard punt return in 1966. In 1965, he led the ACC with 11 punt returns for 161 yards.

"I was able to do pretty well," Bryant said. "We didn't have great success at South Carolina, but I was able to have some pretty good individual success returning kicks especially and playing cornerback."

Bryant also was the first South Carolina baseball player to strike out more than 100 batters in a season, and his dual-sport success made him the Anthony J. McKelvin Award winner as the ACC Athlete of the Year in 1967.

Bryant's career reached even greater heights after he left the Gamecocks. He was drafted in the seventh round of the 1967 NFL-AFL Draft by the Minnesota Vikings and would play the next 14 seasons with one of the NFL's iconic teams.

"[Minnesota head coach Bud Grant] didn't care how big or small you were or what color you were. If you did what he told you to do, were disciplined and did your job, you could play for him a long time," Bryant said. "I played 14 years on some great teams. I went up to Minnesota just hoping I could play one year, and 14 years later I decided I was too little to play."

Bryant started all four Super Bowls the Vikings appeared in during his career, and he was instrumental in getting Minnesota to at least two of them. He had two interceptions against the Dallas Cowboys in the 1973 NFC Championship Game, returning one for a touchdown, and he returned a blocked field goal 90 yards for a touchdown against the Los Angeles Rams in the 1976 conference title game.

Bryant led Minnesota in interceptions four times and is second in team history with 51. He was named to the all-decade teams of the 1960s and 1970s by the *Pioneer Press* in St. Paul, Minnesota. In 2010, Bryant was also named one of the team's top 50 players by the *Pioneer Press*.

Bryant played with NFL legends like Carl Eller, Alan Page, Jim Marshall, Fran Tarkenton, and Paul Krause with the Vikings.

"It all started right here at the University of South Carolina, and I am grateful," said Bryant, who retired in Lancaster, South Carolina.

# 48 The Chicken Curse

If you believe in the Chicken Curse, and there are many South Carolina fans who have at least wondered at times if there was something to it, then you could see the knee injury quarterback Todd Ellis suffered during his senior season in 1989 as another example of buzzard's luck befalling the program.

Ellis, however, decidedly does not believe in the Chicken Curse.

"The players certainly heard it and heard it up until the last four or five years or so, and I can't tell you how much that angered players and coaches," said Ellis, now the team's play-by-play voice on the radio. "The Chicken Curse is nothing more than, 'We don't have good enough players. We don't have good enough facilities, and we're not good enough.' The Chicken Curse has never been a real thing. It's about a commitment to the overall top level that it's going to take to play, recruit, coach, and work at it. I always saw that as a weak excuse for why you have not prevailed."

At times, he has seen it as more than that, however.

"The Chicken Curse I think is a symptom of South Carolina the state and the history to some degree, and sometimes you can have a self-defeating attitude in which you talk so much about losing that you talk yourself into, 'We're not good enough, and we don't compete and other people have us.' I think there is some of that, and

I think Steve Spurrier has helped us get rid of that," Ellis said. "You would never hear me reference, 'Well, that's the Chicken Curse.'"

Thousands of fans have, though. In 1990, Doug Nye, a former sports editor of *The State* newspaper, devoted 2,500 words in the newspaper, detailing all of the examples of the Curse's work.

"True Curse fanatics—and like it or not, there are thousands of them—go even further. Even the slightest connection to South Carolina can spell T-R-O-U-B-L-E.

"Think about it.

"Was it just a coincidence that the 1972 U.S. Olympic basketball team—the first American squad ever to lose a game—had USC's Kevin Joyce on its roster?

"Was it just a coincidence that Dallas Cowboys coach Tom Landry decided to de-activate former USC player Jay Saldi the day before the 1977 Super Bowl, or did someone warn him about The Curse? Without Saldi, the Cowboys won.

"Was it just a coincidence that Elvis died only six months after his concert at Carolina Coliseum?

"Such observations come from years of watching USC athletic teams come so, so close to the gold ring only to fall short. In fact, a major weapon of The Curse is its damnable tendency to tease—to take Gamecock fans to the brink, make them think their team is about to accomplish the ultimate, and then hit 'em with a dream-shattering slam to the gut.

"There are those, of course, who laugh at the idea. They say The Curse is nothing more than the invention of frustrated fans trying to fathom their misery.

"But when someone in authority acknowledges the existence of The Dark Force, well, it's time to take a closer look. King Dixon, director of athletics at USC, did that just last month when he learned that the NCAA would not impose sanctions on the school's athletic program after an investigation into steroid use.

"'I'm delighted with the timing [of the report], that it's in July instead of August or later,' said the relieved Dixon. 'There are a lot of opportunities and options out there for conference affiliation, and by golly, if we continue to go in the direction we're going, we're going to get over this Chicken Curse.'"

Former Gamecocks running back George Rogers, the school's only Heisman Trophy winner, said he was a believer in the Chicken Curse at times during his career.

"I know we had a Chicken Curse when it came to beating Clemson," he said. "If there ever was a form of the Chicken Curse, it definitely could have been that. I never scored on Clemson. They always use that against me."

The history of the Chicken Curse goes deeper than just Ellis and Rogers, though. Don Barton, the school's sports information director from 1950–59, remembers it being muttered during his era.

"Anytime we lost they would assign it to the Chicken Curse," Barton said. "Well, the antidote for the Chicken Curse is blocking and tackling."

# 49 Beating Notre Dame with Black Magic

This was not a Knute Rockne Notre Dame team, make no mistake. But for a South Carolina program looking for respect October 20, 1984, it was a big moment.

There were other big moments for the Gamecocks that season to be sure, but none drew more attention across the country than beating the Fighting Irish 36–32 in South Bend, Indiana.

"Exciting," Coach Joe Morrison told the Associated Press after the game. "Taking Georgia, Pittsburgh, and Notre Dame in one year is damn exciting."

The game, like many in the 1984 season, was a nail-biter. Notre Dame led 17–14 at the half and then 26–14 heading into the fourth quarter thanks to two Gamecocks turnovers in the third quarter.

"I felt our chances were slim then," Morrison said. "I thought going in it would be a good game if we didn't do anything to hurt ourselves. With two turnovers in the second half, I was concerned. I thought to myself, 'Here we go again.' But our guys got back and turned it around."

And in dramatic fashion. South Carolina outscored the Irish 22–6 in the fourth quarter on the strength of two touchdown runs by quarterback Mike Hold, including a 33-yarder that provided the difference

"We just kept fighting," Hold said after the game. "We never let down, [and] we were able to make a lot out of their mistakes."

Milton Richman, sports editor of United Press International, noticed that the Gamecocks were not awed by the Irish image that day. In his column the next day, Richman wrote, "James Seawright, one of the Gamecocks' linebackers, was getting in his work with the rest when Dr. Bill Smith, the team's dentist, mentioned an historic fact to him during a break in the session. 'Do you realize,' Smith said to the 22-year-old Simpsonville, South Carolina, senior, 'you are walking on the same hallowed ground where some of football's most famous immortals played?' Seawright mulled it over a moment. 'That doesn't mean anything because all those guys are dead,' he said."

Notre Dame, which outgained the Gamecocks 415–337 in the game, was not in the middle of one of its many heydays at the time. Gerry Faust's team fell to 3–4 that day. That team would go on to beat No. 14 Southern Cal 19–7 and finish 7–5.

"Those kids played their hearts out today," Faust told the Associated Press after the game. "I'm proud of them. It's different when you play well, it really is. We'll be all right. You guys may think I'm crazy, but I really believe that."

Faust would be fired following the next season, clearing the way for the Irish to hire Lou Holtz. The week after the win, South Carolina, which went into South Bend that day ranked No. 11 in the country, moved into the country's top 10 for the first time in history.

Almost 30 years later, Hold can remember the euphoria of that day like it was yesterday.

"We get on the buses and people are lined up all the way out of the airport, all the way down Knox Abbott Drive for a mile," Hold said. "I think they said 10,000 people. It was crazy. I can remember Danny Smith flipped open the top of the bus and was halfway hanging out, just screaming at the fans."

# 50 Gamecocks in the Super Bowl

The Super Bowl has become as much sizzle as substance. The hype and hysteria have virtually overtaken the game for fans and can even influence the teams involved.

The Washington Redskins, though, were all business in Super Bowl XXVI in January 1993.

"I think the biggest thing for me as an athlete was the tone that was set by Joe Gibbs," former Redskins defensive back Brad Edwards said. "He had been to three and won two of them before the game I played in. I will never forget the first meeting we had after the championship, and he said, 'Our goal is not to go to the

Super Bowl. It's to win it, period.' He was so matter of fact when he said that. I was like, 'Okay, to not win is a huge failure.' It was so business-like. We didn't pay a lot of attention to a lot of the things going on around the game."

Eighteen former South Carolina players have made an appearance in the Super Bowl, but none have had a better game than Edwards, a Lumberton, North Carolina, native who played at South Carolina from 1984–87.

Playing in the Hubert H. Humphrey Metrodome in Minnesota, where he had played the first two seasons of his NFL career with the Minnesota Vikings, Edwards intercepted two passes and returned them for a combined 56 yards, broke up five more passes, and had four tackles. He finished second in MVP voting behind quarterback Mark Rypien, and to this day he doesn't mind saying he wanted that MVP trophy.

In fact, with the Redskins comfortably ahead in a game they would win 37–24, Edwards went after the ball and the award.

"I think I gave the Bills probably 20 points in the fourth quarter going for that third interception because you knew you were going to be the MVP if you got that third interception," he said.

Two of Edwards' big hits from that game, on celebrated Bills receivers Don Beebe and James Lofton, can still be found on YouTube.

"I have never seen Brad Edwards hit like he has hit today," television color commentator John Madden said during the broadcast of the game. "Remember Brad Edwards? He was a quarterback in college. Today, he is a safety possessed."

According to Edwards, Madden had gotten a hint earlier in the week that Edwards and the Redskins were ready to play.

"On the first play of the team session of Wednesday's practice, I had a massive collision with [teammate] Gerald Riggs. I mean massive," he said. "I guess John Madden was standing right there and turned to our sports information director and said, 'This game is over. You guys are going to kill the Bills.' By Friday, Joe Gibbs made us tone it down at practice. It was so physical. I could not tell you anything that was going on around the game other than our preparation to go and win."

In contrast, the Bills, who were on their second Super Bowl of four straight, enjoyed the week's pregame festivities more than the Redskins.

"The Bills were a much looser team that was out a lot, or at least that was the perception," Edwards said.

While Edwards had the best Super Bowl of any Gamecock, he can't compete with South Carolina alum Dan Reeves for number of appearances. Nobody can, in fact. Reeves, a quarterback at South Carolina from 1962–64, has participated in more Super Bowls than any person in history. He played in Super Bowls V and VI with the Dallas Cowboys; he was an assistant coach for the Cowboys in Super Bowls X, XII, and XIII; and he was a head coach in Super Bowls XXI, XXII, XXIV, and XXXIII.

As much success as Reeves had making the final game, his teams have had less luck in them. He is 2–7 in his nine career appearances, including 0–4 as a head coach. Reeves lost three times as the Denver Broncos head coach and then lost to the Broncos as the Atlanta Falcons head coach.

Former Gamecock Bobby Bryant, who played for 14 seasons in the NFL, played for four Super Bowl teams—although he missed the big game two of those times due to injury—with the Minnesota Vikings powerhouse teams of the 1960s and 1970s. Robert Brooks (with Green Bay), Steve Courson (Pittsburgh), Max Runager (Philadelphia and San Francisco), and Jay Saldi (with Dallas) are the only other South Carolina alums to play for multiple Super Bowl teams.

Edwards only played in one, but he'll never forget it.

"You get up that morning, and it is so surreal. It's almost indescribable," he said. "When you realize the enormity of it, how much time you have spent in your life getting to that point, the reality that you are going to be in the most televised event on the planet. You pull up and it's almost surreal, just the enormity and the mounting pressure that builds. You get off the bus and all the cameras are there, people are there. It's an amazing experience. In some ways it feels like yesterday."

# 51 Jeff Grantz—The Perfect Fit

Todd Ellis dominates the South Carolina passing record books, but when it came time to name the school's all-time team of the modern era, the Gamecocks chose a guy who was probably more dangerous with his legs and was a heck of a middle infielder on top of it.

Jeff Grantz came to Columbia from Bel Air, Maryland, in 1972. He sat out his freshman season, as was mandatory in the day, and then got right to work. Grantz led South Carolina in passing in 1973, 1974, and 1975, and he powered the team's run-first veer offense on the ground, as well.

"Jeff was as good a quarterback as I ever saw for what I wanted to do," Jim Carlen told *The State* newspaper. "He came to play. He executed. He had a knack about him. He could make the plays and never made a misread. He was the perfect quarterback."

Grantz was named a second-team All-American in 1975, following a senior season in which he threw for 1,815 yards and scored 72 points. Grantz is 10th in school history in passing with 3,440 career yards and 24th in rushing with 1,577 yards... And he did it all while also playing baseball at South Carolina. He still holds the school's fielding record at shortstop and second base, and

*Sophomore quarterback Jeff Grantz of Bel Air, Maryland, relaxes during a scrimmage break on Tuesday, October 24, 1973, in Columbia, South Carolina.* (AP Photo/Lou Krasky)

## The Roundhouse

When it was built in 1956, it was called the Rex Enright Athletic Center, and it officially bore that name all its life. But it was quickly deemed and will be forever remembered as The Roundhouse.

It was round, after all, and in its day, it was considered cutting edge. But it's day had long past by 2013 when South Carolina's administrative staff finally moved to a new home and the building was torn down.

By that time, it was home not only to the Gamecocks' athletic director but also to "snakes and possums and all kind of bugs," longtime administrative assistant Emily White told *The State* newspaper.

"Every [AD] for years wanted to move, move, move, and Eric [Hyman] was finally able to do something about it," White said. "They did all the renovating and once when they were changing the lobby, Jim Shealy said, 'It's like putting lipstick on a pig.'"

In 1956, though, the building was a big upgrade. Enright, then the school's head football coach and athletic director, plus the school's administrative staff had been housed in a swimming pool building.

"Coach Enright had his office on one side of the pool, and the secretary and assistant coaches had space on the other side," said Don Barton, a former sports information director at the school. "If they wanted to have a staff meeting, they had to go across Sumter Street and use one of the dressing rooms in the old [basketball] Field House."

he played on the 1975 South Carolina team that advanced to the College World Series.

Grantz's baseball career meant he never spent a spring practice with the football team, making his success on the gridiron all the more impressive.

"We lined him up. I made sure he got to the games on time," Carlen said in 1992 on *100 Years of Gamecock Football*. "I made sure he got on the field and played. He's an exceptional youngster."

As for being the best quarterback in school history, Grantz says, "Some people may say that, but I think a quarterback is only as good as the people who surround him. I had a great offensive line. I had receivers who didn't drop the ball. There were a lot of different offenses run through that time. It's really hard to determine who the best quarterback is. It's an honor to be a starting quarterback in major college football. I think every single quarterback who has started is very capable."

Grantz was named Maryland's High School Athlete of the Year in 1972 by the *Baltimore Sun*. And in 2012, *The Aegis* in Bel Air, Maryland, wrote, "There's no pro career to recommend Grantz, who chose a successful business career instead, but many people who saw him play at Bel Air High School in the early 1970s still consider him Maryland's finest high school quarterback ever."

Grantz was drafted by the Miami Dolphins in the 17th round of the NFL draft but never played for the Dolphins, and he still lives in Columbia. Ron Bass, who backed up Grantz before taking the starting role after Grantz's departure, said he learned how to handle the responsibilities of a college quarterback from Grantz.

"I certainly learned from him it's better to give it or pitch it than to keep it," Bass said. "You stay healthy a lot longer that way."

# 52 The SEC—Finding a Home

For the first 100 years of its existence, South Carolina football was something of a vagabond.

The program that began in 1892 first hooked up with a league in 1922 when it joined the venerable Southern Conference, home of Alabama, Auburn, Clemson, Florida, Georgia, Georgia Tech, LSU, North Carolina, and Tennessee, among others. In 1953, the Gamecocks were part of a Southern Conference exodus that saw the school join with Duke, Clemson, Maryland, N.C. State, and Wake Forest to found the ACC.

After 17 years in the ACC, South Carolina coach Paul Dietzel clashed with that lead over academic requirements, and the Gamecocks left to become an independent. After 20 years in the wilderness, South Carolina found its current home in the Southeastern Conference or SEC.

The move to the SEC was a boon for the Gamecocks' finances and eventually for its competitiveness, but it was not an easy transition.

"South Carolina was a good match for the SEC, but it had a long way to go and a lot of things had to be generated to be competitive," former athletics director Mike McGee said. "The bridge between where we were and the SEC was an interesting challenge."

It was also a tremendous opportunity.

"I wouldn't have accepted the job at South Carolina if they were still [independent]," McGee said. "I accepted it because of the challenge that it represented."

The challenge was greatest for the team's coaches.

"I remember everybody was hollering and jumping up and all excited, and we were sitting there in the office going, 'We don't have those kinds of players,'" said Brad Lawing, who was an assistant on Sparky Woods' staff.

"It was a great time to be there, but a scary time, too," Woods told *The State* newspaper.

The first game of the SEC era came against Georgia, and the Bulldogs won easily 28–6 behind 134 rushing yards from one-time South Carolina recruiting target Garrison Hearst.

"I was asked after the game by the media if there had been a particular call that changed the game," Woods told *The State*. "I told them I believe it was when Garrison Hearst called me and said he was going to Georgia."

Marty Simpson, a place-kicker on the 1992 team, well remembers the feeling of joining the SEC.

"When I was playing, there was a huge sign right outside the locker room. It was Williams-Brice, back-lit, 10' by 10' with the words, 'The Best Play Here,'" Simpson told *The State*. "I remember I went to my long-snapper and said, 'Yeah, they do now—Alabama will play here, Florida will play here.'"

South Carolina finished 3–5 in its first SEC season, beating Mississippi State, Vanderbilt, and Tennessee. The Gamecocks didn't manage a winning record in the conference until the 2000 team went 5–3 under Lou Holtz.

The benefits, though, have made up for the rough start. The Gamecocks claimed their first SEC divisional title in 2010, winning the Eastern Division, and the budget has continued to swell in the last 20 years.

In 2012, the SEC distributed more than $20 million to each of its 12 schools, which helped push South Carolina's annual athletics budget to $79 million.

"It was a good move by the university and [a] fortunate opportunity that the university was able to take advantage of," McGee said.

# 53 Earl Clary— The Gaffney Ghost

Eighty years after Earl Clary finished his playing career at South Carolina, little of substance remains when you go looking for him.

Which, according to the legends, is how defenders felt when they went to tackle "The Gaffney Ghost." Clary played for the

Gamecocks from 1931–33. He was given his nickname by head coach Billy Laval, according to an article in the *1952 All South Carolina Football Annual*.

"He was a football ghost from Gaffney and the greatest back I've ever seen," Laval said of the shifty running back.

At 6'1" and 170 lbs., the lean Clary was hard enough to find, much less to catch. Here's how Ed Danforth of the *Atlanta Georgian* described Clary's first collegiate game, a 7–0 win over Duke in the 1931 season-opener:

"Clary went into his first varsity game with 12,000 people expecting him to run away with the show—and he did. Although the Blue Devils of Duke had been coached to stop Clary, they could not do so. It takes more than coaching to stop Clary. It takes clutching—clutching at a straw hat blown by the wind. Clary never gives a tackler more than one chance to grab. He is here today and gone 50 miles tomorrow.

"Clary starts slowly it seems, picks his opening, then bursts away in an explosion of speed. Once underway he sidesteps and dodges in a way no coach can hope to teach. They either can or don't do it.

"The fact that Clary lived up to his army of volunteer press agents stamps him as a genius. Some day he will be stopped, but by no ordinary garden variety of football team."

Jack Wade of the *Charlotte Observer* wrote, "Twelve thousand customers sat in a broiling sun and watched the snake-hipped Gaffney youngster gallop through the vaulted Duke line and around Duke's terminals, ripping the entire visiting combination to so many shreds. Duke nor its millions could have stopped him today!"

The writers of the *1952 All South Carolina Football Annual* claimed onlookers were "spellbound" by Clary's "running magic," and they seemed pretty spellbound themselves.

Here is an excerpt from their story on the Gaffney Ghost: "Clary's will-o'-the-wisp appearance belied his tremendous power.

Running at full speed, he could leap 6' to either side, as frustrated tacklers of those days will tell you. When he swerved, he could cut so hard that the middle cleats on his shoes bent from the force. He needed a new pair of shoes after every game."

After his senior year, Clary was named to the All-Southern team, and he was in the first induction class for the South Carolina Athletics Hall of Fame. Clary was 3–0 against Clemson during his career and, after one of those games, Frank Howard, then an assistant coach for the Tigers, wondered how Clemson let him get away.

"Nobody as good as Clary has any business [being] on the side opposite Tiger folks."

When Clary's South Carolina football career was complete, the *Football Annual* records, Clary moved back to Gaffney and started a laundry business.

"He has changed little from the lithe figure of old, except for a few lines around the familiar smile," the *Football Annual* reported. "As the years roll by and new stars blaze across the football firmament, past players fade into the background. But for Clary and his cohorts—Hambright, Mauney, Shinn, Wolfe, McDougall, all that great team—they are not forgotten. As long as an old timer is around to tell 'about the time when Hambright led the way and Clary ran 97 yards through th' hull d--- team,' the Ghost and his teammates will live—in the hearts of fans who idolized them."

# 54 Derek Watson— Promise Unfulfilled

It could have been a storybook pairing—the legendary coach looking to turn around a dormant program, or the schoolboy star who stayed in state to help.

Instead, the combination of South Carolina coach Lou Holtz and Derek Watson produced little but heartache for all involved. Watson was the Palmetto State's Mr. Football in 1999. In tiny Williamston, South Carolina, he set the state's career record for yardage (6,766) and touchdowns (88). In the postseason Shrine Bowl game, which matches the top senior players from South Carolina and North Carolina in an exhibition game after the season, Watson carried the ball 33 times for 275 yards.

In the 1999 South Carolina media guide, Watson is described this way: "Runs a 4.5 40, bench presses 310 lbs., and squats 520 lbs." He chose to become part of Holtz's first signing class rather than accept scholarship offers from Georgia and Tennessee.

That sounds like every coach's dream. Reality, though, was far from that. The trouble began almost immediately. Watson started to show his promise as a sophomore, rushing for 1,066 yards, but that's when the trouble began, as well.

In December 2000, he wrecked a teammate's car while driving on a suspended license and was suspended from the Outback Bowl for violating an unspecified team rule.

It was then that Holtz uttered his most famous Watson quote: "He can star in NFL stadiums, or sweep them out," Holtz said.

Things went in the wrong direction. In February 2001, Watson shoved a student referee to the floor during an intramural basketball game. In May 2001, he was charged with simple assault for punching a female student in the arm. In July 2001, he was charged with driving on a suspended license. In January 2002, he was arrested and charged with possession of marijuana.

He was dismissed from the team after the last arrest, having compiled 2,051 yards and 16 touchdowns in his career. After a tryout with the New England Patriots wasn't successful, Watson returned home and was working at a car wash when he decided to take another shot at turning around his life.

*Derek Watson (right) is tackled by Clemson's Ryan Hemby during a game on Saturday, November 17, 2001, at Williams-Brice Stadium in Columbia, South Carolina.* (AP Photo/Lou Krasky, file)

"I had a lot of people criticizing me," Watson told *The State* newspaper. "I finally had to deal with the fact that it is my fault, that these things people are saying about me, it hurt my feelings because it was true. I did give everything away. I threw it away. When one of my friends hooked me up with [counseling], I'm thinking, 'What kind of person needs help managing their life?' The more I thought about it, the more I realized I was that person.

Once I realized that, I opened up my mind to suggestions I wasn't open to before. I always thought my way was the best way. I found out I'm just a young guy who didn't know a lot of things."

That comeback attempt came in training camp with the Tampa Bay Buccaneers, but Watson never saw the game field.

In May 2007, Watson was charged with first-degree burglary and grand larceny after a home break-in.

"You feel bad because a whole bunch of coaches had some opportunities to change him around some and didn't get it done," former South Carolina assistant Dave Roberts, who recruited Watson, told *The State* newspaper at the time. "But you are what you are. Breaking and entering—nobody feels sorry for something like that. It's wrong, and people know better."

In February 2011, following an unsuccessful attempt at making the CFL, Watson was arrested on a felony charge of cocaine trafficking and possession of marijuana with intent to distribute. The arrest was the culmination of an investigation that started when he was pulled over in a traffic stop on October 16 and determined to be in possession of between 10 and 28 grams of a "white, rock-like substance."

"When I was younger, I wasn't willing to make sacrifices," Watson told the *Anderson Independent Mail* shortly before that arrest. "You want to do what you want to do, and you don't worry about the consequences. But what you have to realize, and what I really want to stress to younger people, is the choices you make now affect your whole future. Because I did things I shouldn't have done, it basically sidelined all the goals I wanted to reach. I just threw it all away."

# 55 The Prank

If a prank has anniversary parties, you know it was a good prank.

Meet "The Prank." In 1961, the members of South Carolina's Sigma Nu fraternity devised and practiced an elaborate and bold gag in which dozens of them donned uniforms of a local high school football team and bluffed their way onto the field at Williams-Brice Stadium before the Gamecocks' game against Clemson to mock the Tigers.

"We practiced four or five nights. The secrecy was what was surprising," participant Ed Hancock told the school's website in 2011. "It was such a well-kept secret. I had a date, like everyone else did, to the football game, and I just told her I was going to the restroom. I could see all my teammates coming out of the stands, and we met under the left side, which is where Coach [Marvin] Bass gave us permission to use a small room there to dress."

"[Bass] didn't see anything wrong with it, and we needed his okay to get past the cops and onto the field," participant Carroll Gray told *The State* newspaper in 2011. "I was sports editor of the *Gamecock*, and I talked to [Coach] on the flight to the Virginia game. After he said all right, I told [the fraternity members], 'Hey guys, we're on,' and it took a life of its own."

The tricky part was getting onto the field.

"The real teams had been out to warm up, and they'd gone into their locker rooms, and that's when we came out onto the field," Hancock said. "There was a huge, burly looking guard standing there at the gate, and I said, 'I don't know if we're going to get through here,' but since Jack was leading the way and he really looked like a football player, cause he actually was, the [guard]

## The Man Who Would Be King

When King Dixon and Alex Hawkins were teammates at South Carolina in the 1950s, they were the Gamecocks' odd couple. Dixon was the clean-cut, yes-sir, no-sir halfback, while Hawkins was the hard-living halfback, and their careers went on to follow those paths.

While Hawkins played in the NFL and wrote two books detailing a carousing life, Dixon went on to become South Carolina's athletics director from 1988–92.

"King was mature when I first met him," Hawkins said on *100 Years of Gamecock Football*. "He was 18 years old, and he was as mature as most people are at 35. He just had his stuff together early. He was just exceptional. I have never seen him bend a rule, much less break one."

Dixon, a member of the South Carolina Athletic Hall of Fame, once ran back a kickoff 98 yards for a touchdown against Texas. While Dixon's administrative career will probably be best remembered for the ill-fated hiring of football coach Sparky Woods, it would be unfair to remember Dixon for that alone.

He spent 22 years in the Marines after college and earned the Bronze Star, Navy Commendation Medal, and Vietnamese Cross of Gallantry.

swung the gate open and we ran out and as soon as we touched the field the Clemson band just started 'Tiger Rag' and all the stands went crazy. They were all standing, all wearing orange, all screaming and yelling, and the South Carolina side is booing and booing and carrying on."

From there, the players mimed milking a cow, fell to the ground while running simple drills, and generally portrayed their rivals as hapless cowhands.

"We had about ten minutes on the field and then we had to leave regardless, no matter what happened, so we had to start letting them know the hoax was on," Hancock said. "The first thing we did was the 'cow milk,' where I would put my fingers together and point my thumbs down and my partner would 'milk' my thumbs.

We would line up, snap the ball to the quarterback, and everyone would just fall on the ground. We did that three times.

"I was on the sideline nearest Clemson, which I argued not to be, but I was punting facing the north end zone. It would go back over my head, and Dick Melton would let it bounce off his helmet rather than catch it. During our practices, we would time ourselves, and we thought [that if I kicked] it twice and they returned it, we would be pretty close to our time to get off the field. So I kicked twice, [then I] looked over my shoulder at the Clemson stands just to see what was happening, and it looked like someone had taken orange paint and poured it down the stands. The crowd was coming after us, the band stopped playing—literally, the entire stands were coming after us."

Pushing and shoving ensued, but order was restored and South Carolina went on to win the game 21–14.

In 2011, participants in The Prank gathered at a Columbia restaurant to relive their glory day.

Ron Leitch, who impersonated a blustering Clemson coach Frank Howard during The Prank, told *The State* that his Howard outfit "cost me $10.97 at Goodwill." When The Prank made news across the nation, Bass distanced himself from it, according to Gray.

"Coach Bass threw me under the bus," Gray said. "I figured I would at least be suspended or maybe expelled. I spilled my guts and Dr. [William] Patterson listened, then [he] sat there and looked at me for what seemed like 10 minutes. Then he said, 'That was pretty funny, but don't do it again. Now get out of here.'"

# 56 Sparky Woods—A Tumultuous Tenure

Sparky Woods finished his five-year South Carolina coaching career with a 24–28–3 record, so Gamecocks fans are not predisposed to find much sympathy for the man.

Still, consider the hurdles Woods faced in Columbia. He took over for not just a popular coach in Joe Morrison but a popular coach who had died unexpectedly during the offseason. Woods ushered the Gamecocks into the SEC, which they were not prepared for in regard to facilities or personnel. He watched as one of the school's most powerful boosters launched a public campaign to replace him. And he had to tamp down a revolt within his team that saw a group of players threaten publicly to quit.

"I thought he did a good job of handling [the revolt] because it had to be an awfully tough spot," said quarterback Steve Taneyhill who was a freshmen at the time. "Our guys were frustrated because we hadn't won a game and here you are a senior and it's supposed to be your best year, your most memorable, and you are not winning. It just escalated."

It was 1992, South Carolina's first year in the SEC, and the Gamecocks were 0–5. A team meeting turned into a referendum on Woods, and an informal vote was taken by the players. Sixty-two said the coach should go, 24 said he should stay, a Columbia television station reported at the time, although one player told the Associated Press that the vote was less formal than that.

"There was no real firm number you could count," linebacker Ben Hogan said. "You couldn't count hands. You couldn't look at one person and tell how they voted. People were just hollering things out. Basically, it was two hours of chaos. If you could put any one word on it, it was basically mutiny. Guys sign scholarships and they think they become part of the board of trustees, and they want to hire and fire coaches when that's not what we're here for."

Woods, who had been 38–19–2 at Division I-AA Appalachian State before coming to South Carolina, tried too hard to prove himself at the major college football level, said Corey Miller, who was part of Woods' first two teams at the school.

"I think he came in a little stern," Miller said. "When you are coming to a big program from App State, you are trying to earn the respect of guys. A lot of guys didn't know who you were. He was trying to get that respect, and I think he tried a little too hard and kind of turned some guys off. We went from a top 10, top 20 caliber program [under Morrison] to not being good at all. So the memories are not so good because the program kind of took a dip there for two years. There were rough roads. He's a nice guy, but when you are making that transition it's difficult and you had a lot of headstrong guys on this football team that had had some success."

It was so bad in the first half of 1992 that former Gamecock and successful banker Hootie Johnson, who would go on to be the chairman of Augusta National Golf Club, said publicly that Woods should be fired and replaced with former Clemson coach Danny Ford, which led to bumper stickers in the state that read, "It Takes a Ford to Get Out of the Woods."

Woods was not fired, however, and South Carolina turned things around that season under Taneyhill, then a freshman. The Saturday following the players meeting, the Gamecocks upset No. 15 Mississippi State 21–6 and would win five of their final six games, prompting an apology from Johnson, who also sent roses to Woods' wife after the incident.

It never worked out in the long run for Woods, who was fired the following season after going 4–7, but his handling of his team's mutiny made an impact on Taneyhill, who is now a head high school coach with five state titles to his credit.

"I remember him telling us after we beat Mississippi State… we finally get a win and what he said after the game was, 'Who cares who gets the credit? I just want to win,'" Taneyhill said. "That statement—that's important for me now in coaching."

# 57 The Cockaboose Railroad

If you've been to Williams-Brice Stadium for a football game, you've almost certainly seen a Cockaboose, even if you weren't quite sure what it was. Even if you've only watched the Gamecocks on television, you've probably seen the now-trademark railroad cars that sit beside the stadium.

"It has been the subject of a number of opening scenes of Carolina television," South Carolina historian and former sports information director Don Barton said.

The history of the Cockaboose is steeped more in green than in garnet and black. They came to sit beside South Carolina's stadium for no reason other than local businessmen Ed Robinson and Carl Francis "Doc" Howard thought they could turn a profit on the arrangement.

In 1990, Robinson and Howard rolled 22 defunct train cabooses onto the track adjacent Williams-Brice and put up For Sale signs.

"People would look at you and they would give you this kind of wild-eyed look like, 'You're nuts,'" Robinson told *The State* newspaper in1990. "Then they'd say, 'Yeah. I want one.'"

Robinson died in 1998 followed 10 years later by Howard, but not before their idea became a hit. The pair sold 20 of the cabooses for $45,000 each within two days of putting them on the market. They kept two for themselves, and a tradition was born.

"It just happened," Barton said. "Things that catch on are not things that are contrived. They are just things that happen to catch on, and this just happened to be one of them."

The cabooses, which are each 45' by 10' on the outside and 30' by 9' on the inside, have increased in value since that day. In 2012, 16 Cockaboose Road (as the official real estate listing is called) was on the market for $299,000.

"There's really no way to put a price on these things," an original owner, Brian Harrison, told the Associated Press in 2010. "How could you find a more perfect tailgate experience? I have heat and air conditioning, a bathroom. And if it rains, I have a roof."

In 2011, *Parade* magazine dubbed the Cockabooses college football's "Most Luxurious Digs" in its Tailgating Awards.

"In 1990, steel magnate Ed Robinson installed 22 gutted cabooses on the dormant railroad tracks outside Williams-Brice stadium and sold them for $40,000 apiece. Gamecocks devotees snatched up these 'Cockabooses' and decked out the interiors in high style; they're now the site of pregame 'railgating,'" the magazine read.

The Cockabooses have also been featured in *Southern Living* and *Smithsonian*.

Painted garnet with a golden metal cutout of the state of South Carolina and the Gamecocks' mascot on the outside, the Cockabooses are designed on the interior at the owner's discretion. And many go all out.

"Everyone's got $100,000 in them," Columbia auto dealer Sam Jones told *The State* newspaper.

Each Cockaboose has running water, heating and air conditioning, a deck on the roof, interior plumbing, and cable television. The Cockabooses have even inspired imitators. In 2002, other local developers added seven more train cars across the street. However, they cannot claim the name Cockaboose. They are called "Steel Spur cabooses."

# 58 Alshon Jeffery— Service Station Star

Alshon Jeffery was famous in college football circles before he ever stepped foot on South Carolina's campus. But it was for the wrong reason.

In a move deemed over the line even in the cutthroat world of college football recruiting, Tennessee coach Lane Kiffin reportedly told Jeffery during a last-ditch recruiting pitch that Jeffery would end up pumping gas for a living if he chose to sign with the Gamecocks. The news spread quickly, painting Kiffin as an overzealous recruiter and putting a target on Jeffery.

After Jeffery did sign with the Gamecocks, he quickly made people understand why Kiffin wanted to get him out of the state so badly. Despite playing just three years before leaving for the NFL, Jeffery left South Carolina in 2011 as the school's all-time leader in receiving yardage (3,042) and second all-time in catches.

Jeffery grew up in St. Matthews, South Carolina, a tiny town with a Class A high school where Jeffery not only starred on the football field but also packed the basketball gym for four years running. With the 6'4", 237-lb. Jeffery playing any position he wanted, including point guard, St. Matthews won four consecutive state titles, at one point winning 78 games in a row.

"I ain't trying to brag," he said, "but I guess I'm pretty good."

And he brought those basketball skills to the gridiron. Jeffery's signature play was as simple as it was effective—go long, throw it high, and let Alshon do the rest.

"He combines great size, strength, and ball skills," said Derek Dooley, who replaced Kiffin as the Volunteers head coach. "He has everything that you need when the ball is up in the air. He has the physicality not to get pushed around, and he has the ball skills to know where the ball is and get himself in position to catch it. In many ways, in a one-on-one setting when the ball is up high, he is nearly unstoppable."

Dooley was not the only opponent impressed with Jeffery's physical gifts.

"You can't really have the same appreciation for him watching film as you do playing him live, just how big he really is, just how athletic he really is," Auburn coach Gene Chizik said. "You know he's a really good player when you watch the film, but I don't think the film does him justice."

Jeffery set the school record for 100-yard receiving games with 12, catching four passes for 148 yards in the last game of his career despite being thrown out of the Capital One Bowl for fighting in the third quarter.

"If you've got him in anything close to one-on-one coverage, you just put it up there and chances are either he catches it or no one catches it," FOX college football analyst Charles Davis said. "You can't go over him; you can't go through him; you can't go around him."

Jeffery often related his ability to catch the ball with rebounding.

"You just box the guy out and go up and get the ball," he said. "My confidence is like 85 percent that I'm going to get the ball."

Jeffery was named first-team All-American after a sophomore season in which he caught 88 passes for a school-record 1,517 yards. He also scored nine touchdowns. His numbers dropped as a junior in part due to poor conditioning, and he finished the year with 49 catches for 762 yards. Still, he was selected in the second round of the NFL draft in 2012 and had 24 catches for 367 yards in his rookie season with the Chicago Bears.

*Wide receiver Alshon Jeffery (1) catches a touchdown pass over the head of Vanderbilt cornerback Jamie Graham (25) in the fourth quarter a game on Saturday, October 23, 2010, in Nashville, Tennessee. South Carolina defeated Vanderbilt 21–7.* (AP Photo/Frederick Breedon)

Now instead of pumping gas, Jeffery can return to St. Matthews whenever his football career is complete and run for public office.

"Right now, if Alshon were to run for mayor, he could win," Calhoun County High basketball coach Zam Fredrick said in 2010. "As a matter of fact, in the last election, somebody put him on the ballot for a couple of different offices. It means a tremendous amount to everyone in Calhoun County to have one of our own that we know grew up pretty difficult, didn't have a whole lot, and he kind of threw himself into athletics. Everybody [in St. Matthews] more or less takes ownership in Alshon."

# 59 Beating the Big Three

Entering the 2010 season, South Carolina had beaten Florida, Georgia, and Tennessee a combined 22 times in the previous 116 years. From 2010–12, they were 8–1 against those conference rivals.

"Those streaks are massive," said South Carolina play-by-play announcer Todd Ellis, a former Gamecocks quarterback. "The time frame over the last three years has been remarkable and particularly beating those teams. There had been no history of that. People would like to say those programs are down. Well, part of the reason they are down is because we're up, and we're getting those good players, and we have great coaches."

For Gamecocks coach Steve Spurrier, it's that record as much as anything that has signified the turnaround South Carolina has made.

"Every time we play Georgia and Tennessee, I tell the guys this is one reason I came here, so we could coach against Georgia and

Tennessee, because it is always fun if you can beat those guys...
along with winning the SEC," Spurrier said. "The tradition was not
all that great, was not all that super [at South Carolina]. Nowhere
to go but up. I like those situations—a lot of firsts we can achieve
if we keep it going."

## Gamecocks in the Movies

Ron Bass is the most famous South Carolina football player
associated with the movie industry, but he's not the program's only
connection to Hollywood. For starters, there is also *The Program*.

The 1993 movie that starred Halle Berry, James Caan, and Omar
Epps was filmed in and around the Gamecocks' athletic facilities,
including Williams-Brice Stadium. The movie was not a huge
commercial success, but it launched Mike Hold's movie career. Hold
was the quarterback of South Carolina's 1984 Black Magic team, but
he had left Columbia by the time and was back closer to home in
Arizona.

Mark Ellis, the brother of former South Carolina quarterback
Todd Ellis, was an assistant sports coordinator for the movie and
knew Hold matched the physical frame of Craig Sheffer, who played
quarterback Joe Kane in the movie.

"So he called me in Arizona and asked me to come. I said,
'Sure,'" Hold said.

Hold went on to step into the on-field action in *Jerry Maguire* and
for Adam Sandler in *The Waterboy*.

"It's amazing to see a person like Adam Sandler and see how
he is when the lights are on," Hold said. "One day, he just stopped
me out of the blue and we had a conversation. He was a quiet, kind
of reserved guy, but then five minutes later when he was on set, it
was like, 'Boom.' It was neat just to see the real person behind the
scenes."

That movie launched an even longer movie and television
career for Mark Ellis, who has gone on to be the football and sports
coordinator for nearly 50 movies, including blockbusters like *Any
Given Sunday*, *Miracle*, *The Longest Yard*, *We are Marshall*, *The Amazing
Spider-Man*, and *The Dark Knight Rises*. Ellis is currently the football
coordinator for the USA Network's *Necessary Roughness*.

During their winning streaks against the Gators, Bulldogs, and Volunteers, the Gamecocks achieved a number of firsts, such as a first win in Gainesville, Florida, a 36–14 victory in 2010 that clinched the SEC East title. South Carolina's wins over the Volunteers in 2010 and 2011 were the first time they had managed to win back-to-back games in the series, and the Gamecocks had never beaten the Bulldogs three times in a row until 2010–12.

The only blemish on the record against the Big Three from 2010–12 was a 44–11 loss to Florida in 2012.

The Gamecocks' 3–0 record against Georgia during the stretch featured one of the team's most exciting and best games of the last decade. In 2011, South Carolina won a 45–42 shootout that featured a 68-yard fake punt for a touchdown by defensive lineman Melvin Ingram. The next year, Georgia came to Williams-Brice Stadium ranked No. 5 in the country and bent on revenge. Instead, sixth-ranked South Carolina walloped the Bulldogs 35–7.

"I expected it to be a dogfight the whole game, but we came out with a fire we need to come out with every week. We definitely sent a message out to the whole country. This is not the old South Carolina. We can play with anybody," tailback Marcus Lattimore said after that game.

The streak against Tennessee featured two comfortable wins by the Gamecocks (38–24 in 2010 and 14–3 in 2011) and then a squeaker. In 2012, South Carolina defensive end Jadeveon Clowney sacked Tennessee quarterback Tyler Bray, forcing a fumble that stopped a late Volunteer rally inside the 20-yard line to preserve a win in which quarterback Connor Shaw threw for 356 yards.

"Look at that Tennessee game. You talk about a big game," Ellis said. "That was a pretty dang good football team and just finding a way to beat them [was huge]. I can't tell you the times I've been in the booth or been on the sideline where they have a late drive 90 yards to beat us 28–24. For us to stop that with a great play from a great player was just remarkable."

Ellis points out that the record against the Big Three can be extended to even more impressive lengths. From 2010–12, the Gamecocks were 14–1 against Alabama, Florida, Georgia, Michigan, Nebraska, and Tennessee.

"To my knowledge, there is nothing like that record in the history of the program," Ellis said.

# 60 The Nightlife—Five Points and the Vista

When the Gamecocks are done playing on Saturdays during the fall, their fans tend to funnel one of two ways—either to the Vista or to Five Points.

If you've been out of college a few years and your hardest partying days are behind you, you're probably headed to the Vista, a still-developing arts and entertainment center in downtown Columbia.

The corridor, which is centered on Gervais Street, was once part of the city's industrial enterprise. As late as the 1980s, active railroad depots filled the area, serving warehouses and industrial buildings.

The change began in 1984 when the city began taking down the railroad trestle that cut through the district. The departure of the tracks was soon followed by the relocation of the industry it served and a blighted area dotted with empty warehouses.

That vibe then drew art galleries and studios, which led to a swift transformation of the area supported by the city. The Vista, as it is called now, was originally called The Congaree Vista after one of the rivers that runs through downtown Columbia.

In the early 1990s, restaurants like Beulah's and the Blue Marlin were built in old railroad depots, and the transformation was under way in earnest.

"The heart of any city has to be vibrant and expanding and attractive to people," Mayor Bob Coble told *The State* newspaper in 1991. "We've accomplished that to a degree. There is still a long way to go, but the momentum is clearly there."

Colonial Life Arena, home of the Gamecocks men's and women's basketball teams, and the Columbia Metropolitan Convention Center were built on the southern border of the district.

"The influx of that many residents, as well as people coming to the Vista for the arena and the conference center, is going to change the character of the area and create the demand for more and different retail," Fred Delk of the Columbia Development Corp. told *The State* newspaper.

By 2006, the Vista featured more than 45 restaurants and bars and more than 60 shops and galleries.

Five Points also has a deep history in Columbia. It was the city's first neighborhood shopping district, and it was jumpstarted in 1936 when Theodore Dehon opened the Shandon Coal Company on Greene Street. A gas station soon followed, and the area around Harden and Devine streets has not stopped evolving since.

Columbia's first supermarket, first Chinese restaurant, and first bar to serve a mixed drink were built in Five Points, according to research by *The State*.

In order for Five Points to become what it is today, Rocky Branch Creek had to be diverted underground by a Y-shaped tunnel that became a place for the children of the day to traverse on a dare, as Charles Dickerson told *The State* in 2005.

"As I remember, I went through with a bunch of guys my age," he said. "We didn't want the big guys with us."

In 1964, the Five Points Merchants Association listed 182 businesses. In the late 1940s, one of those was an auto parts store that also sold televisions.

"When the World Series would come on, we had this TV sitting up on top of the Coca-Cola box between the front doors and we'd gather about 10 people out front," Kenny Hooks, one of the business' owners, told *The State*. "They had to come [inside] in order to see the picture."

From there the district grew into a popular spot for students at the University of South Carolina, including the football players. In fact, it's not unusual when a Gamecock finds trouble with the city's laws that the offense takes place in Five Points.

The most famous of those incidents came in 2011 when Jadeveon Clowney, who at the time was only a signee with the school but would go on to be a consensus All-American defensive end, was briefly handcuffed in what was reported as a case of mistaken identity.

Coach Steve Spurrier was quick to come to the defense of his prize recruit, staging a scene after practice in which Chief of Police Randy Scott placed Spurrier in handcuffs in front of more than a dozen media members following a spring practice.

"Chief Scott said there was a robbery and somebody called and said it looked like the head ball coach at South Carolina," Spurrier said. "I had to tell him I didn't leave practice all day today, and he said it was okay. It's not embarrassing to be handcuffed. That's what I'm trying to say."

"[Clowney] should not have been around town at two in the morning, but he was with some [high school] teammates," Spurrier said. "Somebody said the guy that was the robber was a tall guy that looked a lot like Jadeveon. So they went in and questioned him. [They] didn't know who he was and cuffed him up the way I just got cuffed up. A lot of people would probably get upset getting handcuffed, but the police have a tough job to do. They don't know who has a gun that's going to shoot them or not."

"I want to make it clear that [Clowney] did nothing wrong," Scott said. "He was not drinking. He was not consuming any alcohol, and hopefully we will see him on the USC football field."

# 61 Melvin Ingram— Out of Nowhere

When defensive end Melvin Ingram stepped onto South Carolina's football field for preseason practice in 2011, he was considered a stalwart senior whose job was soon to be taken by hotshot freshman Jadeveon Clowney.

The last time he performed at Williams-Brice, an NFL Films Crew was filming his every move and he had a line of T-shirts ready to roll off a printing press with his nickname "SupaMelvin" emblazoned on them.

A consensus All-American season will do that. It became clear early in the fall of 2011 that Ingram was going to be something special, something his first three years at South Carolina did not suggest.

He arrived in Columbia from Hamlet, North Carolina, considered a very good but not great high school prospect. And at first, he didn't even live up to that billing. As a freshman, he played in 12 games as a linebacker and totaled 15 tackles. After a season on the shelf due to a broken foot, he returned in 2009 and had another underwhelming season at linebacker, notching 18 tackles this time.

However, a move to defensive end late in the year proved a boon for the Gamecocks, if not immediately. The next year, Ingram led the team with nine sacks despite not starting a game.

*South Carolina's Melvin Ingram (6) sacks Florida's John Brantley (12) during the SEC East battle between the Florida Gators and the South Carolina Gamecocks played at Williams-Brice Stadium in Columbia, South Carolina, on November 12, 2011. South Carolina won the game, 17–12.* (Cal Sport Media via AP Images)

Then came 2011. With Devin Taylor rooted at one defensive end spot and Clowney coming to campus with more hype than any high school player in the country, Ingram was an afterthought… at least from the outside.

"He's the best athlete on our team," All-SEC running back Marcus Lattimore said in preseason camp.

To watch the 268-lb. Ingram stay step for step with the 218-lb. Lattimore in practice drills was to see that Ingram had special ability. He had shown that ability ever since childhood, as stories of his athleticism were legendary in his hometown where he played almost every position on his high school football team. He could do a standing backflip and would prove it without much encouragement. He also worked as a backup long snapper when he arrived in the NFL with the San Diego Chargers.

The foot injury that cost Ingram the 2008 season eventually saved his career, according to South Carolina defensive line coach Brad Lawing.

"Things came so easy to him before, and he didn't know how to work. When he finally learned how to work—and there was a lot of hair- and tooth-pulling to get that done; there were times I'd feel like my head was going to explode to get him [to do] what he needed to do as far as work ethic—but when he learned how to work, that's when things finally came into play for him, and I'm proud of him for that," Lawing said. "Some never learn. Melvin finally bought in."

The results of that work were evident in the Gamecocks' second game of the season, a 45–42 win over Georgia in which Ingram swung the momentum with a 68-yard touchdown run on a fake punt and scored another touchdown on a fumble recovery.

"The plays he made tonight were just unbelievable," defensive coordinator Ellis Johnson said. "The things he did tonight affected the game as much as anyone on the field."

Ingram finished the year with a single-season South Carolina record of 10 sacks, plus 15 tackles-for-loss, two interceptions, two fumble recoveries for touchdowns, and 48 tackles. He was named a consensus All-American, joining George Rogers and Del Wilkes as the only Gamecocks to earn that honor at the time.

From there, Ingram went on to be selected No. 18 overall in the NFL draft, fulfilling a prediction made by his father who died when

Ingram was 9 years old but had told Ingram's mother Nancy when Melvin was a baby that he expected his son to play in the NFL.

For Ingram, the selection capped one of the most unexpected careers in South Carolina football history.

"I am ready to go grind right now," he said as he paced Radio City Music Hall in New York following his selection. "I'm ready to get on a plane right now."

# 62 Doubters Beware—Steve Spurrier's First Year

It was 2004 and Steve Spurrier was ready to get back into coaching. After a disappointing two years in the NFL where he was 12–20 with the Washington Redskins, Spurrier didn't work in the fall of 2004.

He was finally pulled back to the college game in November of that year to replace Lou Holtz as the Gamecocks head coach.

"I wanted to coach again. I got my energy back, and I got my hunger back," Spurrier told the *Atlanta Journal-Constitution* at the time of his hiring. "I looked around, and South Carolina just seemed like the perfect situation for me. [Athletics Director] Mike McGee pursued me and made it clear he wanted me to coach here. And I wanted the opportunity. Everything is here. I'd like to borrow a line from the Boston Red Sox, 'Why not us?' Why can't we win the SEC?"

There were plenty of people ready to list the reasons. At the time of Spurrier's hiring, South Carolina had one title to show for 111 years of football, and that was the 1969 ACC crown.

More shockingly, the Gamecocks had won 10 or more games in a season just once and eight or more in a season only eight times.

"There are some special challenges here," McGee acknowledged at the time to the *Atlanta Journal-Constitution*. "But I got the sense that Steve is really up for those challenges. I wondered if he would still have the passion after his NFL experience, but after one conversation it was very clear that he is excited about what is possible here."

Spurrier might have been the only one. Holtz, who came to the school with a national title, couldn't get the program to a championship and averaged six wins in his final three seasons. The chorus of, "No one can win at South Carolina!" was loud, and the Gamecocks took notice.

Tommy Suggs, a former South Carolina quarterback and 40-year veteran of the school's radio team, remembers the 2005 season as one of his most stressful as a broadcaster.

"The one I remember the most was Steve Spurrier's first year, and the reason I remember that is some of the national media were saying fairly frequently, 'Why would he go to South Carolina? He can't win there,' all this type of stuff," Suggs said. "I was pulling so hard for him to show them wrong and for us to do well, and he did."

It didn't start fast, though. The Gamecocks lost their first three conference games under Spurrier—to traditional powers Georgia, Alabama, and Auburn. Things began to turn around on October 8 with a win over Kentucky. Another win came during the next game, against Vanderbilt, and then came a date with Tennessee in Neyland Stadium on October 29.

The Volunteers were ranked No. 23. South Carolina had never won a football game in Knoxville, Tennessee, and the Gamecocks hadn't beaten Tennessee in the last 12 games.

That changed when place-kicker Josh Brown, normally a short-distance specialist, hit a 49-yard field goal with 2:45 left in the game to give the Gamecocks a 16–15 win.

The next day, the headline in *The State* newspaper read, "Over the Rocky Top." In that story, Spurrier said this: "We've still never beat Florida [as a member of the SEC]. So that could be a historic game, too."

It was nice foreshadowing of the November 12 matchup against the Gators. Spurrier won the Heisman Trophy as Florida's quarterback and then coached the Gators for 12 seasons, including the 1996 national championship season.

To say the game was hyped would be an understatement. Florida led the overall series between the teams 19–3–3 at the time. The last South Carolina win had come in 1939.

Again Spurrier pulled a rabbit out of his hat, coming away with a 30–22 win.

"I told you guys we had a lot of history that we could set at South Carolina," Spurrier said after the game. "I didn't think we'd set this much this year."

It was the first time the Gamecocks had ever beaten Tennessee and Florida in the same season.

"They kept on saying it was like 1930-something. I was like, 'I don't care about football back then.' I wasn't even born," South Carolina defensive tackle Chris Tucker told *The State*. "We were like, 'We can keep on making history,' [and] try to beat Tennessee and Florida the same year. That's what we did."

The Florida game capped a five-game winning streak that was snapped the next week by Clemson with a 13–9 loss, but the message was loud and clear in Columbia—Spurrier really can win here. South Carolina lost its bowl game 38–31 to Missouri and finished 7–5.

"I just felt like that was a critical year—not for him so much but for the reputation of our school," Suggs said. "We needed to put it back in their face and say, 'He came here because he can win.' I thought that was a huge thing for us."

# 63 The Pastor of Pain

He never entered a wrestling ring, but if anyone had a nickname and birthplace combination made for the dramatic announcement, it's "The Pastor of Pain... from Pageland, South Carolina... Corey Miller!"

Miller played linebacker and defensive end for the Gamecocks from 1988–90 and was named All-South Independent in 1989 and 1990. He came along before recruits were ranked by stars, but he was a SuperPrep All-American and one of the most sought players in the South, coming out of Pageland High School.

Miller narrowed his search to schools close to home so that his family, which didn't have much extra money to be traveling on fall Saturdays, could come see him play. He had a final four of South Carolina, Clemson, Georgia, and North Carolina.

The Gamecocks had a big advantage, though. Pageland High School coach Al Usher played football at South Carolina in 1968, 1970, and 1971, and Usher was not shy about telling Miller where he should attend school.

"He kind of brainwashed me," Miller said. "Then I saw [the team come onto the field to] '2001' and fell in love with it."

There was, however, a problem. Miller was a Proposition 48 recruit, which meant he had to sit out his freshman year because he didn't meet the entrance requirements for immediate eligibility.

"It was a difficult transition," Miller said of the time. "I missed my first year [and] just had to work out. The next three years I took full advantage of playing."

Miller was switched from linebacker to defensive end before his junior season because it better suited the Gamecocks' needs, but his 6'2" 250-lb. frame was best suited for outside linebacker, and that's just where the New York Giants put Miller after drafting him in the sixth round of the 1991 NFL Draft.

There Miller joined one of the greatest linebacker groups in the history of the NFL, initially playing behind starters Lawrence Taylor, Carl Banks, and Pepper Johnson.

At South Carolina, he counts his greatest game as a 1989 win over Georgia during which he had 16 tackles and two sacks.

"They were ranked. We went in there and knocked them off," he said. "The other [favorite] one would be my last game, [a] Thursday night game, Thanksgiving game, [when] we played West Virginia here at home. It was my final game as a Gamecock, and having Mom and Dad here was great."

After his NFL career, Miller earned his nickname by becoming a minister. He still speaks at many church events and is a sports talk radio host on 560 AM The Team in Columbia. In 2013, Miller's son Christian, one of the top high school players in the state of South Carolina, made big news by verbally committing to play for the University of Florida.

"It would have been so awesome to see my son put on the garnet and black and run out to '2001,' but it's probably best for him to do it on his own somewhere else," Corey Miller told *The State* newspaper.

Miller is in the conversation of the greatest linebackers in South Carolina history, along with James Seawright, John Abraham, and Kalimba Edwards.

"Some people would say that, but I don't know if I'd say that. There were a lot of good ones," Miller said.

The worst memory of Miller's South Carolina career is a 38–35 loss to The Citadel during his senior season.

"If I could go back in time, I would go back to that Citadel game and I [would] give us a different coach and put him on that sideline," Miller told country music writer and South Carolina fan

Patrick Davis during a series of interviews Davis did with former South Carolina players. "You don't understand, I hear about that today. My wife's father was a Citadel graduate, and he would always hold that over me. He'd go, 'I got the tape if you want to watch that game.' You had myself and Gerald Dixon, two ends who played almost 20 years in the NFL combined, you put us in a wide-9 technique. I never will forget having to stand and address the media. I was so angry. I wanted to sit there and go, 'Sparky Woods, Rick Whitt, it's your fault.' You shouldn't lose a game like that ever. That's going to [stay] with me for the rest of my life."

# 64 Beating No. 1—The Trifecta

Alabama was coming off a national title. It had won its last 19 games, and it was ranked No. 1 in the nation.

South Carolina, meanwhile, was still wondering if it belonged in the upper echelon of the Southeastern Conference. The Gamecocks, who had never beaten a top-ranked opponent, finished 7–6 in 2009. They were 3–1 on October 9, 2010, and coming off a disheartening loss to Auburn.

Steve Spurrier, never known for his rah-rah pregame speeches, had a simple message for his team before they took the field.

"Fellas, let's give fate a chance," he told the Gamecocks. "If fate is going to smile on South Carolina, we've got to give it a chance. Who knows? If you give it a chance, something big may happen. If you don't give it a chance, it's not going to happen."

It happened and in a big way. South Carolina scored five touchdowns on what was the No. 1 scoring defense in the country.

The Crimson Tide had surrendered just three touchdowns in its five previous games combined.

"I think it was just meant to be," Spurrier said. "Fate was on our side."

The victory capped a historic year in South Carolina sports history. The men's basketball team and baseball team had knocked off the No. 1 teams in their respective sports previously in the calendar year, making South Carolina the first school in history to complete that feat.

"We have a lot of guys on our team who haven't lost a game," Alabama coach Nick Saban said. "This is a lesson for everybody about what you have to do to prepare, what it takes to play with consistency in this league."

Junior quarterback Stephen Garcia, who had been benched two weeks prior to the game only to win back his starting job, completed 17-of–20 passes for 210 yards and three touchdowns.

"I think we responded unbelievably to the questions that were asked of us, the questions that were asked of me," Garcia said. "It was an unbelievable feeling. I'm not really sure how to describe the feeling, but it's unbelievable."

Garcia was named the Walter Camp National Offensive Player of the Week, and the victory stands as the high point of his tumultuous career at South Carolina, which included five suspensions and an eventual dismissal from the team.

"Stephen Garcia played the best he's ever played," Spurrier said that day.

The defense didn't play badly, either, holding the reigning Heisman Trophy winner, running back Mark Ingram, to just 41 yards on the ground.

"I think we basically stopped the run, which I did not think we could do," defensive coordinator Ellis Johnson said. "There was a never a time as we managed the running game that we didn't feel like we had control of it."

When the game was over, Alabama quarterback Greg McElroy told Garcia, "We'll see y'all again," anticipating a rematch in the SEC Championship Game.

McElroy was only half right. The Gamecocks would go on to win their first SEC East title and play in the SEC title game, but their opponent was the Crimson Tide's top rival, Auburn, which beat the Gamecocks 56–17 on the way to the national title.

The Gamecocks would lose their next game despite being heavily favored against Kentucky, but the win over Alabama helped establish South Carolina as a contender in the conference and powered them to a three-year period that would see a school-record 31 victories.

The victory gave Spurrier 107 SEC wins, second only to legendary Alabama coach Bear Bryant, who won 159 conference games.

"It's sort of neat to get that [milestone], I have to admit," Spurrier said. "It was neat to get it against Alabama. I didn't think about it until the game was over. Bear Bryant holds the record, which no one will ever catch, which is fine. But to be second to him against Alabama, the No. 1 team in the country…

"I gave myself a game ball. The players wanted to give fate a game ball. I said, 'I'm accepting for fate.'"

# 65 A Brief Bowl History

These days a 2–3–3 record wouldn't qualify for a bowl game, but in 1945 the rules were a little different.

That year a group of Jacksonville, Florida, businessmen had started a new bowl game, the Gator Bowl, and needed somebody to fill it. The Gamecocks and Wake Forest, who at the time were rivals, seemed to fit the bill. South Carolina had played Wake Forest to a 13–13 tie in Charlotte in November, and a rematch seemed like it might sell tickets.

That's how Johnnie McMillan ended up taking South Carolina to its first bowl game in his one season as head coach. Wake Forest prevailed 26–14, kicking off decades of mostly bad bowl experiences for the Gamecocks.

The first bowl trip earned on the field came following the 1969 season when the Peach Bowl in Atlanta invited the Gamecocks to play West Virginia. South Carolina finished the regular season 7–3 in Paul Dietzel's fourth season as head coach. The school filmed Dietzel as he announced the news of the invitation to his team.

"One of the things we said was if you come to Carolina, we don't want you to come here unless you're planning on winning the ACC title, and you've done that and I congratulate you. And the other thing is I didn't want you to come here unless you wanted to play in a bowl game, and I have to tell you the truth that on December 30, the University of South Carolina is the host team in the Peach Bowl," Dietzel said, causing his players, still in uniform, to erupt with joy.

The game wasn't such a happy occasion as a Mountaineer team coached by future South Carolina coach Jim Carlen beat the Gamecocks 14–3 while rushing for 356 yards and throwing for just 3.

The Gamecocks would have a happier bowl result against West Virginia 26 years later, but in between would come six straight bowl losses, giving South Carolina an 0–8 start to its bowl history. South Carolina lost to Miami of Ohio, Missouri, Pittsburgh, Oklahoma State, LSU, and Indiana before the 1995 Carquest Bowl came along to break the curse.

The Gamecocks finished 6–5 in the regular season behind junior quarterback Steve Taneyhill, who threw for 227 yards and a touchdown and rushed for another score in a 24–21 win over the Mountaineers.

Suddenly, the Gamecocks were on a winning streak. They wouldn't go back to a bowl game until 2001, but they won both the 2001 and 2002 Outback Bowls against Ohio State.

"It wasn't one of the best Ohio State teams—I don't want to oversell it—but we were clear underdogs in both of those games that he won," said Mike McGee, who was the athletics director at the time. "I think that more than anything put South Carolina on the map."

The team didn't capitalize on that bowl momentum, however, and dropped three of its next four postseason games. The conclusion of that string was a 20–7 loss to Connecticut in the 2010 PapaJohns.com Bowl that made Steve Spurrier so angry he couldn't quit talking about it for months.

"If we can't get our players to play any better than last Saturday, then we as coaches better find us some new players or pretty soon they're going to find some new coaches around here," Spurrier told *The State* newspaper after the game. "We've got a lot of good players, but we need help."

They got it and won two of their next three bowl games, losing 26–17 to Florida State in the 2010 Chick-fil-A Bowl and then beating tradition-rich programs Nebraska and Michigan in the 2012 Capital One Bowl and 2013 Outback Bowl, respectively.

Spurrier counts those wins over Nebraska and Michigan as some of the most important in his career because they each gave the school 11 wins in a season. They were also signs to Spurrier that South Carolina was closing the gap on more storied programs.

"I told the guys [before the Capital One Bowl], 'We may be 42 conference championships behind Nebraska and five national championships behind them, but when that ball is kicked off, we are going to show them we can play ball at South Carolina,'" he said.

# 66 The Songs of the Gamecocks

Paul Dietzel was a man of many hats at South Carolina.

Not only was Dietzel the Gamecocks' football coach and athletic director from 1966–74, he also found time to write the school's fight song.

Until 1969, South Carolina's athletic teams had been urged on by a number of different fight songs—including "The Carolina Fight Song"—but none of them made enough of an impact on Dietzel to be considered irreplaceable.

"I don't remember if they even had a fight song," Dietzel told *The State* newspaper. "If they had a fight song, I'm not sure I knew about it or whether I was extremely impressed with it. I thought everything about us is kind of new, and it would be kind of nice and new if we had a new fight song, one with a little spring to it."

Dietzel found the beat he was looking for in "Step to the Rear," a musical number from the 1967 Broadway play *How Now, Dow Jones*, which was written by Elmer Bernstein. The play centered on the story of a girl who announces the Dow Jones numbers and was remade in 2009.

South Carolina band director James Pritchard helped arrange the music around Dietzel's words:

Hey, let's give a cheer, Carolina is here,
The Fighting Gamecocks lead the way.
Who gives a care, if the going gets tough,
And when it is rough, that's when the 'Cocks get going.
Hail to our colors of garnet and black,
In Carolina pride have we.
So go, Gamecocks, go—fight!

Drive for the goal—fight!
USC will win today—go Cocks!
So let's give a cheer, Carolina is here.
The Fighting Gamecocks all the way!

(Dietzel was not the only person to borrow from "Step to the Rear." The music was so popular that it appeared in a television commercial for Lincoln-Mercury's 1969 line of cars and in Hubert Humphrey's campaign for president.)

Since Dietzel's work, there have been suggestions he might have been better served sticking to sports. Even former South Carolina coach Lou Holtz publicly lambasted the song.

"I would like to have something that would bind us together, something you could learn and sing if you ever win a game," Holtz told *The State* newspaper after his 0–11 1999 season. "My children could sing the Ohio State fight song when they were 3 years old because I was coaching at Ohio State. 'Fight the team across the field, show them Ohio.' Your players learn it. It's a bonding-type thing. Tell me what song anybody can sing here other than the alma mater. The players don't know it. I don't know it. I've tried. I don't know of anybody who knows it. This is the first place I've ever been where nobody knows it."

Holtz even threatened to write a new song of his own.

"The piece offers a number of problems," William Moody, a University of South Carolina professor and coordinator of conducting, told *The State*. "When you take into account the syncopation and the speed of the piece and the rhythms of this fight song, it is very difficult to sing—even though the words fit."

The Gamecocks' fight song is not to be confused with the school's alma mater, which was written in 1911 by English professor George A. Wauchope, according to *Remembering the Days: An Illustrated History of the University of South Carolina*.

The alma mater, set to the music of "Flow Gently, Sweet Afton," is titled, "We Hail Thee Carolina."

We hail thee, Carolina, and sing thy high praise
With loyal devotion, remembering the days
When proudly we sought thee, thy children to be:
Here's a health, Carolina, forever to thee!
Since pilgrims of learning, we entered thy walls
And found dearest comrades in thy classic halls
We've honored and loved thee as sons faithfully;
Here's a health, Carolina, forever to thee!
Generations of sons have rejoiced to proclaim
Thy watchword of service, thy beauty and fame;
For ages to come shall their rallying cry be:
Here's a health, Carolina, forever to thee!
Fair shrine of high honor and truth, thou shalt still
Blaze forth as a beacon, thy mission fulfill,
And crowned by all hearts in a new jubilee:
Here's a health, Carolina, forever to thee!

Members of the school's athletic teams now stand and face the school's band for the playing of the alma mater after each game. As the last line is sung, athletes raise a cupped right hand to mimic a toast. "Here's a health" was a common refrain in toasts from the 1920s and earlier.

"The fact that our tradition now is to sing the alma mater after the games, I think that is really a special tradition," athletics director Ray Tanner said. "I don't see that with other teams and other schools. I think that's really special."

# 67 "Hot is Who We Are"

In 2008, the city of Columbia finally decided to embrace its identity.

That's when The Midlands Authority for Conventions, Sports, and Tourism signed off on a new marketing slogan—"Famously Hot."

Anyone who has ever been to Columbia to see the Gamecocks play in the early fall, much less spent a summer in the middle of South Carolina, knows exactly what the tagline means. It's just plain hot.

The new motto—which includes the lesser known, "The New Southern Hot Spot"—replaced, "Riverbanks Region: Where Friendliness Flows," a slogan that never caught on.

"This is a very different brand," Lora Prill, who worked for the Columbia advertising agency that came up with the campaign, told *The State* newspaper. "It's vibrant, not passive. 'Hot' is who we are. It takes a perceived negative and turns it on its head."

The average high in Columbia in May, June, July, August, and September is at least 88 degrees, peaking with July's average high of 95. There are several reasons why the city is even hotter than many of its summer neighbors.

"Columbia is an hour and a half from the coast, and yet we're just a few hundred feet above sea level," Ben Tanner, a meteorologist at Columbia's WIS television station, told *The State*. "If you look at a topography map, you'll see that in Richland and Lexington counties, there's a bit of a sink, so we get very little wind. A lot of the systems don't even make it over the mountains."

Columbia also lies on the Fall Line, a geological formation that separates the Piedmont from the sandy Coastal Plain, and that sand

**Emily White**
For 45 years, nine athletic directors came and went at South Carolina, while Emily White was there through it all. White, who retired as an administrative assistant to the Gamecocks athletic directors in 2012, "was the glue that held the athletic department together," men's basketball equipment manager Mac Credile told *The State* newspaper upon White's retirement.

In 2008, White was inducted into the South Carolina Athletics Hall of Fame.

"If someone thinks her job is strictly clerical, then they really don't know the person and her qualifications," former athletic director Bob Marcum told *The State*.

White prided herself on keeping her insider information to herself.

"Some people would like to know and tell things," she told *The State*. "I've always been one to keep it to myself and listen to others talk about something they didn't know."

absorbs and retains heat. And then there is the city itself and all the concrete and steel that comes with it.

"All the development, all the concrete and parking lots mean the city tends not to give up its heat during the night," state climatologist officer Wes Tyler told *The State*. "Also, there is less evaporation, which is a cooling mechanism, in the city because there is so much less plant cover. Instead, you have buildings and parking lots."

Former State Meteorologist John Purvis studied the worst of the stretches in Columbia of consecutive days with 100-degree or higher temperatures.

"Most of the real hot days come when we have a high pressure system in the area," Purvis told *The State*. "That's when we have lots of sunshine and a lot of air subsiding from above, as it typically does with high pressure. And usually we have a weather front that is not quite strong enough to make it across the mountains. That front will then work its way around and along the Eastern

Seaboard. When that happens, it magnifies the downslope effect. That means the air drops down, gets warmer, and we wind up with a big mass of hot air. And if we look back at the high temperatures over the years, we find the big bubble of real hot weather is located right on the Fall Line."

Whatever your position on global warming, it's not debatable that the heat in Columbia is not going anywhere.

The summer of 2011 was the hottest on record in the city. The average daily temperature from June through August was 84.18 degrees, and it's not just hot in the summer in Columbia. On January 12, 2013, the city set a new high for the date when the temperature reached 82 degrees.

"Famously Hot" indeed.

# 68 Joe Morrison's Death

On February 5, 1989, Teddy Heffner was putting the finishing touches on *The State* newspaper's sports section.

"I had the best sports picture I had ever seen," said Heffner, the paper's beat writer for the South Carolina football team. "It was a horse race, and the jockey had been thrown over the horse and [he] hung on to the horse's bridle backward and crossed the finish line to win. So I lay out the paper and blow up this big ol' picture."

Only one edition of *The State*'s readers would ever see that picture because of what happened next. A colleague of Heffner's heard on the office police scanner that an ambulance had been dispatched to the coaches' offices at Williams-Brice Stadium. The stadium was across the street from *The State*, so Heffner drove over to see what was happening.

Joe Morrison, the Gamecocks' seventh-year football coach, had been taken to the hospital. By the time Heffner arrived at the hospital, Morrison was dead.

"Of course we had to completely redo the paper," Heffner said. "I'll never forget that great picture of that horse that only went to one edition."

Morrison had been playing racquetball at the stadium when he began to feel ill.

"He started complaining he couldn't catch his breath, and the doctor who was there told him, 'Do not get [in] the shower,' but [Morrison] said, 'No, I'm not going [to the hospital] all hot and sweaty,'" Heffner said. "So when he got into the shower, according to the doctor, the water caused his blood vessels to constrict and actually brought on the heart attack. He was basically dead before he hit the floor."

That health problems would fell Morrison was not a huge shock. Coaching college football can be a stressful job. Throw in the fact that Morrison was probably on his way to losing his job because of a steroid scandal that had emerged at the school and the fact that Morrison was such a heavy smoker that he used to sneak smoke breaks during the games of his 14-year NFL career, and the recipe wasn't good.

"His doctor told him if he didn't quit smoking he was going to kill himself, so he actually quit smoking in 1984. Then in the 1986 season, Carolina really had a good football team, but they went 3–6–2 and all those good bounces they had in '84 went the other direction in '86. It got him so frazzled he started smoking again."

Former South Carolina quarterback Todd Ellis was recruited by Morrison, and not long before Morrison's death, they had a meeting to discuss whether Ellis would enter the NFL or return to South Carolina for his senior season.

"It was awful on everybody," Ellis said. "It was tough."

At the time of his death, Morrison was the most successful coach in the school's history. He was not far removed from the Black Magic season of 1984, which saw the Gamecocks reach the No. 2 ranking in the country at one point. Morrison was named the National Coach of the Year that season.

"It was hard times because everybody loved Joe, and we were on the brink I think of really turning things around when he passed away," said Corey Miller, who played linebacker for Morrison's Gamecocks.

But Heffner believes that turnaround wouldn't have occurred because Morrison was on his way out as football coach due to the steroid scandal.

"[School president James] Holderman had actually made the statement that he felt like maybe Coach Morrison would have been better off somewhere else," Heffner said. "When I told Joe that, Joe said, 'Hell, I wish he would have told me that a couple weeks ago,' because he was actually approached by the Cincinnati Bengals about coaching their team and turned them down."

Morrison had also considered returning to his alma mater, the University of Cincinnati, that offseason because he could see trouble brewing for him in Columbia, Heffner said. Morrison's defensive coordinator Joe Lee Dunn talked him out of it, according to Heffner.

"Joe Lee said, 'We've come too far to take that kind of a step back,'" Heffner said. "Joe Lee always told me he wonders if they had taken that job if Joe would still be alive, but I don't think so. I just think his heart had reached that point."

# 69 1975—Fits Like a Glove

Jim Carlen's coaching career at South Carolina lasted seven seasons, and the later years saw a 17–14 road win over Michigan and George Rogers' 1980 Heisman season. But the best one of all might have come first.

In 1975, Carlen walked into a great situation when he arrived on South Carolina's campus to find quarterback Jeff Grantz and running backs Clarence Williams and Kevin Long ready to plug into his veer offense.

"It fit us like a glove," Long said. "Everybody had speed, and I think that was something new for the Carolina fans, seeing that much speed on the field at the same time. Clarence ran a 4.4 40-yard dash. I ran a 4.5. I know Jeff ran four-something. We had a pretty potent backfield."

In fact, it was a historic backfield. Long and Williams became the first Gamecocks running backs to each gain more than 1,000 yards in a season. Long finished as the team leader with 1,133, while Williams was right behind with 1,073.

Long, Williams, and Grantz combined for 10 100-yard rushing games. With Grant pulling the trigger on the option pitch, the Gamecocks rolled up single-game rushing totals of 260, 302, 371, 378, 320, 354, and 458 yards that season.

"It was the best offense I played in the entire time I was here," Long said. "We knew each other. Jeff would just hold the ball until the last second. He took some awful hits, but he'd get the ball out there to you perfect. He'd get us the ball 10 or 15 yards downfield. He was always looking to pitch you the ball. We just had fun with it. Jim Carlen just let us run to daylight. We didn't have a lot of designed plays that we stuck to."

*Running back Kevin Long (32) is thrown for a loss by Ron Zook (17) of Ohio during the Tangerine Bowl game on Saturday, December 20, 1975, in Orlando, Florida.* (AP Photo/Bill Hudson)

Long and Williams are eighth and ninth in South Carolina history in career rushing with 2,372 yards and 2,311 yards, respectively.

"When Jim Carlen came in, his philosophy was, 'The best 22 players are going to be on the field.' He stood by that promise," Long said. "He didn't play politics or nothing. If you were a player, he let you play. He didn't worry about outside influences."

The Gamecocks finished the regular season 7–4, and Grantz was named a second-team All-American after the season.

"The community started getting more involved in the team," Long said. "It was a great time."

The season ended with a 20–7 loss to Miami of Ohio in the Tangerine Bowl, but for South Carolina fans it was capped in the regular season finale. Archrival Clemson was coming to Williams-Brice Stadium, and a bowl bid hung in the balance.

The Gamecocks won 56–20, scoring a touchdown on every possession. It remains the fondest memory of the series for many South Carolina fans.

"We should have been 9–2, but it was a special season and it was a great way to go out," Grantz said. "The senior year was very important to me to go out like that, and then, of course, the last game against Clemson."

# 70 Mike Safran—Housing History

Mike Safran is the kind of guy who gives hoarding a good name.

Safran is a fourth-generation antiques dealer in Columbia, and in the last 30 years he has become the unofficial keeper of a South Carolina Gamecocks museum. His collection is not recognized by the university (not that he hasn't tried), but nowhere else on the planet will you find more South Carolina stuff than at 1015 Whaley Street in downtown Columbia—not quite in the shadow of Williams-Brice Stadium but within sight of that shadow.

There, at Safran's Antiques, resides the Gamecock Shop, the name of a 4,000-sq.-ft. section of warehouse that houses nothing but the history of South Carolina athletics. Memorabilia is stacked upon memorabilia, and another 2,000 sq. ft. sits out of site behind a wall.

Safran, a 53-year-old South Carolina graduate, came to be the owner of this collection almost by accident after he was introduced to the sports memorabilia business in his twenties.

"I found right away that sports cards didn't do anything for me. I have always been one who enjoyed having something a little bit different than what everybody else had," he said. "I got to the point where I was thinking, 'What is something [different] you could do?' Everything that you could amass some kind of collection of had been done already. Then I said, 'You know, nobody has ever collected the University of South Carolina. Nobody has ever been dumb enough to collect the University of South Carolina.'"

Safran was. He started by pulling old game programs out of his mother's attic, and it took off from there.

"The fact that it turned into a magnet is a sword that cuts both ways," he said. "It's great that the name has gotten out enough that people know this is the place for stuff to go if you've got stuff. And yet in the last month I've picked up a folder 4 inches deep of just negatives [of photos from games]."

More than once, Safran has tried to get officials from the school to take an interest in his collection and perhaps partner on a more official display setting, but he has now given up on those efforts.

"I started saving it because I saw it wasn't being saved," he said. "I just kept trying to see if I could get a light bulb to go off over somebody's head over there. Without getting too political on it, I just kind of came to the conclusion that it would never happen at the university, and they didn't give much of a care about this past."

When he bought the warehouse where Safran's now sits, which also houses another 5,000 sq. ft. of other antiques, his wife urged him to take the Gamecocks collection from his basement and set it free. The South Carolina section started on one wall of one room but quickly began to take over one half of the store.

"It's taken on a life of its own," he said.

Safran has everything from game-worn jerseys to audio cassettes of legendary play-by-play voice Bob Fulton to tribute videos to stacks and stacks of photos and negatives.

For the last several years, Safran has had students from University 101 freshman classes in his building.

"I'll walk them around for 15–20 minutes and try to teach them enough Gamecock sports history that they could go back and write a paper," he said.

And he's quick to give the same history lesson to anyone who asks. The massive building is heated and cooled only by the elements Mother Nature provides each day. And in the winter, Safran offers visitors "the guest coat," an old South Carolina soccer sideline cape.

"It's toasty," he said.

At least five televisions are running in the Gamecock Shop every moment the store is open. Two are devoted to highlights and replays from the baseball team's back-to-back national titles. One is a look back at Frank McGuire's basketball heyday. One is a football highlight tape, and another is raw footage of Lou Sossamon, the school's first All-American, and his teammate from the 1940s, Dom Fusci, discussing their days with the Gamecocks.

The back and forth between Sossamon and Fusci alone is worth a trip to Safran's. The video has been running on a loop since Fusci's death in February 2012.

"After Dom died, I just said, 'I've got that thing. I'll let them talk for the rest of the week,'" Safran said. "Then I'll let them talk for the rest of the month. Now they've been talking for more than a year."

It is the relationships Safran has built with the Sossamons and the Fuscis and the Tatum Gressettes and the George Rogers that have made his "labor of love" even more rewarding, he said.

"It's turned into a magnet for the legends," Safran said. "They love to come around and tell the stories. I think my record is six or seven [South Carolina athletics] Hall of Famers here at one time. Some Hall of Fame inductions don't bring that many Hall of Famers. My most precious thing is the relationship [I've] been able to make with the greats."

# 71 Alex Hawkins—A Life Lived

Alex Hawkins has already written two books with stories from his life, and he might write a third.

He could probably fill three more with original material if he had the time. The 76-year-old Hawkins is one of South Carolina's greatest players, but he's probably better known for his lifestyle off the field. Hawkins was a schoolboy star in South Charleston, West Virginia, in the early 1950s, and he had offers to play basketball and football at more than two dozen schools.

He chose the Gamecocks, he often told people, because Rex Enright offered him a new car, a new wardrobe, and $1,500 a semester in extra benefits.

"I never did get the clothes or the automobile, and I only got the money for one semester," he told *Georgia Trend* magazine. "Then Warren Giese replaced Enright as head football coach and said no one was going to get anything but a scholarship."

Giese and Hawkins would butt heads throughout Hawkins' career despite the fact that Hawkins was one of the team's captains.

In one meeting, "I slammed a football on his desk and I said, 'I quit,'" Hawkins said in 1992. "I stormed out of his office, and he called the other two captains, and he said, 'There's a problem with one of our captains.' Well, they surmised who it was since I was the only one not there. He said, 'One of our captains is either having a nervous breakdown or he's gone crazy.' They looked at each other and said, 'You're probably talking about Hawkins.'"

Hawkins never did quit and was named the Atlantic Coast Conference Player of the Year in 1958 when he played halfback and defensive back for the Gamecocks. He is 25th in school history in rushing with 1,490 yards.

Hawkins was a popular topic in the school's *100 Years of Gamecock Football* video, produced in 1992.

"Alex Hawkins was a great two-way player," said Don Barton, who was South Carolina's sports information director during Hawkins' career. "At one time or another he led Carolina in rushing, passing, and receiving. He also kicked extra points, and he was our best defensive back."

"I think if you look at both sides—without a doubt, I think most people would agree with me—he was the best football player Carolina ever had," said Bob Fulton, the school's longtime play-by-play voice.

King Dixon, a teammate of Hawkins who was his polar opposite in temperament and would go on to be South Carolina's athletics director, said, "Alex was as tremendous a competitor as I've ever met in my life, one dedicated to winning and giving 105 percent [on the field]. We have always wondered what it would have been like if Alex really worked hard during the week."

From South Carolina, Hawkins went on to play for the iconic Baltimore Colts teams of 1959–65. He also played for the Colts in 1967 and 1968 and the Atlanta Falcons in 1966 and 1967. His carousing ways did not stop in pro football. He once shot out a light at the Falcons practice facility with a B.B. gun just for fun, and he told *The Post (Charleston, SC) and Courier* that he got three DUIs in one week while he was a member of the Falcons.

"But I was a jock and got out of them," he said. "Thankfully, nobody got hurt."

Hawkins detailed his many adventures in *That's My Story and I'm Sticking to It* and *Then Came Brain Damage*. Legendary sportswriter Dan Jenkins wrote the forward for one of Hawkins' books.

"The first time I ever saw Alex was when he came down to Austin, Texas, in 1957 and tore the Longhorns' [behinds] up in a game South Carolina won 27–21," Jenkins wrote. "It was Coach

Darrell Royal's first season at Texas. It was the first time I ever heard of Alex Hawkins or a Gamecock. 'Who was that Hawkins?' I asked Darrell after the game. 'Hell, I don't know,' said Royal. 'We ain't tackled him enough times to find out.'"

Hawkins retired to Denmark, South Carolina, and on the verge of his 70th birthday, Hawkins told *The Post and Courier* that he was still smoking three packs of cigarettes a day and drinking a gallon of vodka a week.

"I'd say that when I was 18 years old, the odds of me making it to 70 were about 10,000-to-1," he said. "It's nearly unbelievable that I'm still alive."

# 72. The End for Marcus Lattimore

One of the greatest careers in South Carolina football history ended in a gruesome flash.

With 4:50 left in the second quarter of a game against Tennessee on October 27, 2012, junior running back Marcus Lattimore took a handoff from quarterback Connor Shaw, looked for room up the middle, and then broke left to daylight. The same thing had happened 554 times before at South Carolina, usually with great results.

This time things went very badly. With a Tennessee player draped on his shoulders and his right foot planted in the ground, another Tennessee player dove directly into the front of Lattimore's right knee. The knee dislocated, tearing three ligaments and leaving Lattimore lying on the field in shock as a previously raucous crowd in Williams-Brice Stadium sat stunned and silent.

Many people—including Lattimore, he would say later—thought his football career was finished. It turned out that only his Gamecocks career ended that day.

Coach Steve Spurrier and Lattimore's teammates couldn't help but wonder after the game if Lattimore, who had torn the ACL in his left knee the previous year, would ever play again.

"Maybe he'll be back next year, and maybe it won't be quite as severe as it appeared on the field out there," Spurrier said in his postgame news conference. "We will all pray for him, and hopefully he'll be back. He's such a good young man. Good things are going to happen to Marcus. I don't know exactly where or how, but good things are going to happen for Marcus Lattimore."

"He went out there and he gave us everything, and that might have been his last snap," wide receiver Ace Sanders said. "It's real sad it had to end that way, but sometimes you just have to face reality."

Lattimore said he thought his football career was over as he was wheeled off the Williams-Brice turf on a medical cart. The sight of South Carolina's players and most of the opposing Volunteers gathered on the field at Williams-Brice Stadium as he was loaded onto a cart will remain one of the most poignant in the school's football history.

Spurrier called the scene "touching" and talked of the respect that even South Carolina's foes had for Lattimore.

"I truly believe that Marcus could very possibly be the most popular South Carolina football player that has ever been here," Spurrier said. "Not only his ability on the field, but off the field, community work, hospital visits. He's a special young man that everybody appreciates."

Although the injury was devastating, Lattimore did not suffer the two types of damage that could have ended his career—vascular damage and nerve damage—said team physician Dr. Jeff Guy. Rather than attempt a return to South Carolina, Lattimore decided to forego his final year of eligibility and enter the 2013 NFL Draft.

He finished his career as the sixth-leading rusher in school history with 2,677 yards.

"I wouldn't change anything that happened these last three years because it made me a better person, made me a better man, and it's going to make me a better person in the future, knowing I can get through anything, and I will get through this," Lattimore said when he announced his departure from the school.

Two months later, he stood at a podium at the NFL Combine in Indianapolis, Indiana, and pronounced himself well on the road to recovery.

"It's a blessing to be here, no doubt. I will not take this opportunity I have for granted," he said. "I just think about guys who are less fortunate than me, guys who would kill to be in my shoes right now, even with the injury. That's what keeps me going. At this point it really doesn't matter where I get drafted because I am going to do what I do," he said. "I am going to do what I've been doing my whole career, and that's just be myself. If I get a chance to play this year, I am going to make the most of it, and I think I will."

He was taken in the fourth round by the San Francisco 49ers.

# 73 Sarge Frye— Grooming the Grounds

Sarge Frye never played a snap of football for South Carolina. He never called a play, and he never hired a coach.

But there are few men who had more impact on Gamecock athletes than Frye, a retired army master sergeant who became the school's head groundskeeper in 1953. In the ensuing 50 years, Frye would have the baseball field named in his honor, and he would be promoted to care for all the school's grounds.

When current Gamecocks athletics director Ray Tanner was hired as the school's baseball coach in 1997, he sought Frye's advice on most things Gamecock.

"When I took the job, I asked to meet with Sarge," Tanner told *The State* newspaper after Frye died in 2003. "I told him, 'I know who you are, but you don't know a lot about me. I want you to help me in transition, teach me the ropes.' He laughed a little and said, 'I'll help you out, Bubba.' He more than lived up to that promise. Some days when you were down, I'd seek out Sarge, or he'd stop by and I'd grab him for a few minutes. And he'd make everything better. He had that sort of influence on people. He was a friend to everyone—not just coaches and administrators. I'm talking about janitors, assistant coaches. He was such an inspiration."

Frye officially retired in 1997 but was a constant presence around Gamecock athletics.

"When you think of someone who was revered by the entire Carolina program, you think of Sarge Frye," former athletics director Mike McGee told *The State*. "Sarge was a tradition around our department. His contributions to Carolina will last an eternity. Sarge Frye was a remarkable person by almost any means of evaluation. I used his background and wisdom as a consultant on many things. He had a calming effect on this Irishman, and we had a lot of great times. I will value those conversations forever."

The school's baseball field was renamed in Frye's honor in 1980, a virtually unheard-of honor for a groundskeeper. The move was made at the suggestion of head football coach and athletics director Jim Carlen.

"Everyone went along with it," Carlen told *The State*. "They needed to be aware of people who served [the school], not just coaches. That was the name that needed to be on there. He's an institution."

From that point until the stadium's destruction in 2010, it was known simply as "The Sarge." Part of Frye's job was to maintain the field at Williams-Brice Stadium and the football team's practice fields.

"We had the best baseball field I ever played on," two-sport star Jeff Grantz told *The State*. "In football, our practice fields were as nice as most teams' stadiums."

Frye never made much of his touch with turf.

"I felt I had the responsibility to have a good place for them to practice and play," he told *The State*. "I noticed a long time ago in trying to grow cotton and corn that where I spilled fertilizer, grass grew."

Bob Fulton, the longtime play-by-play voice of the football team, even asked Frye to lend him a hand in his own yard, Fulton told *The State*.

"I told him one time that I was having trouble with my yard," Fulton said, "and I asked him what I should do. He said, 'Invite me over and we'll see.' Well, he came and did a lot of work and, in no time, I had grass. He considered my offer to pay him an insult."

Frye's tenure at South Carolina spanned eight baseball coaches, nine football coaches, and 10 athletics directors. And his impact in Columbia would live on even longer. His son Jerry lettered three years on the Gamecocks' football team, and his grandson Jay also played for South Carolina and went on to be the head coach at Richland Northeast High School in Columbia.

Frye, who was named the National Groundskeeper of the Year by the American Baseball Coaches Association in 1980, was once asked if he wanted his ashes spread across the field at The Sarge.

"I don't know if that would help the grass," he said.

# 74 The Early Years

"It is doubtful there is a college in the state that takes as little interest in athletics as we do."

Those were the words a South Carolina student penned in the campus newspaper in 1891 as part of a plea for his university to add football to the official list of extracurricular activities. The sport was growing in popularity across the United States, but the economy was decidedly not growing. With the country going through a recession, South Carolina's enrollment in 1892 dipped to 73 students.

Still, some of those 73 students were determined to play football, so on December 24, 1892, South Carolina students played their first football game without faculty consent in Charleston against Furman.

Some of the students probably wondered right away if they had made a mistake because Furman's Mountain Boys pulled away easily for a 44–0 win.

The next day's newspaper read: "Furman's Champions Easily Defeat the South Carolina College Football Team."

"Charleston yesterday afternoon witnessed her first game of real football—the game as played by the great kickers of the North. There was a fair-sized audience at the Base Ball Park at 3:00,'" read the story's first sentence.

*The Carolinian* newspaper put it this way:

"Of all sad words of tongue or pen,

The saddest are these: it might have been.

But the most consoling, and just as terse,

Are these few words: it might have been worse."

It would get worse before it got better. Although the school did sign off on the addition of football, allowing South Carolina to play its first official game against Georgia on November 3, 1894, the school lost that game 40–0 and its only other game that season 16–4 to the Augusta (Georgia) YMCA club team.

South Carolina's first college football victory would have to wait until November 2, 1895, when the team, which played its first three seasons without a coach, beat Columbia AA 20–0 in Columbia. The next week brought a 14–10 victory over Furman that jumpstarted South Carolina's first official rivalry.

It did not take long for the team to adopt the university's official colors—the colors it still wears today.

Part of the story from the victory over Furman points out, "The garnet and black came off victorious."

The 1896 season was historic for two reasons. The school named W.H. Whaley its first coach (although the hiring of an official football man would take another 24 years), and it won the inaugural game of the Clemson series, prevailing 12–6 in Charleston.

By the 1903 season, South Carolina had adopted the Gamecocks mascot. (The team was often referred to in its early years as the Birds.) The 1903 season was also noteworthy because South Carolina won eight games that year, the most it would be credited with in a single year until 1979.

"There were a lot of 'howevers' in there," said Don Barton, a former sports information director at South Carolina and a Gamecock historian. "They played teams like Welsh Neck and Columbia Y."

There was also a win over Guilford, but the victories weren't all easy. The Gamecocks also topped Georgia, Tennessee, and Georgia Tech that season.

In 1920, South Carolina hired its first honest-to-goodness football coach, Sol Metzger, a Pennsylvanian who had previously coached at Baylor, Pennsylvania, Oregon State, West Virginia, Washington & Jefferson, and Union College.

Metzger, who also served as the school's basketball coach for one season, stayed on for five seasons, the longest tenure of any coach at the time, compiling a 26–18 record in football.

The school's rivalry with Furman dominated the team's early years. After Furman beat the Gamecocks five straight games between 1923–27, South Carolina hired away its coach, "Tricky" Billy Laval.

Laval did help turn around the series, beating Furman four of the seven times he faced them and tying them in another game. He was also the first Gamecocks coach to tinker with the team's uniform, which to that point had been canvas pants and a plain garnet sweater. In 1932, Laval introduced a distinctive bull's eye jersey, which was red with a large circular symbol on the chest.

Laval worked seven seasons at the school, the most by any coach until Rex Enright showed up on campus in 1938 and helped usher in the modern era of Gamecocks football.

# 75 The Gift of Gab

From 1999 all the way through the 2012 season, no college football team in the country has had a more quotable head coach than South Carolina.

While Steve Spurrier holds the title now, it started with Lou Holtz. Where Spurrier's best one-liners are often zingers directed at opponents and even his own players, Holtz livened up press conferences throughout his career as a sort of modern-day Yogi Berra.

In fact, when the Gamecocks hired Holtz in 1999, the school devoted almost an entire page of his biography in the media guide for a section titled, "Coach Holtz Said It!"

Here are a few of the highlights:

- At the press conference announcing his hiring, Holtz was asked how long he planned to stay at the school. "I'll stay as long as I have to, until I answer all your questions."
- When asked for his impressions of the Palmetto State, he gave mostly positive comments but added a barb about excessive litter. "We must have the cleanest cars in America… because all of the trash is out along the highways."
- When Holtz was asked what assistant coach Buddy Pough's title would be, he replied, "I think we'll call him, 'Coach.'"
- On a schedule that included Tennessee and Florida in back-to-back weeks, he said, "I don't know what they are paying us to play those games, but [I] doubt if the guarantees will cover hospital bills."
- After the first contact work of his first spring practice, Holtz said, "I told our team we either must improve our tackling or we need to find some way to get it outlawed."
- When asked about his team's depth: "We could never get on Noah's Ark… We don't have two of anything."
- Holtz said he had a list of 107 things he wanted to do in his life and that he had accomplished most of them. When asked what he had not crossed off the list, he said, "I haven't been on an African safari. I've taken a camera to the zoo before, but I don't think that counts. And I'm still looking for someone slower than me so I can run with the bulls at Pamplona."
- When explaining his decision-making process before taking the South Carolina job after two years off, he said, "I went back and forth. One day I thought I would get away from everything, so I went and played golf. Man, did I play poorly. I had to quit after eight holes, I played so bad. I said to myself, 'If I'm going to play this bad, maybe it's time

to get back into coaching.' I went back and discussed the situation with my wife and decided to take the job. I went out and played [golf] the next day and played great."

- On living in a college town, Holtz said, "I don't think there's a better environment than a university setting. I don't want to live in a place where the average age is deceased. I want to be involved."

It's important to remember that this covered only the first few months of Holtz's tenure with the Gamecocks. After his coaching career, Holtz was hired by ESPN as a college football analyst, and his folksy sayings earned him a segment on the network's college football shows in which "Dr. Lou" delivered Holtz's version of wit and wisdom.

# 76 Dom Fusci—The Class Clown

Dom Fusci was an All-Southern Conference lineman in 1943 and he is a member of the school's pre–World War II all-time team, but he was never one of the school's biggest stars on the gridiron.

He was one of its greatest characters off the field, though, and that's why his name is still well remembered 70 years after his playing career ended.

"He was one of a kind," said Don Barton, a former sports information director at the school and the athletic department's unofficial historian. "He got people's attention."

Fusci got Clemson coach Frank Howard's attention during the teams' annual Big Thursday rivalry game in 1943.

"We had them 24–6, and we had about five minutes left in the ballgame," Fusci said. "The coach went ahead and sent in some ballplayers. I said to one of them, 'Who'd you come in for?' He said, 'You.' I said, 'You come in for me? Why didn't you tell me?' He said, 'I thought you'd get mad.' I said, 'You must be crazy.' When I looked up I saw the umpire start counting [the players on the field], so I said, 'I better get out of here.' I was only 20 yards from [Clemson's] bench and I was 60 from our bench. I'd never get off the field without a penalty, so I ran as hard as I could for the Clemson bench. When I get off the field, I dove and we got the ball off just as I was going through the air. And whose feet do I land at? I land at Coach Howard's feet. He's yelling to the officials, 'He was on the field! He was on the field!' As I dust myself off, I say, 'Coach, I wasn't on the field. You know that.' With that, he told me where to go, and it was a pretty hot place. So I started off into the end zone. I said, 'Well, the game is over. I may as well get me a hot dog and a Coca-Cola,' so the guy gave me a hot dog and a Coca-Cola and he said, 'That'll be 35 cents.' I said, 'Thirty-five cents? Where am I going to get it? We don't have any pockets on these pants.' So I went around and I was eating in on the bench."

According to Barton, Fusci also once picked up an official's flag on him and moved it down the field, resulting in an improper spot that benefited the Gamecocks. He also once convinced an official to pick up a flag despite the fact he had committed a penalty.

When Barton put together a "This is Your Life" sketch to honor Fusci at the Columbia Touchdown Club, one of the voices Fusci heard was the first official to throw a 15-yard penalty flag on him.

Fusci played for the Gamecocks in 1942 and 1943 and then again in 1946 after a break to serve in World War II. The war did nothing to damper Fusci's spirit.

"I was in the navy on a PT boat out of Okinawa in 1945 and got this letter from the Redskins telling me they had drafted me," Fusci told *The State* newspaper. "I took the letter to my commanding officer and told him, 'I'm needed in Washington. Cut the orders.' He said the navy should have notified him, then asked for the letter. He took one look and told me to get my butt back on that boat."

Fusci came to the Gamecocks from Brooklyn, New York, but he adopted South Carolina as his home and lived there (while having a predictably successful career as a salesman) for the rest of his life after a brief attempt at a pro football career.

He was a staple in Columbia life and a factor in South Carolina athletics throughout his life. He was a friend of legendary South Carolina basketball coach Frank McGuire, and in 2004 Fusci crowned the Corkball Queen during a minor Columbia traditional corkball tournament behind a local bar.

In short, Fusci lived up to his nickname "Dynamite" throughout his life. When he died at age 89 in 2012, his son Dom Fusci Jr. told *The State* newspaper he once asked his father if he had any regrets.

"Let me tell you something," his father replied. "I'm the happiest guy there could be. I've done everything I possibly could do. I did everything I wanted to do. I married a beautiful woman. I have three great kids. I've got a job that's outstanding. I played football for a prestigious college. I've done everything I've wanted to do, and there is not one thing I would change. And when I die, do not mourn my death—celebrate my life because I've had one hell of a life."

Family and friends took that to heart and followed through on that request, playing Frank Sinatra's "My Way" at Fusci's memorial service in a local American Legion Post.

"Dom's funeral," Barton said, "was the most fun funeral I have ever been to."

# They Fought the Law and the Law Won

There are plenty of schools in the country who have found more trouble with the NCAA than South Carolina, but it hasn't all been smooth sailing from a compliance standpoint for the Gamecocks.

Four times in the school's history, South Carolina's football team has had to face the music for violations of the NCAA's rules. The most recent penalties came down in 2012 when South Carolina was forced to give up six football scholarships, pay an $18,500 fine, and begin three years of probation after the NCAA ruled athletes or prospective athletes were given more than $55,000 worth of recruiting inducements or improper benefits.

The NCAA determined 12 athletes, including 10 football players, got reduced rates at a local luxury hotel that were worth more than $50,000 and that a Philadelphia-based organization provided $8,000 worth of improper benefits and recruiting inducements to Gamecocks or potential Gamecocks.

The case was the first time during Steve Spurrier's 23 years as head coach that violations were found in one of his programs.

"Sometimes crap happens. You just have to deal with it," Spurrier said, "[and] find out who was at fault."

Even in handing out the punishment, the NCAA praised South Carolina's handling of the matter.

"This has been one of the best cases I have seen from a process standpoint," said Britton Banowsky, chairman of the infractions committee. "When information comes to their attention, a university really has a choice to make. It either decides to fully develop an investigation or tries to manage information in a way to protect itself. In this case, it was obvious to the committee that the university wanted to get to the truth. We see that less than we see the other approach."

The NCAA had not been as pleased the last time it dealt with the Gamecocks. That came in 2005 during Lou Holtz's tenure at the school. South Carolina was found guilty of five major infractions, including providing improper tutoring to two junior-college transfers before they were enrolled at South Carolina; ethical misconduct by a former senior associate athletics director who arranged the tutoring and allowed an inaccurate report to be submitted to the SEC and NCAA; improper reinstatement of a player on academic suspension; providing transportation for star tailback Derek Watson to get to class, practice, and other locations; and lack of institutional control.

Holtz never took responsibility for the incident.

"Most of the infractions... occurred in the academic office," he told *The State* newspaper after leaving the school. "I'm not in charge of the academic office. I was never consulted [about academics]. I'm not passing the buck. When I visited with the academic office, all I wanted to know was who was going to class and what was their attitude."

The NCAA claimed during that case that South Carolina officials were not as cooperative as they could have been.

"It's not a process that anyone would sign up for. Nobody wants to go through that," faculty athletics representative Russ Pate said. "If you find yourself as an institution in that situation, all you can do is work as hard as you can to be responsive and at the same time try to ensure the university is fairly represented in the process. Even though it did take a long time, I think in the end the outcome was a fair one and the university accepted it and moved on."

The Gamecocks lost four scholarships and were put on a three-year probationary period. Those two incidents were the only time South Carolina lost scholarships due to violations.

The school was also called out by the NCAA in 1991 after four assistant football coaches were indicted on charges stemming from a steroid scandal at the school in the 1980s. However, the only penalty that time was a six-month extension of a previous probation involving the men's basketball program.

The school's first appearance before the NCAA's punishment division came in 1967 and may have been the most costly of all incidents. In January 1967, the NCAA ruled that head coach Marvin Bass had provided or helped provide cash, meals, and books to three unnamed players and had a secret fund to entertain recruits.

The school was placed on a two-year postseason and television ban and forced to forfeit all wins in 1965. That meant the ACC title clinched in a dramatic 17–16 win over Clemson in the season finale was forfeited.

South Carolina's first title of any kind would have to wait another four years until the 1969 team captured the ACC title in a violations-free season.

# 78 A Smile Vanishes

Steve Spurrier was stunned on the evening of September 20, 2010. As South Carolina's football team was taking the field for its usual Monday evening practice, terrible news was beginning to make its way to the players and the coaching staff.

Kenny McKinley, a Gamecock wide receiver from 2005–08, had been found dead earlier that day. He was 23 years old, and the cause of death was a self-inflicted gunshot wound.

"I guess it is true," Spurrier said. "Kenny McKinley is dead."

It was hard for anyone who had ever met McKinley to understand it, that it could happen at such a young age, and that it could happen that way. Spurrier always remembered McKinley for two things—the expert way he ran a slant pattern and his smile.

Everyone remembered that smile. Many of the Gamecocks had seen McKinley nine days earlier, and he had seemed like the old Kenny.

"[He] seemed in good spirits; [he had that] great smile like he always had. I don't understand it if it happened the way they say. It's hard to comprehend," Spurrier said. "Kenny was certainly one of my favorite all-time players. He was one of them. Wonderful guy. It's hard to figure how or why this happened. It's a sad day."

McKinley was a zip-quick slot receiver whose blazing speed made up for a relative lack of size. (He was 6' and weighed 187 lbs.) As a junior, he caught at least seven passes in each of the final four games, including 14 catches for 151 yards against Tennessee to set what was then a school record for single-season receptions with 77.

At the time of his death, McKinley was the school's career leader in catches (207), receiving yards (2,781), and consecutive games with a reception (43).

He was selected by the Denver Broncos in the fifth round of the 2009 NFL Draft, and his death occurred in his Denver home not far from the Broncos practice facility.

An investigation by the Arapahoe County Sheriff's Department after McKinley's death revealed the young receiver was dealing with several issues, including injury and debt, and had recently purchased a gun from teammate Jabar Gaffney, who played for Spurrier at Florida.

McKinley had suffered a season-ending knee injury in the first week of Denver's training camp that year, injuring the same knee he had hurt late in the 2009 season. He had also borrowed $65,000 from former teammate Tom Brandstater and owed $40,000 at Las Vegas casinos, according to the sheriff's department investigation.

Still, the death stunned his current and former teammates.

"We've all seen him recently. He's been the same person every time we see him. [He] liked junk food and chips and things like that," Denver head coach Josh McDaniels told the Associated Press. "He was in the cafeteria, or in the training room, when we were seeing him the last so many weeks here. [There was] nothing that would alarm us to anything like this."

More than 1,000 people, including more than 100 with South Carolina ties, attended McKinley's funeral in his hometown outside Atlanta.

"Kenny was not only one of the best receivers I've ever coached but one of the most competitive, greatest kids I've ever had the privilege to coach," Spurrier said at the funeral. "It's hard to understand how all this happened. All of his buddies were here today. He was a very loved young man that we are all going to miss."

South Carolina businessman John Barbour, who employed McKinley while he was a Gamecock, also spoke at the funeral.

"Kenny McKinley is probably the one kid that people remember more than the big-name guys simply because Kenny had that smile," Barbour said. "There is no way I could ever, ever tell you just how much he was endeared by the Carolina people."

A year after his death, McKinley's Broncos teammates still couldn't forget "that smile."

"That's the only thing that everybody remembers. He showed all 32 of his teeth," Denver linebacker Wesley Woodyard told the Associated Press on the anniversary of McKinley's death. "It was just a wonderful thing to be around every day—seeing that smile, listening to that laugh, hearing those jokes. It was pretty good to have him around. We always think about him. Kenny was the type of guy who always wanted to make sure that everybody had a good day. So every day you come to work, that's the kind of attitude you have to have. You've got to take Kenny McKinley's attitude—have fun and enjoy your work."

In 2009 when Spurrier was leading a movement to retire McKinley's No. 11 jersey, McKinley wrote a letter to the team's fans and sent it to *The State* newspaper in Columbia.

"I will never forget while in high school during my recruitment, I attended a spring game and the Gamecock Nation made me feel as though I was already a part of the team," McKinley wrote. "This was well before I made my first reception or scored my first touchdown. Because of your support I was able to exceed my expectations and achieve record-breaking numbers!"

# 79 The Patriot

When Del Wilkes' family went to the grocery store, young Del immediately camped out in the magazine aisle and poured through every wrestling magazine he could find.

"When I was a kid, there were two things—football and pro wrestling—that occupied my every waking thought," Wilkes said. "I just devoured it."

Wilkes went on to be an All-American offensive lineman at South Carolina in 1984 before taking a shot at his next childhood dream.

"I had always said that whenever football ended, whenever that was, that I wanted to see if I could have a career as a professional wrestler," Wilkes said.

Wilkes' football career ended in 1986 after unsuccessful attempts to make the Tampa Bay Buccaneers and Atlanta Falcons. So Wilkes returned home and enrolled in a Columbia wresting school run by Mary Lillian Ellison, better known as the Fabulous Moolah. Ellison was an iconic figure in women's wrestling and was involved in the sport as a participant, promoter, or trainer for more than 50 years. Later in her life, she ran a training school for female wrestlers in Columbia, but there were a few spots for men, and that's where Wilkes got his shot.

It skyrocketed from there.

"I sort of equate it to minor league baseball. You've got Single A, Double A, Triple A, and you just sort of work your way up," Wilkes said. "I was fortunate that I got in front of some people who had the ability to get me in front of some people, and it just worked out."

One of the people he got in front of was Wahoo McDaniel, another former offensive lineman who went on to achieve wrestling fame. McDaniel worked for Verne Gagne, who ran the NWA wrestling company in Minneapolis, Minnesota.

"Their TV show came on ESPN every day Monday through Friday 4:00 PM to 5:00 PM," Wilkes said. "That got me on nationwide TV, which is very important."

Wilkes' career took off from there, and at the high point of his career he was one of the world's most popular wrestlers as The Patriot in the World Championship Wrestling (WCW) and the World Wrestling Federation (WWF).

"I had a very good career, a very successful career that ended a little early due to a [torn triceps] injury," Wilkes said.

Wilkes has been very open since his retirement in 1997 about his use of steroids during his wrestling career, and he has appeared on CNN calling for the sport to take action to get steroids out of the business.

"When you make a living with your body, the way you look is very important," he said. "At that time, that was part of what sold a particular wrestler was that look, that big, thick, sculptured look. If you weren't on steroids, then you didn't have a chance to compete. Just look at the guys you are trying to fight for TV time. Boy, they looked great. You want people to buy your T-shirts and your video games and your action figures. Well, you have to do the same thing. It was just part of it. Everybody I worked with did them, so you didn't think anything of it."

Wilkes, who lives in Newberry, South Carolina, and works in Columbia, recently had his right knee replaced and will have his left replaced at some point, he said.

"I think considering everything that I have done to my body, I think I'm in pretty good health," Wilkes said. The knee replacement "has made things a lot better. I don't limp around anymore. I put my body through a great deal. Wrestling was tougher on my body than football was because there was no offseason. There is no chance to recover from injury or recuperate."

# 80 Meet Sunshine

In 1971, Alexandria, Virginia—like much of the South—was still sorting out the realities of racial integration. But Ron Bass and his teammates at T.C. Williams High School were just playing football.

They had no idea that their story would be turned into the based-on-a-true-story Hollywood blockbuster *Remember the Titans* in 2000.

"Any of the players who said, 'Yeah, we knew we were doing something special,' would be lying. We were just there," Bass said. "We were in the moment. We just happened to be in a place that was desegregating. We were doing it at a time a lot of other cities were, too. I have heard many people say, 'We were going through the same thing in Orangeburg (South Carolina),' or in Charlotte, wherever—especially around the South."

Bass played quarterback for South Carolina from 1973–74 and 1976–77, but in 1971 he was the quarterback at T.C. Williams, and he would go on to be immortalized as the character Sunshine in *Remember the Titans*. Bass' role in the history that became the movie was a long-forgotten part of his past until then.

"My wife didn't even know," he said. "She knew I went to school in Virginia and then came to South Carolina to play, but she had no idea what happened in Virginia. For me, it was just high school football. That was a part of the history that was gone. I had gone on to South Carolina and played football, and that was my identity until this movie came out. Then all of a sudden the previous identity came back to life."

Including the nickname. Bass had been happy to leave it behind at T.C. Williams, but for 13 years now his daughters have called him Sunshine.

"Affectionately, I think," he joked. "It did bring that darn nickname back to life."

Bass still has the blond hair that was part of the Sunshine persona in the movie, but he insists it was never down to his shoulders as the movie suggests. According to Bass, there were other parts of the film with which screenwriter Gregory Allen Howard, director Boaz Yakin, and producers Jerry Bruckheimer and Chad Oman took dramatic liberties.

"I never kissed that guy in the locker room," he said. "We didn't dance. We didn't dance coming onto the field, and we certainly didn't dance during warm-ups and all that stuff. All that was Hollywood. We were a basic football team. It wasn't nearly as exciting as they made it look."

Still, not everyone gets to be the inspiration for a movie that grosses more than $130 million worldwide.

"It was an interesting thing to be a part of," Bass said. "We had no idea it would grow into what it was, but the way I hear it the writer was in a barber shop [in Washington, D.C.] and started hearing about this team. We were lucky the right guy was in the right barber shop at the right time when the story was being told."

At South Carolina, Bass started as a junior and a senior, but his most memorable season came as a sophomore when he filled in for injured starter Jeff Grantz. He had filled in for Grantz once the previous year, but that had been against Florida State in a 1 PM game.

"So you got up, had breakfast, and started playing," Bass said. "[But the] North Carolina game was going to be a home game, [and] it was going to be a night game. You had all day to think about it. That didn't help. I remember being nervous most of the day."

He shouldn't have been. The Tar Heels decided their best strategy was to make the young quarterback beat them, and he did, rushing for 211 yards in the Gamecocks' option offense and being named *Sports Illustrated*'s National Offensive Back of the Week.

"They took away the dive. They took away the pitch. That only leaves the third option, and that's to keep it and run. So we did," Bass said. "We called a few passes and had an instant read where the defensive end would drop into pass coverage, which he did when we rolled out. Their defensive end the whole game would drop into the flat, I'd yell go, and the back would run and we were picking up yards left and right. They never adjusted the whole game. Go figure.

"It looked like Ron was hogging the ball, but it wasn't Ron's option. Or I guess it was the option because they took away the other two."

# 81 The Historians

Together they served South Carolina's athletic program for more than 40 years, and together they have chronicled more Gamecocks history than anyone.

It started with Don Barton, who grew up a Clemson fan of all things but converted as a student at South Carolina and became the school's sports information director in 1950. Barton left that job in 1959 but never left the school.

After getting into the advertising business, Barton stuck around to keep statistics for the basketball team. From there he was asked to write a book about the South Carolina–Clemson football series, and a second career was born.

Barton's *The Carolina-Clemson Game* was later updated by him to *Big Thursdays and Super Saturdays*. He went on to write a book with longtime play-by-play radio announcer Bob Fulton about legendary Gamecocks basketball coach Frank McGuire. ("Actually, I wrote every word in it," Barton said. "Sportswriters can't talk, and announcers can't write.") He also wrote a book about Fulton as well as *They Wore Garnet & Black: Inside Carolina's Quest for Gridiron Glory*.

Barton's home in the venerable Forest Hills neighborhood still features file cabinets packed with Gamecocks history, and he remains a go-to interview for anyone researching the school's history. He should also be remembered by anyone who remembers Tom Price because Barton hired Price before leaving his job at the school.

"I was one person acting alone. [I] didn't even have a secretary, and so I had all these spring sports and when Tom Price came out of the navy, he was interested in baseball," Barton said.

Barton quickly found a place for Price—with one catch.

"I said, 'Okay, you can have the job for no pay,'" Barton said. "Tom Price became a historian in his own right. His heart was always in Carolina, so when the opening came as sports information director, he jumped at the job."

That was in 1962, and Price would remain as the school's sports information director until 1992. After his official retirement, he remained a fixture at South Carolina and served in an emeritus capacity until his death in 2008.

His name, which is now on the press box at Williams-Brice Stadium, is still synonymous with South Carolina history, and his influence in his industry is still felt.

"He gave me the foundation that has allowed me to have success in Major League Baseball," Rob Matwick, vice president for communications for the Detroit Tigers and a former Price assistant, told *The State* newspaper after Price's death. "Tom was as old-school as it gets. He taught me those fundamentals of preparation, accuracy, [and] building relationships."

Kerry Tharp, also hired by Price, went on to be South Carolina's sports information director and then a communications director for NASCAR.

"He instilled in me a passion for the Gamecocks that I'll carry the rest of my life," Tharp told *The State*. "He used to say, 'My two favorite words in the English language are, 'Cocks win.'"

Like Barton, Price marveled people with his memory of South Carolina sports.

"For about three seasons in the 1960s, we couldn't find any information [about the football team]," former Price assistant Jamie Kimbrough told *The State*. "Finally I said, 'T.P., 1962 Carolina-Duke game, any recollection at all?' He tipped those half-moon eyeglasses up on his head and said, 'Played in Durham, final score was so-and-so, so-and-so had so many yards rushing.' The same with the rest; he knew every game, the scores, the stats. I was dumbfounded."

Price added to the South Carolina library with *Tales from the Gamecocks' Roost* and *The '84 Gamecocks: Fire Ants and Black Magic*, among others.

He was especially attached to South Carolina's baseball team, and he once paid $37 to make a phone call from Tokyo, where he was on a trip with the basketball team, to check the score of an NCAA regional game between the Gamecocks and West Virginia.

"If you listen to Tom's half-million stories—and I've heard about 100,000 of them—it's amazing what he's seen," Mike Morgan, a former baseball play-by-play announcer, told *The State*. "I have people ask me what's it like working with that 'old guy,' and I tell them, 'Fascinating.'"

# 82 Ryan Brewer Gets the Last Laugh

Ryan Brewer has always believed that everything happens for a reason. Given his college football career, it's easy to see why.

Brewer was Mr. Football in Ohio in 1998. He set the single-season high school rushing record in the football-rich state with 2,864 yards as a senior. In four years at Troy High School, he rushed for 7,656 yards and scored 761 points. *Ohio Prep Magazine* named him the Ohio High School Player of the 1990s.

It seemed the perfect story. The schoolboy hero would take all those awards to Ohio State, but Buckeyes head coach John Cooper never offered the 5'10", 215-lb. hometown hero a scholarship.

"They came to my school and they would invite me to the games, and my recruiting coordinator, who was the running backs coach, would say, 'He's going to offer you, he's going to offer you,' and every time he'd come up to me and give me a little swim move

## The Great White North?

As 1959 was turning to 1960, the Big Thursday tradition of the South Carolina–Clemson series was coming to an end. The Tigers and their supporters were tired of playing the game every year in Columbia and watching all of the revenues associated with the game go to the Gamecocks.

When options for the site of the game were being discussed, South Carolina athletics director Rex Enright was asked his opinion.

"Someone asked him where he thought the game should be played, and Rex said, 'It belongs to the people of South Carolina. If they want to play it in Nome, Alaska, I'll play it up there,'" said Don Barton, South Carolina's former sports information director.

"The next week they got a telegram from the chamber of commerce in Nome, Alaska, offering to host the game if they wanted to move it up there," Barton said.

The schools declined Nome's offer and decided on a home-and-home rotation for the game. Considering the average high temperature in late November in Nome is 17 degrees, it was probably a sound decision.

and go on to the next guy," Brewer said of Cooper. "It got to the point where me and my family and my brother said, 'To heck with this. Let's figure out something else.'"

About the time Cooper was giving Brewer the cold shoulder, South Carolina was rolling out the welcome mat for new coach Lou Holtz, who had previously won a national championship at Notre Dame. Brewer, a Notre Dame fan growing up, suddenly realized why his hopes of playing for the Buckeyes had been thwarted.

"It was just magical," Brewer said.

Not only did Holtz offer a scholarship, he also offered early playing time. Brewer played all over the field in his true freshman season, leading the Gamecocks in punt returns with 14 for 143 yards, finishing third on the team with 163 yards on 35 carries, and catching six passes for 67 yards.

The next season Brewer's career took a real storybook turn. The Gamecocks engineered the second-best turnaround in NCAA history, going from 0–11 in 1999 to 7–4 in the regular season in 2000. Their reward was a trip to the Outback Bowl against, of all people, the Buckeyes of Ohio State.

Brewer—who started 10 games as a sophomore, catching 36 passes, rushing 33 times, returning punts, and even punting three times—would have a chance for revenge. But it looked like that payback would have to come mostly as a complementary player. The Gamecocks had an emerging star at tailback in Derek Watson, one of the best players in South Carolina high school history.

However, Watson was suspended from the Outback Bowl in what would be the first of many issues for the talented player. The result this time was that Brewer started the game against the Buckeyes. South Carolina fans will never forget it.

Brewer had 214 all-purpose yards, three touchdowns, and was named the game's MVP. He rushed for 109 yards and two touchdowns. He added 92 yards receiving and another score, and he had 13 yards in punt returns.

"It was just one of those magical moments," Brewer said. "To be honest with you, I don't want to say [it was] an out-of-body experience, but you don't realize what's going on in the game until you go back and watch it the next day. I had no idea what happened that game. If I didn't have film of it, I would have no idea."

South Carolina won the game 24–7. It was the last game of Cooper's career.

"I was Mr. Football of Ohio, and when the [state's] head football coach doesn't offer you a scholarship [yet] he tells you every game he is going to… It just seemed fitting be able to play them," Brewer said.

Brewer continued his Swiss Army knife routine the next two years of his career, and he left the Gamecocks with 102 catches for 1,027 yards, 100 carries for 385 yards, 65 punt returns for 477 yards, and three punts for 121 yards.

# 83

# 56–20...Enough Said

It was the fall of 1975, and R.J. Moore was nervous. The next day would be the annual rivalry game between South Carolina and Clemson and, like any Gamecock fan of his day, Moore was expecting the worst.

South Carolina had won six games to that point. Clemson had only won two. Still, a bowl bid, which would be only the third in school history, hung in the balance, and the Gamecocks were all too accustomed to having their seasons ruined by Tigers.

"At the pep rally the night before, [Moore] was walking around, and I was like, 'R.J. why are you worried?'" remembered South Carolina quarterback Jeff Grantz, then a senior. "He said, 'We have to win this game to go to a bowl game.' I said, 'R.J. we are going to score every time we've got the ball. I feel confident about that.'"

Bold for sure—and accurate. The next day the Gamecocks trounced the Tigers 56–20. Every South Carolina possession ended with a touchdown, and it remains the most the Gamecocks have ever scored on their rival. In fact, it's the only time they have ever posted more than 38 points against Clemson.

"To this day [Moore] says, 'Jeff, you lied to me. You didn't tell me we were going to score touchdowns every time we had the ball,'" Grantz said.

Grantz's prediction was more than just idle boasting, he said. He had reason to believe, thanks to a wrinkle in the Gamecocks' run-first veer offense installed that week by assistant coaches Jack Fligg and Bob Gatling.

"We had a motion with one of our backs, and we felt like they couldn't adjust to it in the secondary," Grantz said. "We worked on it all week. Our guys who were used to playing against it couldn't figure it out, either. It would almost put us into a spread offense before its time."

Grantz completed nine passes, and five of them went for touchdowns. He threw for 158 yards and added 122 rushing yards on 12 carries.

"I threw five touchdowns. Three of them were off that formation," Grantz said. "They never adjusted to it."

South Carolina gained 616 yards, including 458 on the ground.

"Once the game started, we seemed to do whatever we wanted at will," running back Kevin Long told *The State* newspaper. "It was one of those fantasy games you only dream of. It was unbelievable. We were just having a lot of fun."

And they had fun right to the very end. Late in the fourth quarter, with 49 points already on the board and facing a fourth down inside Clemson's 10-yard line, South Carolina coach Jim Carlen called a rollout pass and Grantz got his fifth touchdown pass of the day for the final bit of salt in Clemson's wound.

Tigers coach Red Parker accused the Gamecocks of running up the score, but Carlen said he simply couldn't call off Grantz with the day he was having.

"When you're a competitor like him, I can't put him down," Carlen told *The State* newspaper. "I hurt for that other team. I hope people don't think I ran the score up."

# 84 Milestone Moments

Soon after he was hired at South Carolina in 2004, Steve Spurrier told the Sumter Gamecock Club that he planned to become the school's winningest football coach.

According to Spurrier, it was meant less as a boast and more as an indication to the team's fan base that he planned to be around for a while rather than cash a few checks and head off to retirement.

"That will give me a good goal to shoot for," Spurrier told *The State* newspaper in 2005. "That will give me an individual goal that I think we can achieve. If we average eight wins a year for eight years, we'll get there."

At the time, Rex Enright, who worked at South Carolina for 15 years in two different stints, held the record with 64 wins.

In the early years of Spurrier's tenure, when he wasn't averaging the eight wins a year he had hoped for, he wondered if the milestone would ever come. Things started to heat up in 2010, and Spurrier did reach the mark in the final regular season game of 2012 against none other than archrival Clemson.

The Gamecocks beat the Tigers 27–17 in Clemson's Death Valley behind backup quarterback Dylan Thompson to make Spurrier 65–37 at South Carolina.

"That's sort of neat that it came against our instate rival," Spurrier said. "It's interesting some of my other so-called big numbers came against Georgia. To have this as No. 65 makes it special. The [game] ball's worth keeping, put it that way."

Enright needed 140 career games to set the mark, while Spurrier needed only 102.

It was not the first milestone victory for Spurrier during his South Carolina tenure. Earlier that season, Spurrier became the

*Head coach Steve Spurrier (right) shakes hands with Clemson head coach Dabo Swinney after a game on Saturday, November 24, 2012, in Clemson, South Carolina. The Gamecocks won 27–17.* (AP Photo/Rainier Ehrhardt)

22nd coach in major college football history to win 200 games as a head coach when the Gamecocks beat UAB 49–6 on September 15 in Williams-Brice Stadium.

But Spurrier said that victory did not have as much significance for him.

"There are a bunch of dudes who have won 200 games. I don't know how you brag about that too much," he said. "That means you've coached quite a few years and been fortunate enough to stay healthy and not get fired. Those are the guys who win 200 in college. I am hoping for 201 next week. That's what I told our guys."

## A Vocal Fan

All four members of rock band Hootie and the Blowfish are South Carolina alumni, but it is the band's front man Darius Rucker who has become most closely associated with the team.

Rucker, who went on to more fame as a solo country music artist, is not shy about sharing his love for the Gamecocks. He has performed the national anthem before games at Williams-Brice Stadium and before South Carolina appeared in the Outback Bowl on January 1, 2013.

In 2012, Rucker served as the celebrity guest picker on ESPN's *College GameDay* when it filmed in Columbia.

"I have watched this show since they started it, and I have wanted to do that since they started it," Rucker told the network that day.

Rucker also revealed that quarterback Mike Hold, who quarterbacked the 1984 Black Magic team, is his favorite Gamecock.

"For me, it's Mike Hold because he was there when I was in school, and we had some fun times watching Mike Hold bring us back in games," Hold said.

After running back Marcus Lattimore was injured later that season, Rucker sent a message to Lattimore on Twitter.

"@LattTwoOne. Marcus Lattimore, Ur a class act my friend. Get well u r in my prayers. Much Much Love. #Gamecocknation," Rucker wrote.

Rucker, Mark Bryan, Jim Sonefeld, and Dean Felber formed Hootie and the Blowfish while students at South Carolina.

---

Spurrier is one of only three active FBS coaches with 200 victories, and his colleagues were much more willing to praise the achievement.

"That's a phenomenal number," former Auburn coach Gene Chizik said. "To be able to be in this profession that long and be that successful is amazing. He's a great coach. His body of work would say that without me saying it. Coach Spurrier is great at what he does. He loves the game. He's very good at it. He's got

South Carolina in a position right now where it's probably as good as they've been, maybe ever, in terms of consistency and winning. Steve is a dang good ball coach. He loves the game, and he's great at what he does."

"Congratulations to the ol' ball coach," LSU's Les Miles said. "How wonderful. It lets you know he's been at it a number of years. It lets you know that he's done it right. He's sustained a very high level of competition for a long time. I can remember when I first got in the league, my wife and kids needed to meet the old coach. You followed Coach Spurrier because he seemed to have an entertaining way of communicating, and he played and coached for some very fine football teams."

Will Muschamp, who was in his second year at Spurrier's former school Florida when Spurrier won his 200th game, said he still lived in Spurrier's shadow in Gainesville, Florida.

"The guy will go down as one of the best coaches in college football history," Muschamp said. "I'm 193 [wins] away."

One of the reasons the 200th victory didn't resonate as much with Spurrier is that he has always counted his years as a professional coach in the USFL in his victory total. Using that formula, he earned win No. 250 overall against Georgia on October 6, 2012, with a 35–7 win in Williams-Brice Stadium.

"Having it against the Georgia Bulldogs was special, too," Spurrier said. "They are a team that used to beat my alma mater pretty well. I have been very fortunate against them as a coach—not so much as a player, but as coach—so that was special."

# 85 The Streaks

Uninterrupted periods of success against Clemson don't come around too often for South Carolina. So when they do, the Gamecocks enjoy them.

The Tigers lead the series 65–41–4 all-time, and there have been some bleak runs since the Gamecocks first met Clemson in 1896. The Gamecocks won just twice from 1897 until 1920. The Tigers took seven straight from 1934–40. From 1976–83, South Carolina won once, and Clemson won eight out of nine from 1997–2006.

Twice in the rivalry, the Gamecocks have won four straight, and those years stand as their best streaks of the series. The first South Carolina teams to do it were Rex Enright's clubs from 1951–54. The Tigers never scored in double figures during that time frame, and the Gamecocks won the games by a combined score of 53–15.

South Carolina would manage only one more winning streak of more than two games against the Tigers until Steve Spurrier arrived on campus. In fact, of the nine Gamecocks coaches between Enright and Spurrier, only one—Paul Dietzel—managed to beat Clemson four times during their coaching career, much less four in a row.

By the time Spurrier got around to the feat, the Gamecocks were due. From 1988–2008, a period that included the first four years of Spurrier's tenure at the school, South Carolina was 5–16 against Clemson.

The 2008 game might have been the worst of the bunch. Clemson won 31–14, Spurrier fell to 1–3 against the Tigers, and Memorial Stadium in Clemson rang out with cheers of "Dabo

Swinney" as the game ended. The victory is credited with moving Swinney from interim head coach at Clemson to the full-time position, a job he still holds today.

"We just got smashed," Spurrier said following the game.

It all turned around from there, though. South Carolina had lost four of five, including three straight, heading into the 2009 Clemson game. When the Gamecocks pulled out a 34–17 win, *The State* newspaper headline simply said, "Season Saver."

Freshman cornerback Stephon Gilmore was the star, playing one series at quarterback out of the WildCock formation, rushing for 20 yards, and throwing a 39-yard pass. He also had four tackles, recovered a fumble, and returned three punts for 31 yards.

In 2010, Clemson stopped South Carolina's star freshman tailback Marcus Lattimore, holding him to 48 yards on 23 carries, but they couldn't do much with sophomore wide receiver Alshon Jeffery, who had five catches for 141 yards and a touchdown as the Gamecocks prevailed 29–7. The win marked the first back-to-back victories over the Tigers since 1969–70.

"I am 3–3 with Clemson now. And two in a row, I guess, is good because it hasn't happened in a long time," Spurrier said. "You would have thought that would have happened in the last 40 years. But anyway, we've done some firsts this year."

In 2011, quarterback Connor Shaw started his first South Carolina–Clemson game and directed a 34–13 victory by completing 14-of-20 passes for 210 yards and three touchdowns and leading South Carolina in rushing with 107 yards and one touchdown. The win gave the Gamecocks 10 victories for just the second time in school history.

In 2012, Shaw was sidelined by a foot injury and backup Dylan Thompson took over, throwing for 310 yards and rushing for another 38 in a 27–17 win.

"We were very fortunate again," Spurrier said. "It seems like when we play Clemson they don't play very well."

The win gave the Gamecocks another 10-win season and set them up for a spot in the Outback Bowl, but no one wanted to talk about that after the game.

"I am not worried about [the bowl game] right now," Thompson said. "We just beat Clemson for the fourth time in a row. I am just happy right now, and I'm going to celebrate this one."

The Gamecocks will enter the 2013 season looking for an unprecedented fifth straight win over the Tigers.

# 86 Mike McGee—The Man Who Made the Hires

On October 30, 2004, Lou Holtz called South Carolina athletic director Mike McGee.

The Gamecocks had just been walloped 43–29 by Tennessee in Williams-Brice Stadium, and Holtz had seen enough.

"The season had gone reasonably well, and he thought we had a great opportunity to beat Tennessee… We just didn't play well, and Tennessee was a very good football team—a better football team than they are today," McGee said.

That night Holtz told McGee that 2004 would be his last season as a college coach.

"I then set about hiring [Steve] Spurrier," McGee said.

Spurrier would go on to be the most successful coach in Gamecocks history. While his tenure is most closely associated with that of athletics director Eric Hyman, it was McGee, with a little help from Holtz, who brought Spurrier to Columbia.

McGee said Spurrier and Holtz were friends and had spent a few days playing golf at Augusta National Golf Club, where Holtz is a member, the summer before Holtz's retirement.

The timing couldn't have been better for McGee and South Carolina. Not only did Holtz give the school a head start on its coaching search by calling McGee following the Tennessee game, but Spurrier was out of work that season, having resigned from the Washington Redskins following the 2003 season. With Spurrier unattached, there was no red tape for McGee to fight and he was able to get ahead of other would-be suitors such as LSU, which would soon be looking to replace Nick Saban and would eventually land on Les Miles.

"There were other people, LSU and other people, that Steve's name had been associated with, so we took the route of going after an early decision with Steve," McGee said.

Within three days of Holtz's first phone call, McGee had called Spurrier and set up a face-to-face meeting. McGee would soon meet with Spurrier and wife Jerri and bond over their connection to Duke University. McGee was an All-American football player at Duke and went on to be the Blue Devils head coach from 1971–78. Spurrier coached the Blue Devils from 1987–89.

"We had a number of mutual friends, so there was an immediate rapport that played into the process," McGee said.

Before the 2004 season was complete, McGee and Spurrier had signed a letter of intent. McGee would retire from the school the following year, ending a long and varied career in athletics.

McGee won the 1959 Outland Trophy as the nation's outstanding lineman and was chosen in the second round of the NFL draft by the St. Louis Cardinals in 1960. A neck injury ended his playing career in 1962, and he then went on to serve as assistant coach at Duke, Wisconsin, and Minnesota before landing his first head coaching job at East Carolina in 1970.

From there, McGee went back to Duke as the head coach and stayed for eight seasons, compiling a record of 37–47–4. After leaving Duke, McGee went into athletic administration, and he served as the athletic director at Cincinnati and Southern Cal before taking over the Gamecocks' program.

With South Carolina, McGee not only hired Holtz and Spurrier but also tabbed Ray Tanner to run the baseball program. Tanner would go on to win two national titles in baseball before taking over the athletics director position in 2012. The school's athletic budget increased from less than $20 million annually to more than $50 million annually in McGee's tenure, as well.

"We were fortunate to have the opportunity at South Carolina," said McGee, who retired with his wife to Colorado. "We loved the people there. We're from North Carolina, so it was familiar territory to us. We had a wonderful time and have good friends who will be lifetime good friends from Columbia and the university. Our family all became Gamecocks. We had a really good time, good experience."

# 87 Hootie Johnson

Hootie Johnson was not sure he belonged in this book, and if it was based solely on what he did on the football field, he would be right.

Johnson lettered as a running back at South Carolina from 1950–52, and the early 1950s wasn't the time to be a running back for the Gamecocks unless your name was Steve Wadiak. Johnson's first two years were spent as a backup to Wadiak at tailback, but his final year saw a switch to fullback, where he earned South Carolina's Jacobs Blocking Trophy.

Johnson was recruited to his home state school by Coach Rex Enright, who had to fight off both Georgia and Tennessee for the star

*Augusta National Golf Club Chairman Hootie Johnson listens to a quesiton during the chairman's annual press conference on Wednesday, April 7, 2004, at the club in Augusta, Georgia.* (AP Photo/The Augusta Chronicle, Rob Carr)

runner from Greenwood, South Carolina. Johnson won a state title at Greenwood High playing for Palmetto State legend Pinky Babb.

"I don't know that I learned all that much playing football," Johnson said. "I learned most of my stuff from my mother and father."

It's not football that Johnson is known for, however—it's golf. After his South Carolina football career, Johnson returned to Greenwood, where his father had started the Bank of Greenwood, and began a career that would take him to the heights of American banking and eventually into the crosshairs of a very public national battle.

Under Johnson's leadership, the Bank of Greenwood became Bankers Trust, a regional fixture, and Johnson would go on to chair the executive committee for Bank of America. Along with that professional ascent came a social one.

Johnson was invited into the Augusta National Golf Club by founder Bobby Jones in 1968, and he rose to the club's chairmanship in 1998. He oversaw two major renovations of the golf course during his time in charge. But that's not what made him famous, either.

Martha Burk is the reason William Woodward Johnson became not just a name known in Southern power circles. In 2002, Burk and the National Council of Women's Organizations protested Augusta National's all-male membership, saying it was time for a woman to be invited.

Johnson and the club did not agree.

"We do not intend to become a trophy in their display case," Johnson wrote to media members at the time. "There may well come a day when women will be invited to join our membership, but that timetable will be ours and not at the point of a bayonet."

"At the point of a bayonet" became part of the golf lexicon, and Johnson was cast as the typical Southern powerbroker despite a history of progressive actions in his home state.

"I don't think it's a contradiction at all," Johnson said in a 2003 interview with *Sports Illustrated*. "You know, I have stood up for doing the right thing my whole life, but not to be a member at [South Carolina golf club] Forest Lake because it doesn't have any Jews? To suggest it's a contradiction to my moral integrity, I'm offended. All you have to do is look at the details of my life to know what I stand for."

While Johnson said most of his lessons didn't come from the football field, he did take one from his parents that translated perfectly to football—"Don't ever give up."

Johnson now maintains residences in Columbia and in Greenwood.

# 88 Graveyard of Coaches

After Steve Spurrier took the South Carolina job, he flipped through the Gamecocks' coaching records.

Like most people, he shook his head.

"I guess Rex Enright is the only coach who has really coached more than about 10 years or so," Spurrier said. "Coach Enright overall did not have a winning record, but he is the winningest coach here… It is always interesting looking at history [to] sort of see what's happened."

At South Carolina what has happened is that coaches have come and gone. In fact, the school has been called a "graveyard for coaches" in print and off the tongues of its faithful fans.

From 1943 until the end of Lou Holtz's career in 2004, the Gamecocks had 13 head coaches. That's an average of not quite five years per coach, and Enright was the coach in 10 of those seasons. Take away his service from 1946–55 (his second stint at the school), and Gamecocks coaches averaged 4.25 years on the job.

More tellingly, since World War II no coach has held another head coaching job after leaving the Gamecocks' sideline. The legacy of chewing up careers is so widespread that Brad Scott was asked when he took the job in 1994 why he would come to such a place. A sought-after assistant coach at national power Florida State, Scott could have waited on a softer landing spot, but he chose the Gamecocks.

"I guess I'm not smart enough to know any better," Scott said at the time.

Scott was fired five seasons later with an education of sorts. He was 23–32–1 overall and was 1–10 overall and 0–8 in the SEC his final season. His career is only one example of a supposed savior flaming out in famously hot Columbia.

Eight of South Carolina's last 12 head coaches left with losing records, and two of those came to the school with national championship rings on their fingers.

Paul Dietzel won a national title at LSU, but he was 42–53–1 at South Carolina. Holtz was a legend after winning a championship at Notre Dame, but he was 33–37 at South Carolina, a record that included an 0–11 season. He called the Gamecocks job the hardest of his career.

"[This] is a little bit different than most situations," he told *The State.*

It's different for several reasons, said Sparky Woods, who was 24–28–3 from 1989–93.

"It has always been a very political job, with the state capital right there," Woods told *The State.* "When I was there, how many [former] coaches were they paying? Richard Bell [who only coached one season, 1982]? Jim Carlen? I think it's a great place. But I think the lack of [coaching] stability has killed them."

Longtime South Carolina sports columnist Ken Burger declared in the late '90s that "Fire the coach!" should be the new state motto due to the Gamecocks' and rival Clemson's penchant for dispatching football coaches with great proficiency.

Burger wrote, "Hiring and firing football coaches, of course, is an age-old ritual here in the Palmetto State. We've had a lot of practice. Which would make you think we're good at it, but we're not.

"In a way, we handle success and failure of our favorite college football programs the way we handle our state politics—if you don't like the bum you've got, heck, fire him and get another bum just like him.

"In our politics as well as our football, we have never learned to look far beyond the surface of the people we put in charge. We just run somebody out and run somebody else in. Sooner or later we're bound to get a good one."

Well, that may be true in some blood sports. Unfortunately, it doesn't always work in politics or football.

That's why South Carolina, one of the poorest states in the country, is home to some of the world's richest ex-politicians and ex-football coaches in the world."

# 89 Rick Sanford— First First-Rounder

When Rick Sanford came out of high school in Rock Hill, South Carolina, he had options—and not just options of where to play football.

In addition to being a highly sought football player, Sanford also had several major college basketball scholarships. In fact, it looked at one point like that's the direction he would take.

"If it had come down to basketball, I would have probably gone to Wake Forest because I liked the school and I really liked their coaching staff," he said.

On the football side, home state South Carolina and Clemson were the top two suitors. In the end, Gamecocks coach Jim Carlen convinced Sanford that not only was football his future but football at South Carolina was his future.

"Coach Carlen made a very vivid point in my mind," Sanford said. "He said, 'You know son, there are a lot of 6'2" shooting guards in college basketball that never make it to the professional level. But there aren't a lot of 6'2" guys with your kind of speed as a defensive back that don't get in the NFL. I think that's your best shot.' That really kind of made my decision."

It played out exactly as Carlen suggested it would. With the Gamecocks, Sanford was named an All-American by *The Sporting News* after leading South Carolina in interceptions (four) in 1978. After lettering from 1975–78, Sanford became the first Gamecock selected in the first round of the NFL draft, going No. 25 overall to the New England Patriots in the 1979 draft.

The 6'2", 192-lb. defensive back is a member of the South Carolina Athletic Hall of Fame.

Sanford played six seasons with the Patriots, intercepting seven passes in 1983. He played his final season in 1985 with the Seattle Seahawks before returning to Columbia where he became a chiropractor and sports talk radio host.

In 2012, Sanford became one of more than 1,800 former NFL players, including former South Carolina stars like George Rogers and Terry Cousin, to sue the NFL in relation to concussions suffered during their career.

"It absolutely scares me," said Sanford of concerns about his long-term mental health.

At the time, there were stories across the nation about former football stars such as Junior Seau, Andre Waters, and Dave Duerson

*Miami Dolphins wide receiver Nat Moore (89) is upended by the New England Patriots Rick Sanford (25) after Moore caught the ball from Dolphins quarterback Dan Marino during second half of NFL action at Sullivan Stadium in Foxboro, Massachusetts, on November 13, 1983. The Pats downed the Dolphins, 17–6.* (AP Photo/Mike F. Kullen)

committing suicide in events that were later linked to brain damage suffered while playing football.

"I look at those and I go, 'Am I next? Who's the next guy? Am I going to wake up one day and be somebody different?'" Sanford said. "It really is a scary thought. I am very concerned about it as I continue to age."

Sanford said he saw "notable" changes in his mental function after his playing career.

"I'm not quite as quick as I used to be in my thinking, and [there has been] some impulsive thinking," he said. "I've seen things that have happened to myself. It's very scary where it may end up down the road."

The precautions football players take now to avoid head injuries were never a thought during Sanford's playing career, he said.

"Back when we had a head injury or a concussion, there was no such thing as, 'You're not going to play next week,'" he said. "I can only recall one concussion when I even came off the field. Why would there be this many people having as many problems as they are having if there wasn't a correlation with head injuries? There has to be some kind of correlation, and for years and years the league denied it. If there weren't problems, why would they be so careful now with these guys?"

# 90 Sideline Stalwart

In the modern era of college football, it's become commonplace for assistant coaches to change jobs with frequency and it rarely makes big news, especially if the coach is not a high-profile offensive or defensive coordinator.

It was different when Brad Lawing left South Carolina in 2013. Lawing, the Gamecocks' defensive line coach, had become synonymous with the program after 17 seasons as an assistant coach under three different head coaches.

Lawing, a North Carolina native, first came to Columbia as a member of Sparky Woods' first staff in 1989. He was retained by Brad Scott after Woods was fired and remained with the Gamecocks through Scott's tenure, which ended after the 1998 season. When Lawing was not retained by Lou Holtz, he went to Michigan State, where he worked with Nick Saban, and then North Carolina before

## The Phantom

Ed Dew, who lettered at South Carolina from 1946–48, was never an All-Conference or All-America player, but he'll always have a place in Gamecocks history as "The Phantom."

Dew was a defensive lineman, and during a game against Clemson in the 1940s, he left the field mistakenly thinking a substitute was taking his place. With only 10 defenders on the field, South Carolina allowed a Clemson runner to get around them and take off down the sideline near the Gamecocks' sideline.

"Rex Enright looked and said, 'Ed, what are you doing here?' [Ed] said, 'I thought you sent for me,'" said Don Barton, the school's former sports information director. "About that time they ran that single wing and they were running a sweep toward our sideline, and Ed Dew ran off our sideline and made the tackle for a loss."

At the time, no one noticed, but Clemson coach Frank Howard saw it later on game film.

"The next week Frank Howard called Coach Enright and said, 'Rex, I found out where that phantom tackler came from,'" Barton said.

returning to the Gamecocks in time for Steve Spurrier's second season in 2006.

In that time, it's almost certain Lawing set a school record with 106 wins as an assistant coach. South Carolina does not keep records of its assistant coaches before 1972, but it's doubtful anyone has won more games on South Carolina's sideline as Lawing, who has been involved in almost 20 percent of the school's football victories in history.

"That's called longevity," Lawing said.

That longevity gave Lawing a unique perspective on South Carolina football. He was there during the darkest days of Woods' tenure and also from 2010–12 when the Gamecocks won a school-record 31 games.

"There were some days you realized it was going to take a while [to win at South Carolina]," he said. "I always expected to win.

We've got better players, and they've responded better to it. It's just a better opportunity to win now."

Lawing's first tenure at South Carolina spanned 10 years and saw 47 wins. His second stint was just seven years but saw 59 wins. Lawing credited Spurrier for much of that turnaround.

"Coach Spurrier has brought a level of expectation," he said. "He expects to win, and our players have taken on that same mentality. They are not happy with just a good effort."

Lawing said at the time of that interview in December 2012, "This is where I want to be."

Which made it all the more surprising when three months later he left the school to take an assistant coaching position at rival Florida.

"It was a surprise to a certain extent," South Carolina defensive coordinator Lorenzo Ward said. "I think Brad's reason to leave here was way beyond football, and that's between him and his family. I think there were a lot of other things going on beside football."

Ward was not surprised, though, that Lawing got an offer from the Gators.

"People don't know it, but Nick Saban called Brad all the time about coming to work for him at Alabama, but Brad never wavered. I think this was a lot deeper than that. I wish him and his family the best," Ward said. "I don't think money had anything to do with it at all."

Many South Carolina assistants have gone on to head coaching jobs, including Ellis Johnson (Southern Miss), Charlie Strong (Louisville), Skip Holtz (South Florida), Buddy Pough (South Carolina State), Al Groh (Virginia), Ray Goff (Georgia), and Charlie Weis (Notre Dame).

The most famous Gamecocks assistant coach has to be Holtz, who was on Paul Dietzel's first two staffs at South Carolina in 1966 and 1967.

Holtz went on to be the head coach at William & Mary, North Carolina State, the New York Jets, Arkansas, Minnesota, Notre Dame (where he won a national championship), and finally with the Gamecocks from 1999–2004.

# 91 The Hit

It was midway through the fourth quarter of the 2013 Outback Bowl. South Carolina trailed Michigan 22–21, and the Wolverines had just converted a fourth-down attempt with the help of a questionable call by the referee.

On the television broadcast of the game, ESPN color analyst Jon Gruden said this as Michigan lined up for the next play: "You have to learn to forget about it when it doesn't go your own way and finish."

But South Carolina defensive end Jadeveon Clowney had not forgotten. The Gamecocks' sophomore defensive end, who was wrapping up a consensus All-American season, said later that he was angry at the injustice of the whole thing.

ESPN play-by-play announcer Mike Tirico picked up after Gruden left off. "Michigan at the 41. What a hit. Ball's free, on the ground. South Carolina deserves to have it, and they do."

What had happened—and happened so quickly that Tirico hadn't even finished enunciating "41" by the time it was all over—was that Clowney had taken advantage of a blown blocking assignment by the Wolverines offensive line and gotten into the Michigan backfield at the same time running back Vincent Smith took the handoff from quarterback Devin Gardner.

*Michigan quarterback Devin Gardner (12) loses his helmet as he is hit by South Carolina defensive ends Devin Taylor (98) and Jadeveon Clowney (7) during the second quarter of the Outback Bowl on Tuesday, January 1, 2013, in Tampa, Florida.* (AP Photo/Chris O'Meara)

Before Smith could react, Clowney hit him with such force that Smith's helmet flew back 4 yards and the ball fell to the ground. Clowney reached out his left hand and picked up the ball, giving the Gamecocks the ball at the Michigan 31-yard line and sparking a 33–28 comeback win.

"Clowney just says I'll take care of business right here… How about that quickness and get off?" said Gruden, a former NFL head coach. "Not many guys I've ever seen can get off the ball and rock people like Clowney."

The play instantly became known as The Hit, and before the game was over a YouTube clip of the play was moving like wildfire through the college football internet community. LeBron James tweeted about it. ESPN's *SportsNation* asked if it was the best hit its viewers had ever seen. Two months later, the various YouTube highlights of the play had been viewed more than six million times.

Even Smith watched it more than once with a grudging respect, he told ESPN.com.

"I saw it and was like, 'Dang,'" Smith said. "I saw it coming, and I couldn't do anything about it. I couldn't duck or try anything. My head wasn't even down, and that's why my helmet popped off."

South Carolina defensive coordinator Lorenzo Ward and several of Clowney's teammates said the play sounded like two cars colliding.

"When he doesn't want to be blocked, he can't be blocked. That's all I can tell you," Ward said. "His speed and quickness out of his stance are unbelievable. I would be scared if I played against him."

The Hit served as the unofficial start of Clowney's 2013 Heisman campaign, Gamecocks athletics director Ray Tanner acknowledged.

"He sort of took care of everything initially that could have been done, would have been done [from a marketing standpoint] to a level that we couldn't have satisfied," Tanner said. "I think he shot the first arrow."

The play got so much attention that South Carolina head coach Steve Spurrier felt like he had to come to the defense of the rest of the game's plays, which had included several big plays by the offense.

"I get home and I'm watching the local news, and all they show is Clowney's hit. They must have shown it five, six, seven times," Spurrier said. "I said, 'When are they going to show Ace Sanders' catch in the back of the end zone? When are they going to show Damiere [Byrd]? When are they going to show Ace's punt return? When are they going to show that fourth-and-3? When are they going to show Connor [Shaw] and Dylan [Thompson] escaping a sack?' There was a whole bunch of big plays, and Clowney's was just one of them."

But it was a spectacular one.

# 92 Willie Scott

Two times in its history, South Carolina has seen two of its players picked in the first round of the NFL draft.

Three of those four names—running back George Rogers, cornerback Stephon Gilmore, and defensive lineman Melvin Ingram—probably roll easily off the tongues of most Gamecocks fans. The fourth is probably a little trickier.

He played with Rogers, helping to clear the way for the tailback to win the 1980 Heisman Trophy, and he caught a few passes along the way. Willie Scott, a Newberry, South Carolina, native who caught 63 passes at South Carolina, was the 14th overall player selected in 1981, taken by the Kansas City Chiefs.

"I really didn't think Willie would last until the 14th pick in the draft," South Carolina coach Jim Carlen told United Press International at the time. "I think he might be the most underrated player I've ever seen. We are going to miss him at least as much, if not more, than we're going to miss George Rogers.'"

Scott had 360 receiving yards as a senior and was considered a dominating blocker coming out of college.

"Willie has a great shot at being a starter," Chiefs coach Marv Levy told UPI. "But everyone has to earn their way into the lineup. It usually takes a tight end a couple of years to develop, but guys like Kellen Winslow [in San Diego] and Ozzie Newsome [in Cleveland] have had success very quickly.'"

Scott was one of two tight ends that Kansas City selected that year, along with Southern Miss product Marvin Harvey, an accomplished pass catcher.

"Why two tight ends?" Levy said. "We felt tight end was our prime need going into the draft. Having two tight ends doesn't hurt the situation—it helps it. With Scott and Harvey, we've now got two different dimensions at the same position."

Scott went on to play eight seasons in the NFL, although he never panned out to the level the Chiefs had hoped. His best seasons came in 1983 and 1984 when he combined to catch 57 passes for 500 yards combined. In 1986, the Chiefs traded Scott to the New England Patriots.

"Whatever [the Patriots] want me to do is fine," Scott told the *Boston Globe* at the time. "I'm just happy to be able to contribute."

He attributed his relative lack of production in Kansas City to "circumstances."

"My first year there, I fractured my finger in training camp, and that set me back. Then they changed coaches the next year and put in a whole new system," he said.

In one exhibition game with the Patriots, Scott moved from tight end to offensive line during the game.

"I changed jerseys at halftime [from No. 88 to No. 71]," he said. "I had some friends in the stands, and they couldn't find me. They thought something had happened."

He finished his career with three seasons as a role player in New England before returning to his South Carolina roots. Scott served as a graduate assistant coach on Sparky Woods' coaching staff with the Gamecocks and went on to a career as a coach at Pelion High School just outside Columbia.

In 2012, as Gilmore and Ingram were on the verge of matching the accomplishment of Rogers and Scott in the NFL draft, Scott wished them luck.

"Records are made to be broken," he said. "You have to be in the right place at the right time. Usually when you have a group of guys together, you push each other."

# 93 Knocking the Lid Off

When South Carolina's baseball team took the field at Rosenblatt Stadium in Omaha, Nebraska, on the night of June 29, 2010, the wind was in its face.

The Gamecocks had been competing in athletics for 118 years, and all that time they had not produced a national title in any men's sports. There had only been six national titles in school history, and five of them had come in equestrian events, which is nothing to sneeze at but not exactly a feather in the big-time athletics cap, either. The only time South Carolina had won it all in a major NCAA sport was in 2002 when its women's track and field team captured the national title.

Baseball coach Ray Tanner and his team had beaten plenty of odds to get to that night, rallying after dropping their first game in the College World Series and then winning five straight to set up a decisive game against UCLA. In the bottom of the eleventh inning, Whit Merrifield singled to score Scott Wingo and give South Carolina a 2–1 win and the national title.

The impact of that night was felt throughout the state of South Carolina.

"I think it had a positive effect on our city, on our state, on our other sports teams," said Tanner, who would win the 2011 national title as well and then advance to the final game of the 2012 College World Series before retiring to become the school's athletics director. "I am not patting myself on the back or our baseball team. [It's] just the result had even a greater magnitude than I would have guessed. Winning a national championship is very special by itself. I didn't realize the impact that it has had throughout."

It certainly made an impact on head football coach Steve Spurrier, who placed rows of pictures of the baseball team's celebration dog pile throughout the football locker room. The month after the baseball team's title, Spurrier stood before hundreds of media members at the SEC's football media days and talked about the psychological impact of the victory.

"Our baseball team certainly proved you can win a big championship at the University of South Carolina," he said. "We believe that will rub off on the other sports, and we're the next one up. Hopefully, we can take a cue from those guys and have a good run as we go through the season."

Five months later, the Gamecocks captured their first SEC East title in history.

The baseball team's title "was not only super and great for our university and for the baseball program, but it sort of sends a message to all the other sports, 'Hey, it can be done at South Carolina,'" Spurrier said.

For a school that had long thought itself doomed by the Chicken Curse and had reluctantly adopted, "Wait 'til next year," as its sporting motto, the baseball team's national title was a shot over the bow at mediocrity, a signal that winning was possible after all at South Carolina.

"I think it removed maybe some questions that some people may have, some athletes may have, some coaches may have," Tanner said. "You extinguish that. At the University of South Carolina, all things are possible."

In February 2013, South Carolina opened its first baseball season in 17 years without Tanner in the dugout. The school honored him by retiring his No. 1 baseball jersey and designating part of the street that passes by Carolina Stadium, where the baseball team plays its home games, as Tanner Way. After the game, Gene Warr, the chairman of the school's board of trustees, thanked Tanner for his service to the school—and for breaking through the Gamecocks' personal glass ceiling.

"When [Tanner] was hired, I think all of us were very hopeful [and] had high expectations, but as we look back now, I just think, 'Who would have seen that coming?'" Warr said. "For however long I will live, I will never forget exactly where I was and how I felt in June 2010 and June 2011. Coach Tanner brought the kind of success to us that we had always dreamed of here in sports but had never had before. You have changed the way we see ourselves and what we think we can accomplish. You have changed many things and reset many standards."

# 94 Perfect Recall

It was impossible to say as the 2012 season ended when Steve Spurrier's tenure at South Carolina might end. After his eighth season with the Gamecocks, Spurrier signed an extension and talked about sticking around for a while.

What we can say with a good deal of confidence is that whenever it ends, Spurrier will remember almost every moment of what happened on the field.

"He remembers the third inning of his high school baseball game and who was on base," Spurrier's wife Jerri said.

She is barely joking. Whether it is football or golf or his stellar high school baseball career, Spurrier has a stunning recall of his athletic history. Take this example, related by Spurrier in 2011, from Duke's 21–17 win over Clemson in 1989.

"We are down 14–0 at half, nothing good is happening much, but our guys are playing hard…. So we get the ball early in the second half, and we get sacked, and we get a penalty and it's third-and-30. Third-and-30. Back in those days, I'd call a 30-yard pass [and] just throw it down there and hope somebody catches it. Every now and then we'd hit them. We call an 'everybody take off,' one of those patterns, and a guy ran a comeback. Our receiver got confused. The week before we had him run a comeback on that particular play. So he runs a comeback and stops, and their defensive back, Dexter Davis, catches it on a dead run, of course, going the wrong way for Clemson. He runs to midfield [and] stops. He's going to reverse field and drops the ball, the ball slips out of his hands, and our kid dove on it at about the 30-, 35-yard line. We went down and scored, Randy Cuthbert scored off left tackle. And now it's 14–7, and now all of a sudden it's a ballgame. Danny Ford started pacing that sideline in a different mood than he was in earlier. So anyway, the game rocked around. We got a couple more TDs. You want to know how we got them? The 67-year-old Spurrier has used his memory to impress recruits many years younger than him. His office wall at the University of Florida was filled with plaques recognizing each team and listing the score of every game.

"Every now and then I'd ask a recruit, 'Just pick out a game and a year and see if I can tell the score.' I'd get most of them," he said.

NFL assistant coach Brian Schottenheimer, who played quarterback for Spurrier for three seasons at Florida, believes Spurrier's memory is an invaluable part of his ability to successfully call plays.

"He would always go back and talk about things, a play that maybe had won a game back in the mid-1960s," Schottenheimer said. "He's the best play-caller I have ever been around, and so much of that is based on feel and instincts. There is no question it helps, and it helps him more than anybody because he has such an amazing feel for calling the game and getting into the right play."

"He's got what I call a compartmentalized photographic memory," said Noah Brindise, who played for Spurrier at Florida and coached for him in the NFL. "There are a few topics where he can rattle off things like they just happened yesterday, and those are things that happened in games with play-calling, and he's like that with golf. As far as those two things go, it's like a computer."

After a round of golf, Spurrier can recite every shot he took and every shot taken by the three other members of his foursome.

"I can almost tell you the next month what I did on that day if it was like a best round of the year or things like that," he said.

Spurrier's family members tease him about that memory not extending to other areas. During one conversation, his daughter Amy Moody challenged him to remember her age.

"I said, I bet my dad doesn't know how old I am.' He said, 'You were born when I was playing for the 49ers. You were born on a Friday, and the 49ers won only four games that year. That was the season I threw my longest NFL pass, 75 yards. That was 1969, so you are 24 years old."

Jerri Spurrier is so used to her husband's sport-centric recall that it doesn't amaze her anymore, she said.

"If I have a question, I just know he remembers it all. I am not amazed by it. I'm just used to it. [Steve Spurrier Jr.] said the other day, 'You have no idea how amazing it is that he remembers everything about everything.' Now, he has a selective memory, which means there are a lot of things he doesn't put in his brain that he doesn't think are valuable. He doesn't remember plenty of things."

# 95 The Michigan "Series"

It is tradition with a capital T against… well, whatever the opposite of that might be.

The series between South Carolina and Michigan has been very brief, but it has produced enough highlights in that time to deserve a spot in the Gamecocks' annals. The first time the teams ever met was in 1980. South Carolina was unranked and coming off a 23–13 loss to Southern Cal. The mighty Wolverines, college football's winningest program, were ranked No. 17 in the country. The game was played in Michigan's venerable Big House, and few people doubted the outcome.

Everyone was surprised when the Gamecocks came away with a 17–14 win that would vault them into the national rankings at No. 18.

While the defense, and a pair of timely plays by cornerback Chuck Finney, probably deserves the bulk of the credit for the day, senior tailback George Rogers may be most closely associated with the win. Rogers carried the ball 36 times for 142 yards, and the game is credited with starting his march to the Heisman Trophy that season.

"The Michigan game was huge for George," said Don Barton, the school's longtime sports information director and foremost historian. "He did his own hype."

In a video celebrating the first 100 years of South Carolina football, Rogers remembered that the Wolverines players had intentionally run into the Gamecocks as both teams returned to the field for the second half.

"Everybody on that team said, 'We're going to kick their butt,' and that's what we did. We went out there and beat them," Rogers said.

That Michigan team would not lose again and would finish the season as the No. 4 team in America after a 23–6 pasting of Washington in the Rose Bowl.

"Back then they didn't rank recruits like they do now with stars, but apart from a couple of players, they had what would now be a bunch of five stars and we had a lot of one stars," South Carolina defensive tackle Andrew Provence told *The State* newspaper. "But our team had a special chemistry, and we proved something that day."

The victory was such a monumental moment for the Gamecocks that fans packed the Columbia airport to welcome home the team, and *The State* newspaper featured a photo the next day of 2-year-old Toni Kirkland Day in a South Carolina jersey, cheering for her favorite team. When the Gamecocks and Wolverines met 32 seasons later in the Outback Bowl played on January 1, 2013, *The State* newspaper tracked down Day. Where was she? Still in Columbia and an employee of the Gamecock Club.

The second game of the series resulted in Michigan's revenge, a 34–3 Wolverines win in Williams-Brice Stadium in 1985. (Ahem, moving right along.)

When the teams got together for the third and most recent time, it came following the 2012 season. South Carolina was looking for its second straight 11-win season, while Michigan was hoping to return to its former glory with Coach Brady Hoke at the helm.

The Outback Bowl was played in Raymond James Stadium in Tampa, Florida, and when it was over, Gamecocks head coach

*Cornerback Akeem Auguste (3) breaks up a pass intended for Michigan wide receiver Joe Reynolds (85) during the first quarter of the Outback Bowl game on Tuesday, January 1, 2013, in Tampa, Florida.* (AP Photo/Chris O'Meara)

Steve Spurrier said, "[It] might have been one of the most exciting games I've ever coached; it might be the most exciting."

South Carolina had to come from behind in the fourth quarter to win that game. While the comeback was sparked by a now-famous hit by defensive end Jadeveon Clowney, Spurrier said he will always remember the day for the big plays on offense.

The Gamecocks had five offensive plays of more than 30 yards, plus a 63-yard punt return for a touchdown by Ace Sanders. Backup quarterback Dylan Thompson replaced injured starter Connor Shaw during the final drive of the game and threw a 32-yard touchdown pass to Bruce Ellington with 11 seconds left to give the Gamecocks a 33–28 win.

"For a minute I thought we are going to kick a field goal to win from being behind, something that has never happened in all my coaching career," Spurrier said.

After the 2012 season, the tally stood thus: Michigan (with its NCAA record 903 all-time wins) 1, South Carolina (with its 565) 2.

# 96 Charlie Strong—Made Good

Charlie Strong only spent four years at South Carolina, but where he has gone is a story all Gamecocks should know.

Strong was Notre Dame's defensive line coach when Lou Holtz took the head coaching job in Columbia in 1999. Holtz quickly called Strong to offer him the defensive coordinator's position.

"Charlie and his wife used to stop in and see [my wife] Beth when she was struggling," Holtz told *The State* newspaper. "He would ask me if I was ever going to get back into coaching. I said,

'No, but if I ever do, you'll have a chance to tell me no to defensive coordinator.' I always liked Charlie. I liked his demeanor."

The Strong hire proved a good one for Holtz as the Arkansas native slowly turned around the South Carolina defense, placing the Gamecocks No. 16 in the nation in total defense in 2000 and No. 27 in 2001.

His performance was good enough to get interviews for head coaching jobs but apparently not good enough to get those jobs. In 2001, Strong interviewed at California, Kansas, and Vanderbilt. In 2002, he received interest from Tulsa, East Carolina, Kentucky, and Louisville.

Eventually he told *The Tim Brando Show* in a revealing interview in 2013 that he began to wonder if the color of his skin was the reason none of those interviews turned into jobs. In fact, Strong, who is black, told another member of the staff that he didn't want to put himself through the torture of the interview process anymore.

"I can remember at South Carolina, I was going through all these interviews, and I wasn't getting any jobs," he said. "I sat down with a coach, him and I were talking, and I got frustrated. I said to him, 'I'm sick of these interviews. I'm not getting a shot. I think the guys are just bringing me in to bring me. They just want to say they interviewed a minority candidate.' I said to him, 'I'm done with this. I don't want to do this anymore.' He looked at me and said, ' Charlie, you can't." I said, 'Why can't I?' He said, 'There are so many guys out there counting on you. There are so many minorities counting on you, because they want you to get an opportunity so that you can open the door for them.' He told me that. I said then, as frustrated as I get, I can't quit now. I have to continue.

"I said I would keep working hard. Even if it doesn't happen for me, maybe I can work well enough where my work can be noticed and it would happen for someone else. It is good when you hear coaches say, 'You inspire us. You are the reason why I do what I do.'"

## Letter of the Law

The people of the Palmetto State take the South Carolina–Clemson game seriously. So seriously, in fact, that it is state law that the two teams play annually.

The story dates back to 1951 and is the result of Clemson and Maryland running afoul of Southern Conference policy. The Tigers and Terrapins accepted bowl bids that year despite the conference saying they should not.

The Southern Conference then ruled that Clemson and Maryland could not play any other conference members the following year, which would have nixed the 1952 Carolina-Clemson game because the Gamecocks were also Southern Conference members at the time.

South Carolina coach Rex Enright, thinking on his feet, said at the time, "I believe that there's a law in South Carolina requiring Carolina and Clemson to play each other," according to *The State* newspaper. Conference officials agreed that their ruling could not supersede state law, so Enright quickly went about making his proclamation the truth.

On February 27, 1952, the South Carolina General Assembly enacted a resolution "to require the football teams of the University of South Carolina and Clemson College to play their annual game on Thursday of Fair Week, 1952."

South Carolina won the game 6–0.

Strong left South Carolina shortly after that conversation to become defensive coordinator at Florida before the 2003 season. The rumors that he and Holtz were at odds were strong enough that Holtz felt the need to dismiss them without being asked in a press conference after Strong's decision was announced. The move was strictly business, Holtz said—a chance for Strong to expand his profile and work toward his ultimate goal.

"If he felt that this was something he needed to do, then he should do it," Holtz told *The State* newspaper. "I have the utmost respect for Charlie, both as a coach and as a person. I really hate for Charlie to leave. It's like losing a member of your family."

Strong's success with the Gamecocks continued with the Gators. He spent seven seasons there, spanning the tenures of head coaches Ron Zook and Urban Meyer. On December 9, 2009, he was announced as the head coach at the University of Louisville, becoming the 11th black head coach in Football Bowl Subdivision history.

"When we were offered this job, my wife [Victoria] and I looked at each other," Strong said that day, "because you just never thought it was going to happen."

After waiting so long to be a head coach, Strong didn't waste the chance. In his third season at Louisville in 2012, Strong led the Cardinals to 11 wins and a Sugar Bowl victory. He was no longer going after jobs. They were coming after him. After being the man who couldn't get an offer in 10 years, he could now turn down a lucrative offer from the venerable University of Tennessee in 2013.

# 97 A 0–0 Win

When South Carolina opened its 1942 season against Tennessee, there was no reason to think the year would get off to a good start.

The Gamecocks had lost three of their last four games to end the 1941 season. The Volunteers, meanwhile, had won six straight to end the previous campaign. South Carolina's Dom Fusci, a sophomore lineman making his first collegiate start, remembers that his club was a 21-point underdog.

From here the action is best described by Fusci, whose telling of the story comes from archival video footage shot when he was in his eighties:

"The coach told me, 'A lot depends on you today.' As the first game, it kind of worried me, and I walked around the locker room and I saw all these Southern boys chewing tobacco and looking mean and nasty, spitting all over the place. I said, 'By God, let me get a chew of that tobacco. I want to get some courage, too.' I was all excited about the game. I thought it would boost my morale a little bit. I got the tobacco and took a bite, and they said, 'Freshman.' They still called me freshman. They said, 'Freshman, are you sure you have taken this stuff before?' I said, 'Oh yeah.' They said, 'You took a pretty big bite there.' So I put it in my mouth and I start chewing it, trying to look as mean as them other boys. Finally it was time to get out on the field. We get out on the field, we kick off, and I am running down for the kickoff and somebody hit me and flipped me over on my back. And that tobacco didn't go down all the way—it went about halfway down and stuck in my chest. All I could do was go, 'Ooohhh, ooohhh, ooohhh.' So I got in the huddle and I was going, 'Ooohhh, ooohhh, ooohhh,' and the quarterback said, 'Get out of the huddle. We can't hear the plays.' So I was out there trying to get it up [and] couldn't get it.

"Finally Lou Sossamon came out of the huddle and he said, 'The play is fullback up the middle on three.' I lined up with them Tennessee linemen up in front of me and I started going, 'Ooohhh, ooohhh, ooohhh.' The guy in front of me says, 'Holy mackerel, this guy is having a heart attack! Look at all the black stuff coming out of his mouth. He's going to die!' And Lou Sossamon says to him, 'Don't worry, he's been acting that way ever since that dog bit him on Monday.' They all started scattering, [and] nobody wanted to touch me for three or four plays. Finally they got a towel and I went ahead and upchucked in the towel and played the rest of the game.

"By the way, we tied them 0–0."

The Volunteers would lose only once that season—8–0 to No. 4 Alabama. The Gamecocks, on the other hand, had a hard time mustering that kind of effort again that season. Their only win that year came against The Citadel (14–0), and they finished 1–7–1. The game was also one of the few high points of the first 100 years of the Tennessee series for South Carolina. Until the Gamecocks beat the Volunteers three straight times from 2010–12, South Carolina was 4–22–2 all-time against Tennessee.

"They lost respect when we tied them nothing-nothing," Fusci said.

# 98 Jerri Spurrier

The story of South Carolina football is not complete without Steve Spurrier, and the story of Steve Spurrier is not complete without Jerri Spurrier.

"I've heard some of them say she's the best [coach's wife]," Steve said. "I'd rather you quote somebody else, though. I'd be prejudiced."

The line of people forms quickly to take up where Steve would rather not.

"I think Jerri has been a very important part of Steve's success," said Oklahoma coach Bob Stoops, who coached for Spurrier at Florida before moving on to take over the Sooners program. "She is as committed and dedicated as anybody on the staff in terms of helping and encouraging and bringing a positive energy and attitude."

Former Georgia coach and athletic director Vince Dooley calls Jerri's outgoing personality "a tremendous balance" to her husband.

For the 12 seasons Steve served as Florida's head coach and the eight he has been at South Carolina, Jerri has been a consistent presence at games, on the practice field, and pretty much anywhere Steve is. Of the 431 games Steve has coached as the head coach or an assistant, Jerri has seen all but two in person.

**Famous Graduates**

South Carolina has produced more than football players. The university, founded in 1801, counts television host Leeza Gibbons, Houston Texans founder and CEO Robert McNair, U.S. Senator Lindsey Graham, former White House Chief of Staff Andrew Card, former governor Fritz Hollings, Lowe's Motor Speedway president Howard "Humpy" Wheeler, professional basketball Hall of Famer Alex English, and former NBA player and coach Mike Dunleavy as alumni.

"She's seen a lot of ball," he said.

She's seen a lot of pretty much everything that has gone on in the SEC, as she attends most major offseason coaching and publicity events with her husband.

"I figured I better be there. That's how it started out, and then I just never got out of the habit of going," she said. "Somebody told me a long time ago, the lady who used to babysit for my children, she said, 'There are a lot of people who can take care of your children, but you're the only one who should be taking care of your husband.'"

Steve and Jerri met at the University of Florida where he was the Heisman Trophy–winning quarterback and she was a big sister for his fraternity, where she also shepherded over future PGA golfer Steve Melnyk.

"We started going out pretty soon, but like most of them we would halfway break up sometimes and get back together," Steve said.

Jerri traveled abroad the summer after the couple's junior year in Florida but not before Steve gave her a ring, although not an engagement ring.

"That's when he invited me to all the football games his senior year. I thought that was kind of interesting. That wasn't like him," she said. "Then he gave me a little ruby ring and he said, 'Now, this is not an engagement ring. This is not an engagement ring.'"

It turns out it was, though, and the couple drove across the border to Kingsland, Georgia, the week before the football season began and married in a small service in a Presbyterian church.

"We just didn't want to have a lot of people there, so we didn't," Jerri said. "Plus it was football season."

Steve went to football practice that afternoon, and his new wife went to a sorority rush event, she said. The $10 wedding ring they bought at a bait and tackle store on the drive to the church remains on her finger.

"So far, it has served the purpose," she said.

Jerri stopped taking classes after her marriage to Steve but finished her degree during his coaching career with the Gators and has not stopped taking classes since.

"She likes learning," Steve said. "She makes better grades in her fifties and sixties than she did in her teens and twenties."

The secret to their marital success is simple, Jerri said.

"We both love the same thing—the game," she said. "That's [the secret] since the beginning."

# 99 Those $@!*# Trains

You can't truly say you've been to Columbia, whether it be for a football game or any other reason, until you've been stuck for an annoyingly long time at one of the city's many railroad crossings.

The town the trestle forgot is a landmine of delays if you come through at the wrong time. The problem is not only that almost all of Columbia's train tracks are at street level. The city also has two switching stations—one operated by Norfolk Southern and the other by CSX—right on its borders.

Track and freight car switches at those switching stations can cause trains to stop dead in their tracks or even back up in the middle of intersections. The results can be maddening.

Columbia and the state of South Carolina each have laws limiting the amount of time a train can be stopped blocking traffic to five minutes, but the fines can be as low as $5 and are not often imposed, according to *The State* newspaper in Columbia.

Think you can outsmart the trains by working around their travel schedule? Think again. For security purposes, the railroads do not provide schedules of their trains movements.

The city has requested that both of the rail operators schedule their travel around Gamecocks game days, and both have indicated they would try to adhere to the request but they make no promises.

There are sometimes ways for savvy veterans of the town's traffic to backtrack and find a way around the train, but in most cases it just leads to another blocked pass and another delay.

In 2012, one train managed to block three of the city's major intersections at the same time for more than an hour. Delays of that length not only cause aggravation but can also be a public safety issue, Columbia-Richland Fire Chief Aubrey Jenkins told *The State*.

"Especially with responding to USC," he said. "It all depends on which track the train is coming down. We can call for another unit if the train is stopped on the track and the truck can't get through, or we can maneuver around it. But it would still be a delay in getting to that call."

Since 2005, the city has been working to alleviate part of the problem in the busiest parts of Columbia along Assembly Street, but so far none of those plans, which would cost millions of dollars, has made it from boardroom to implementation.

"If I don't get two or three calls on any given week about trains blocking Assembly, it's a good week," South Carolina Department of Transportation commissioner John Hardee told *The State* in 2005 when the issue seemed to be working toward a conclusion.

Later that week, *The State* ran an editorial titled, "Moving Assembly Tracks Would Be a Dream Come True." So far it is still a dream.

The railroads, of course, are a necessary evil in the development of Columbia. The city, named the state's capital in 1786 due in part to its central location, was supported by those same rail lines, or at least their predecessors in the 1840s and 1850s as cotton flowed in and out of Columbia as one of the city's most vital economic engines.

The rails are still vital to the city's economic ecosystem, so for now Columbia is simply stuck with train delays. So if you find yourself pounding the steering wheel and staring at a jet black rail car standing still in front of you, just take a deep breath and consider yourself an official resident.

# 100 Ray Tanner— Taking Over

Few people have seen South Carolina athletics from all the angles Ray Tanner has.

The school's baseball coach for 16 years was named the Gamecocks athletics director in July 2012. Tanner, who throughout his baseball coaching career had dabbled in the administrative side of college athletics, was named to his position after a short search.

"Sometimes you can search the world over for the perfect candidate, and at times you know you have the right leader within your organization," school president Harris Pastides said. "For USC, we knew we had the right person on our team already. When Coach Tanner approached me two years ago and sought more administrative responsibilities, I clearly knew that this was an individual who was seeking a way to lead, to take our great university to the next level. Ray exemplifies all the qualities I am seeking in an athletics director: integrity, a winning attitude, a confident leader and manager, and an individual who puts the well-being of our student athletes above and beyond all other things."

One of the most interesting aspects of Tanner's move was going from a colleague of football coach Steve Spurrier to the boss of the athletic department's most high-profile employee.

"I felt like we had a very good relationship prior to me moving into this position," Tanner said. "I think a lot of people have recognized [that Coach Spurrier] supports everybody. He goes to [women's basketball coach Dawn] Staley's games. He goes to [men's basketball coach] Frank Martin's games. He goes to baseball games. He embraced the other coaches and the other sports, so I felt like I had a good relationship. Moving into this position, I don't think it's a lot different. I don't like the word boss. We are all part of a team here, trying to work together to be successful.

"He's been tremendous to work with. I sought him out soon after I got this job just to say, 'I'm a new AD. I'm not interested in having to go out and hire a football coach right away.' I needed to get his reaction personally, and his reaction was, 'If we're winning football games and I'm healthy, I'm going to keep coaching football.' I loved that answer."

Tanner took over the South Carolina program at its height, with Spurrier's program in the midst of a 31-wins-in-three-years span, the baseball team coming off three straight finals appearances in the College World Series, and both basketball programs seemingly headed in the right direction even if the men's team had a long way to go.

"I feel like I have experienced [the evolution] personally," Tanner said. "This is my 17th year and having been here and been part of the evolution, where we were, where we are, and hopefully where we're going. We are enjoying a very successful period. It's my job that continues. I feel that it's a major part of my daily operation to not only keep us going in the right direction but also to elevate. We have some room to grow. Thirty-one wins in the last three years in football is a heck of a statement, but we have some other sports that have room to grow. And we play in the best conference in the country."

Tanner took over the athletics director position from Eric Hyman, who left the Gamecocks to become athletics director at Texas A&M.

"I was immediately surrounded by tremendous experience here, and I lean on those people daily," Tanner said. "[This] was an influence of my dad growing up—no matter what your position is, you are very important. If you're at the top, you're no more important than the people you are with. And if you're not at the top, you're just as important as the person at the top. I learned that at an early age. I know a lot of people talk about team, and sometimes it's too much of a catchphrase, but I believe strongly in that. I've got a wonderful team that I am a part of here. I feel very fortunate."

Tanner's biggest test as South Carolina's athletics director remains ahead of him. That will come when Spurrier retires as head coach and Tanner has to hire a new football coach.

"[The search] will be thorough and, football coach or otherwise, my involvement will be to hire someone that I feel fits very well in the framework of the University of South Carolina and Columbia. I feel that's a very important component. We're a destination," Tanner said. "We're not a school that coaches should come [to] and move on years later. We're a destination as far as I'm concerned. It is my responsibility on an ongoing basis to be prepared for the future. Again, not only with football but with other coaches, as well. We've got 20 coaches here. I have looked at the head coaches in each of those programs, anticipating who might be long term and who may not be here. I have to do my due diligence to be prepared when that time comes."

# Sources

## Books

Price, Tom. *Tales from the Gamecocks' Roost.* Sports Publishing, 2001.

*South Carolina Gamecocks Media Guide 2011.*
*South Carolina Gamecocks Media Guide 1999.*
*South Carolina Gamecocks Media Guide 1985.*
*South Carolina Gamecocks Media Guide 1984.*
*South Carolina Gamecocks Media Guide 1977.*
*South Carolina Gamecocks Media Guide 1970.*
*South Carolina Gamecocks Media Guide 1969.*

## Videos

*100 Years of Gamecock Football*

## Newspapers

*The (Columbia, SC) State* (from *The State* digital archives)
*Birmingham (AL) News* (from Nexis-Lexis archives)
*Chattanooga (TN) Times Free Press* (from Nexis-Lexis archives)
*Rome (GA) News-Tribune* (from Google archives)
*Atlanta Journal-Constitution* (from Nexis-Lexis archives)
*The Columbia (SC) Record* (from *The State* digital archives)
*The (Macon, GA) Telegraph* (from Macon.com)
*The Raleigh (NC) News & Observer* (from Nexis-Lexis digital archives)
*The Los Angeles Times* (from Nexis-Lexis digital archives)
*The Charleston (SC) Post and Courier* (from Nexis-Lexis digital archives)

*The Lexington (KY) Herald-Leader* (from Nexis-Lexis digital archives)

*USA Today* (from Nexis-Lexis digital archives)

*The (Athens, GA) Banner-Herald* (from OnlineAthens.com)

*The Christian Science Monitor* (from Nexis-Lexis digital archives)

*The (St. Paul, MN) Pioneer Press* (from Nexis-Lexis digital archives)

*The Denver Post* (from Nexis-Lexis digital archives)

**Magazines**

*Sports Illustrated* (from SI.com)

*1952 All South Carolina Football Annual*

**News Services**

The Associated Press

United Press International

**Websites**

GamecocksOnline.com

NFL.com

CoachPaulDietzel.com

YouTube.com

ArenaFootball.com

IMDB.com